Take Hold

Embracing Our Divine Inheritance With Israel

Take Hold

Embracing Our Divine Inheritance With Israel

A Ministry of First Fruits of Zion

First Fruits of Zion
PO Box 620099
Littleton, Colorado 80162-0099
E-mail: ffoz_israel@ffoz.org

Cover by: Boaz Michael. All rights reserved.

Scripture taken from the NEW AMERICAN STANDARD BIBLE®, ©copyright The Lockman Foundation 1960, 1962, 1963, 1968, 1971, 1972, 1973, 1975, 1977. Used by permission. Throughout this publication the name *Jesus* is rendered Yeshua and *Christ* rendered Messiah.

First edition May 1998, Published in Israel
Revised edition June 1999, Published in Israel

ISBN# 1-892124-01-7

First Fruits of Zion, Inc.
Distribution and Mailing Office
PO Box 620099
Littleton, Colorado 80162-0099 USA

Phone: (303) 933-2119 or (800) 775-4807, Fax: (303) 933-0997

Israel Office
E-mail: ffoz_israel@ffoz.org

About the Authors
Ariel (Rick) Berkowitz (B.S., West Chester State College and Philadelphia College of the Bible, M.Div. from Biblical Theological Seminary.) Ariel also co-leads Kehilat Neve T'zion, a Messianic Jewish synagogue in Jerusalem. D'vorah (Michele) has taught and discipled women for the past 22 years. Currently in Israel, she leads women's groups and seminars. Together with their four children, Ariel and D'vorah reside near Jerusalem.

Dedication

We dedicate this book to *Tony* and *Linda*, who always believed what the Scriptures had to say about their connection to the Land, the People, and the Scriptures of Israel. Good friends, you were right! Thank you for helping us to know ourselves as new creations in Messiah.

We would also like to dedicate this book to the precious folks of our *kehilah* here in Jerusalem. Their dedication to the message being written and going forth from Zion has been expressed through their love and support for us as we wrote this book.

In addition, the staff of First Fruits of Zion would like to dedicate this book to all of the faithful supporters who share in the vision and endeavors of our ministry. Our heart's desire in this book is to encourage those of you who have backed this project through your financial support and your prayers. You have helped enable this work to go forth from Zion. We want you to know that your quest to know the truth about our relationship with Israel was a major encouragement to us in the production of this book.

Contents

Unit Four
Taking Hold According to the
Letters of Sha'ul of Tarsus

Unit Five
Taking Hold Through a
Knowledge of the Believer's Identity

Foreword

Today's Messianic believer faces a number of challenges. Our previous book, *Torah Rediscovered*, explored a number of these issues; *Take Hold* is a continuation of the process. It has been our goal in each of these works to make a contribution to the body of Messiah by examining potentially divisive issues in a responsible and gracious manner.

Many believers have been introduced to the "Jewish roots" of their faith in Yeshua. In this, their understanding of His words and His life will be forever changed. They have been encouraged to learn and study, sing and dance. Beyond that, however, they most often are met with unwelcome words, and with theologies intended to discourage them from the burning desire of their hearts. One of the foremost desires of their hearts is to be fully accepted as equals, in every sense of the word, with their brothers and sisters from the remnant of Israel. It is our desire through this work to see all believers come to understand and realize the important relationships they truly have with the God of Israel and His covenant, the Torah.

Take Hold lays a Biblical foundation for all believers to stand upon together, as one new man. This book is a solid biblical presentation of the Scriptures' declaration that anyone who is born into the kingdom of God is born again as a new creation, a fellow citizen and fellow heir with Israel, and therefore a full partaker of the covenants between God and Israel.

May the Lord bless you,

Bon Michael

Boaz Michael
Founder and Director
First Fruits of Zion
Jerusalem, Israel

Acknowledgments

Although D'vorah and I are the authors of this book, we certainly were not the only ones involved in its production. We have the entire staff of First Fruits of Zion, both full time and dedicated volunteers, to thank for all their sacrificial efforts in publishing *Take Hold*! This book grew in quality and quantity as our tireless and gifted staff made their contributions through editing and proofing.

It is difficult for us to express in writing how we here at First Fruits of Zion work. First Fruits of Zion is a real team of professionals who love Messiah. Each member of this ministry makes significant contributions to the production and distribution of all our material.

We are especially grateful to the Director of First Fruits of Zion, Boaz and his wife Amber, for their inspiration and encouragement to write this book.

But, most of all, we are eternally grateful...

To Him who loves us and released us from our sins by His blood and has made us to be a kingdom of priests to His God and Father, to Him be the glory and the dominion forever and ever. (Revelation 1:5–6)

Prologue

The Visitor

Outside, gusts of wind and rain were battering the streets of Jerusalem. Inside, the First Fruits of Zion staff were diligently at work on our daily writing and publishing tasks. Suddenly, the phone rang and a man with a pleasant foreign accent introduced himself as a pastor from India visiting here in Israel and requested an opportunity to come and see us. Boaz asked him where he was. "Right across the street!" returned the eager voice. He continued, "I need only ten minutes of your time."

Of course we invited him up to our sixth floor office. Just moments later we were introduced to this precious native-born Indian pastor. After introductions, this servant of a congregation of believers at the foot of the Himalayan Mountains, now standing eagerly in our Jerusalem office, began telling his story. Sipping tea together, we listened with great interest.

We soon learned that after a lengthy search, this highly educated man of God from India had finally found someone of whom he could ask the questions that clearly came from the depths of his heart. It quickly became obvious to us that this man had truly been on a long journey, searching for biblical truths that he knew were somewhere to be found.

A few years ago, he started having dreams from the Lord about Israel. These dreams were vivid and persistent. Eventually he felt that he had to come here to seek the Lord about the nature of these dreams. The dreams were what God had used to bring him to the Land of Israel and to meet the people of Israel. He began to grapple with the Scriptures of Israel. Questions of great magnitude flooded his mind—questions of his relationship as a non-Jewish believer in Yeshua to this Land, to this people and to these Scriptures.

Determined to find out answers, he cautiously but forthrightly asked one simple question: "How does the Torah relate to me? To the people of my congregation?" His question left us in awe. It was a confirmation of what we and the staff of First Fruits of Zion have witnessed increasingly for some time, that is, God is raising up a remnant of people from among the nations who are trying to understand their relationship with Israel.

The case of the pastor from India, by himself, is a significant occurrence. But we can multiply his example many times over.

The Prospective Readers

Of course, we would be delighted if everyone would read this book! We know many of you who will read this are just like this dear brother from India. Perhaps you are a believer in Yeshua from among the nations and your heart is asking the same questions as his. We are in communication with believers from literally all over the world. We know from speaking at conferences, from receiving letters from the 49 different nations of the world who receive the periodical *First Fruits of Zion*, and from conversing with the multitude of people who visit us in Israel, that there is a profound desire from people like yourselves to know more specifically how you relate to the Land, the People, and the Scriptures of Israel. *Take Hold* does not purport to have all of the answers to that question. But we do have some important input to share with you.

The Plea

This was not an easy book to write. For many, the topic itself can be controversial. Knowing this, we have made every attempt to clarify those ideas we consider to be truth/ accurate, and those which are simply our opinions. We have tried to demonstrate grace to those who differ from us. We hope you will show us the same courtesy.

There were several things continually running through our minds as we wrote *Take Hold*. It is helpful for you, the reader, to know these things about us. First, no matter what you may think you are reading, we firmly believe that personal trust in the person and finished atoning work of Yeshua of Nazareth is the only way for anyone, both Jewish and non-Jewish, to receive the free gift of God's righteousness and to be acquitted for his/her sins. Those of you who are not familiar with our theology concerning the Torah might think otherwise about us. Please give us the benefit of the doubt. It means a lot to us!

Second, we urge you to read our previous work entitled *Torah Rediscovered* in order to understand our viewpoint about the nature of the first five books of the Bible, the Torah. There are a number of assumptions in *Take Hold* that are more fully explained in *Torah Rediscovered*. Foremost among these is the fact that we consider a Torah-positive lifestyle by believers in Yeshua to be a valid expression of our biblical faith. In *Torah Rediscovered* we went to great lengths to demonstrate from the Scriptures that this kind of lifestyle is not legalism, but rather, the visible expression of the grace of God.

Third, carefully woven throughout all of our writings is our firm belief in the spiritual rebirth of a person through personal faith in Yeshua the Messiah. This whole issue is very important to us. But many people have misunderstood it. We believe that when a person becomes a believer in Yeshua, God makes that person into a new creation. We take Romans 6:1–6 literally when it refers to the fact that the old man really died on the cross with Yeshua and the believer is now a brand new person with Messiah's life in him. Moreover, his identity has been changed, from a sinner to a saint. Having Messiah's life in him, he is changed from being constituted a sinner to being constituted a righteous person, according to Romans 5:19. The basic identity of that person was, therefore, changed the moment that person was changed and granted new life from above by God.

Some people misunderstand this viewpoint when they do not take time to listen, thinking we believe that a believer does not sin. Of course he does! However, we believe that his relationship to sin has entirely changed. He is no longer a slave to sin. Sin does not constitute his identity; righteousness does. Sin is relegated to what is known as the "flesh," which is circumcised from him. His responsibility is to yield his members to Messiah in him, not to sin.

This last paragraph is important. Please take time to notice what we are saying. It is our conviction that *having a grip on the nature of the new birth opens the door to understanding* our relationship to God, to all of His Word (therefore, including the Torah), and to other believers. We see it as a matter of great importance that forms the main argument for much of our teaching.[1] When you read this book, please do not read so quickly that you gloss over this important truth.

The Purpose

Take Hold is built around a series of Scripture verses that were chosen to support one simple point, that is, that believers in Yeshua who are from the nations share in a meaningful relationship with the believing remnant of the physical people of Israel. We are not referring only to the modern State of Israel, but to the continual stream of the physical descendants of Abraham, Isaac, and Jacob. Moreover, since there is a significant relationship between the two groups, we are attempting to demonstrate that the non-Israelite believers have divine permission to freely and fully participate in the lifestyle taught in the Torah that was sovereignly bestowed as a gift upon the people of Israel.

The Plan

We have attempted to organize *Take Hold* to follow the pattern that theologians might refer to as "Biblical Theology," although it is not a true Biblical Theology in the strict sense of the term. This means that beginning with the Torah, the most ancient revelation from God, we take a peek into each of the succeeding historical periods of revelation in order to learn what that part of the Scripture teaches about the nature of a non-Jewish person's relationship to Israel. Accordingly, we will look at what most of the Scriptures reveal about the question at hand.

You are now ready to start reading *Take Hold*. May the grace of God go with you as you travel through the pages of this book. And may the Spirit of God confirm in you the truth of His Word whenever it is accurately exegeted herein. May *Take Hold* encourage many of you believers in the Messiah to confidently and joyfully take hold of that which the Scriptures define as your inheritance with Israel.

Introduction

Consider the Star of David. The menorah. Hanukkah. Matzah ball soup! What do these have in common? They are uniquely Jewish. However, for most people, the Torah is particularly characteristic of the people of Israel. The mere mention of the word "Torah" brings to mind images of men with white beards, wearing black yarmulkes and dancing with velvet-covered scrolls in a synagogue. In fact, it is very common for non-Jews to dismiss the Torah completely, as culturally belonging to the people of Israel alone, and as being antiquated theologically.

Indeed, for centuries the people of Israel have been the best-known caretakers of those sacred books of the Bible. Moreover, the descendants of Jacob are unparalleled in helping us to understand the Torah's teachings. It is not surprising, then, that the very word *Torah* has always been associated with the Jewish people.

We do not intend to minimize in any way the importance of these ancient scrolls to the people of Israel. Rather, we would ask, what about those people not physically associated with the people of Israel? Do they have any relationship to the Torah? Is the Torah intended for such people?

A Heated Debate

This can be quite a difficult subject, with widely differing opinions coming from both Jewish and Christian sources.

On the negative side, some ancient sages are quoted as saying, "A gentile who occupies himself with the study of Torah is deserving of death."[2] However, statements such as this probably arose during the era of intense anti-Jewish rhetoric emanating from the Church (2nd through 5th centuries), which claimed that, as the sole recipient of God's grace, it was the divine replacement of Israel.[3]

Most believers in Yeshua also have reservations about embracing the Torah. Many within the Church are convinced that Messiah's death rendered the Torah obsolete; that it has very little place, if any, in the life of the true believer. At best, they feel, it is a rigid code of law which can only reveal how sinful we are when we cannot obey it.[4]

However, both Jewish and non-Jewish viewpoints include moderate positions as well. From the Jewish side we hear, "According to the Talmud, even the Torah is not only for the Jews, but part of the Torah is seen as God's will for all people. This is the part known as 'the seven mitzvot of the sons of Noah.'" Moreover, "any non-Jew who behaves properly by keeping the seven mitzvot is known as one of the righteous of the nations of the world and will enjoy eternal bliss in the Hereafter."[5]

On the other hand, some within the Church suggest that gentiles are responsible for keeping part of the Torah, often advocating the Ten Commandments. However, even within this viewpoint there is some variation: many believe that the commandment for Shabbat now applies to Sunday.

What About All Those People?

By the grace of God, we received an overwhelmingly favorable response to *Torah Rediscovered*, wherein we explored the basic theology of the nature of Torah. This response came, however, from some very unexpected quarters. We had anticipated a warm reception from the Messianic Jewish community; what we could *not* have predicted was the volume of positive feedback we received from believers in small fellowships, home study groups, and churches which traditionally have not embraced the viewpoints espoused therein. Moreover, we have been impressed at the sheer number of people responding to this message. It seems that many evangelicals today are hungry to know more about the Torah. Moreover, beyond that many of these believers have expressed a deep desire not only to know the Torah, but also to learn to live it. Living the Torah is a major part of what it means to take hold of our inheritance with Israel. Accordingly, we have much to say about the non-Jewish believer's relationship to the Torah.

Definitions

Before proceeding any further, let us define certain key words that will be used throughout this book.

1. Torah

In traditional Jewish thinking the word *Torah* refers, in a broad sense, to all authoritative teachings of the rabbis. Other definitions in common use include:

- All Jewish law, as recorded in both the Bible and the *Talmud* (a compendium of oral Torah)
- The *Tanakh* (the complete Old Testament)
- The first five books of the Bible, Genesis through Deuteronomy (also called the *Chumash*)

- The covenant which God gave to Moses on Mount Sinai (because it contains individual teachings, or "torahs")
- Any teaching of the first five books of the Bible

In rabbinic Jewish thinking there are two Torahs: written and oral. When the rabbis speak in these terms, they usually define the written Torah as the Chumash (Pentateuch, or first five books of the Bible). This Torah was written by Moses as he received it from God on Mount Sinai. On the other hand, the rabbis claim that the oral Torah was also received by Moses from God on Mount Sinai—and carries just about as much authority. However, this Torah was passed down through the centuries by word of mouth rather than the written word. Eventually this oral material was written down, beginning around the year 200 CE under the authority of Rabbi Yehuda haNasi. Furthermore, many additions have been made to the oral Torah which, by virtue of the teaching found in Deuteronomy 17:8-13 (according to rabbinic interpretation), are authoritative and originated on Mount Sinai. The capstone of the written oral Torah is the Talmud, which consists of the Mishnah of R. Yehudah haNasi and its authoritative commentary, the Gamarah.[6]

While there is undeniable value in reading and studying the Talmud and other rabbinic writings, we hold the position that the oral Torah is not the spiritual authority for believers in Messiah. [A more complete discussion of this subject is found in Chapter 6 of *Torah Rediscovered*.]

In this book, we will use the word *Torah* in three basic ways: 1) to refer to the first five books of the Bible—all of which, we assert, are from the mouth of God and written with perfect accuracy by the hand of Moses; 2) in reference to specific teachings within the five books of Moses; 3) and on occasion as a synonym for the whole of the Scriptures, the teachings on the truth and righteousness of God for the holy community.

For the most part, we will use the word "Torah" to mean the first five books of the Bible. However, there will be occasions when it will also be used to refer to all of God's teachings. Unless we specify, we will never use it in this book to refer to rabbinic teaching.

It is our hope to demonstrate that the non-Jewish believer in Yeshua possesses a significant relationship both to the remnant of Israel and to its Torah.

2. Israel

Throughout *Take Hold* we will be using the term "Israel." What do we mean by it? Most of the time, unless we state otherwise, by the term "Israel," we are referring to the physical descendants of Abraham, Isaac, and Jacob. This, of course, would include the citizens of the modern political entity called "The State of Israel," but it is not limited to this political state.

Furthermore, whenever we assert that gentile believers in Yeshua are one with the people of Israel, we will always be referring to that special part of this ancient people called "the remnant." We recognize the remnant to be those of the people of Israel who believe in Yeshua of Nazareth. However, we are still defining them as part of their ancient people called Israel.

3. Gentile

The word "gentile"—in Hebrew, *goy* (גוי), singular, and *goyim* (גויים), plural—in the Scriptures simply means people of the nations who are not Israel. In fact, there are places in the Bible that even refer to Israel as a goy. Contrary to what some people think, the word "gentile" in the Scripture is not always a term designating a pagan or an unbeliever. (See, for example, Romans 11:13.) It simply means non-Israel.

Given that definition, however, we also recognize that there are many gentile believers in Yeshua who think of the word "gentile" as something of a derogatory term. Technically, that is not true. But the definition of a word is sometimes as good as its usage. Accordingly, we will attempt to refrain from using the word "gentile" when we are speaking about non-Jewish believers in Yeshua. Sometimes, because of the context and syntax, it will not be possible. When the word is used in this book, please understand that we do not intend to use it in any kind of a demeaning sense.

4. Jew/Jewish

This is a much more difficult term to define. Even those who call themselves Jewish cannot agree on how to define this word. Originally, the word "Jew" is derived from the word "Judah." In the Hebrew, there is a definite linguistic connection. "Jew" is therefore a shortened form of Judah. According to this definition, Jewish people are descendants of the Israelites who were associated with the tribe of Judah.

The Orthodox Jews, for the most part, say that a Jew is a person who descended from Abraham, Isaac, and Jacob. A Jew must either have a Jewish mother or be converted by an Orthodox religious authority. There are some Orthodox who even rquire people to adhere to the tenets of the religion called Judaism, specifically rabbinical or Orthodox Judaism. However, some Conservative, Reconstructionist, and most Reform rabbis have slightly different definitions of the word "Jew."

As we can see, it is not always easy to define words. There is a difference between the modern and the original usage of this word. Most people use "Jew" to refer to the people who are descended from the people of Israel. Thus, it is used synonymously with the word "Israelite." Unless otherwise stated, this is how we will use the words "Jew" and "Jewish."

One last remark: It is culturally acceptable for one Jewish person to call another Jewish person "a Jew." But due to historical anti-Semitic connotations, it can have negative overtones if a non-Jew refers to them as "a Jew." The better term is "Jewish person/people."

5. Christian

This word is almost as difficult to define as the other words above. On the broadest scale, it is a term that is used to refer to the religion, whose adherents believe in Yeshua, whatever that means to each individual. In its most narrow usage, the word Christian can refer to only those of an "evangelical" expression, that is, only those people who are trusting in the person of Yeshua the Messiah and in His atoning sacrificial death and glorious bodily resurrection to receive justification from God.

There is, yet, a third usage of the word "Christian." It is not so much a religious usage, but a cultural one. There is a certain culture that is regarded by the rest of the world as decidedly Christian. Such a culture is one which celebrates holidays such as Easter or Christmas (and others) because it is the social thing to do.

We wish to avoid confusion when using the term "Christian." Because of that, whenever we use it, unless we state otherwise, we mean evangelical believers in Yeshua. To aid us in our attempt to be clear, we tend to employ the term "believer" for such people.

Words that Come From the Heart—Enter the Heart

Before we finish this introduction, we would like to share some of our hesitations in presenting this book. We do so because we fully realize that there may be several topics and ideas that we have written in *Take Hold* that may easily be misunderstood. This may be due to a lack of clarity on our part, confusion or unresolved questions on the reader's part, or a combination of both. In that light, we implore you, the reader, to lend your ears to the message of our hearts as we attempt to clarify some of the important themes in this book.

Saved By Grace and Grace Alone

Since the subject matter of this book will largely be "the Torah," we need to clarify something extremely important. Traditionally many people have perceived the Torah as a set of rules to be followed in order to gain salvation. Not only do we intend to demonstrate the error of that perception of the Torah, but we also intend to proclaim the opposite. Consequently, we earnestly desire you to know from the start that we believe that no one, Jewish or non-Jewish, may earn or keep his eternal salvation by following the Torah. If you think that you are hearing otherwise, please know that we are definitely not perpetrators of such a concept! In short, we fervently believe that all are saved only by the unmerited grace of God through personal faith in the person and work of Yeshua the Messiah.

"Must," "Should," or "Have To"

Our hearts want to communicate something else that we think is important. In this exploration of the non-Jewish person's relationship to the Torah we have scrupulously avoided the use of "must," "should," and "have to," as these ideas are completely inappropriate to the issues at hand. The use of such words tends to open the door wide to the possibility of legalism. By "legalism," we mean the belief that adherence to the Torah is a requirement for obtaining and maintaining one's justification before God. Let it be stated once again for emphasis: We believe there is only one way to be forgiven for one's sin and to stand before the one true God as justified and righteous. That one way is through personal belief in the finished atonement accomplished in the death and resurrection of Yeshua of Nazareth, the Messiah. He is the way, the truth, and the life, and no one goes to the Father except through Him. (John 14:6)

Our teaching on the Torah is not about a way of salvation through obedience to its commandments, but rather biblical instruction for those who have been redeemed by Messiah. The Scriptures clearly define God's holy community as a people whom He Himself has set apart as a light to the nations. We refer to those teachings of righteousness, those instructions for living as a Redeemed community, as Torah. Therefore, if we take up the Torah as it truly is and live it, we are the holy community, living out who we are as God Himself defines us by His Word.

One may ask, "How can we engage in a meaningful exploration of this subject without once saying 'should,' 'must,' or 'have to'?" We can do so by examining a series of biblical passages that suggest that, at the very least, the relationship of the non-Jewish person to the Torah is one of *divine permission* and *encouragement*. That is, we believe that there is sufficient evidence in the Bible to show that God gives His permission for all gentile believers in Yeshua to fully identify with the Land, the People, and the Scriptures of Israel. Moreover, in granting such permission, He also provides all of the encouragement necessary for anyone who so desires to express outwardly their connection with the believing remnant of Israel.

The Uniqueness of the Jewish People

Our hearts want to say something else that is very important. We would like to remind our readers that although most of this book will focus on the unity between Jewish and non-Jewish believers, we need to remember that the physical descendants of Jacob are a unique people.

We will deal with some of this theological uniqueness in chapter 12. For now, let us simply say that we recognize that the physical descendants of Abraham, Isaac, and Jacob have a calling from God that sets them apart from the other peoples of the earth. This calling, in brief, has to do with the fact that the nation of Israel is to function as a teaching picture, instructing all of the peoples of the earth about the reality of the two spiritual kingdoms. One is the kingdom of darkness (Satan's kingdom) and the other is the Kingdom of God. We will expand on this later in the book. Moreover, it is clear that the people of Israel were also called to function as a light to the nations, shining forth the truth about the one and only God.

In addition, through the millennia, the people of Israel have also developed communities that, at their core, have attempted to reflect their Torah-based values. No other people in the world have survived so long, been through so much, and yet remained desirous of following the Torah. To be sure, sometimes their interpretation of the Torah can be criticized. Moreover, even the Messiah of Israel has some harsh words to say about some of the traditional teachings of some of the rabbis. However, do not let those pitfalls take away from the fact that it is the Torah that has kept this wonderful people together and it is they who have been the best guardians of the Torah.

Furthermore, during their wanderings throughout the face of the earth, the Jewish people have also developed a richly blended culture of their own. In fact, there are several Jewish cultures—Sephardic, Oriental, and Ashkenazic. These Jewish cultures are unique blends of Torah practices mixed with rabbinic applications and served in the appearance of the culture of the lands in which God has scattered them. Thus, we have everything from bagels to black hats, all of which are "Jewish."

Take Hold does not in any way intend to diminish the importance of Jewishness as a culture. Nor does it suggest—nor necessarily encourage—that a non-Jewish expression of Torah observance looks like any particular aspect of Jewish culture. The non-Jew's participation in the Land, the People, and the Scriptures of Israel does not necessarily mean that he adopts any aspect of Jewish culture.

This is a book in which gentile believers will be encouraged to "take hold" of their rightful equality with the remnant from Israel and learn how to live out their inheritance as fellow citizens with Israel. However, that does not mean that we are saying that such gentile believers are Jewish, nor even "spiritual Jews." They simply are not. To claim such a title diminishes the importance and honor of being from among the nations, and of being Jewish. We hope that the rest of the book will further clarify what we have briefly introduced here.

So, How Do We Do It?

Some may read this book and go away asking something like, "Fine. Thank you for encouraging me to take hold of the Land, the People, and the Scriptures of Israel. But *how* do I do so?" The answer to that question begins with establishing a biblical theology which, in turn, will provide a solid basis for any practical application that may follow. This book is our attempt to contribute to the establishment of such a biblical theology. More practical implications will have to wait for future books! We thought that it would be best at this point to provide the biblical basis for "taking hold" rather than describing *how* to "take hold."

For those of you who cannot wait for that next book, we strongly encourage you to seek out other literature being produced through the various authors and ministries of the Messianic movement worldwide. If it is important to you to pursue your "how to's" from the theological foundation which is presented in this book, you can seek out literature being produced by the First Fruits of Zion ministry. In the magazine, in the Torah Club, and in booklets, First Fruits of Zion's literature is designed specifically to provide some of those sought-after "how to's." Particularly helpful is a series of booklets called *Mayim Hayim*, which give practical ways for both Jewish and non-Jewish believers to live out the Torah from the standpoint of our being a new creation in Messiah. For further information, please refer to the final section of this book.

The introduction is now complete. You are now ready to work through the pages of this book. The following chapters are intended to demonstrate that throughout the different divisions of Scripture runs a common thread of understanding concerning the relationship of non-Jews to the Land, the People, and the Scriptures of Israel. While these passages originate from quite diverse locations in the Scriptures, we have been careful not to violate their context or intended meaning. We submit these teachings for your prayerful consideration.

Unit One

Taking Hold
According to the Torah

See, I have taught you statutes and judgments just as the Lord my God commanded me, that you should do thus in the land where you are entering to possess it. So keep and do [them] for that is your wisdom and your understanding in the sight of the peoples who will hear all these statutes and say, 'Surely this great nation is a wise and understanding people.' For what great nation is there that has a god so near to it as is the Lord our God whenever we call on Him? Or what great nation is there that has statutes and judgments as righteous as this whole [Torah] which I am setting before you today?

Deuteronomy 4:5–8

Chapter 1
The Covenants

Legally Binding Divine Relationships

The Bible is a unique history book. It records the factual story of not only the origin of the entire universe, but also of many of the people groups that inhabit the earth, specifically the people of Israel. But the Bible is concerned with more than just the history of people and human events. It is also the history of redemption. It tells the story of why people need redemption and how redemption is accomplished. Moreover, "the history of redemption in the Old Testament is marked by the ratification of covenants in which God affirmed His will for His people. A covenantal structure underlies the program of redemption."[7]

Thus, beginning with Genesis and scattered throughout the entire Tanakh are records of those legally binding agreements between God and His people that we call "covenants." These agreements are the basis upon which all relationships with the Holy One are built and maintained. The very existence of the nation of Israel is connected to a series of covenants with God. All of the other Scriptures that we will study find their fullest meaning within the context of the covenants that God made with Israel. As we examine these covenants, we will pay particular attention to how others besides Israel are involved with them. We have placed our discussion on the covenants in this part of the book because they are first revealed in the Torah.

Let us examine what is meant by the concept of "covenant" from both a historical and theological perspective. A better understanding of the biblical covenants will help us to see how non-Israelites may relate to Israel and the covenant of Torah.

A Covenant Primer

The Hebrew word for covenant is *brit* (ברית). While the original meaning of this word is somewhat debated, we do know that "the term *brit* came to mean that which bound two parties together."[8] In biblical times, there were several types of covenants. Some functioned between people, such as personal loans or wedding covenants; others, commonly known as treaties, bound together two or more nations. The covenants in the Bible itself represent agreements between man and God.

Common Features

By studying documents written in cuneiform on Ancient Near Eastern tablets, scholars have discovered that these ancient covenants have a great deal in common with those found in the Bible.

One such feature is a common language. For example, the covenants of ancient Mari, dating from the 18th century BCE, contain the phrase "to kill an ass in peace." This is reminiscent of the statement in Ezekiel 34:25 and 37:26, "to make a covenant of peace." We also learn that the Hebrew word for covenant, *brit*, had its equivalent in Akkadian, the language of many of the Mari documents. Furthermore, the ancient suzerainty treaties (international covenants) employed such phrases as "stipulations," "oath," "blessing and curse," and "witnesses." These same terms are essential to many of the important covenants in the Tanakh.

Another feature of many Ancient Near Eastern covenants was the *religious element*. "Fundamentally, most if not all of them had religious sanctions of some kind."[9] One identifying characteristic of religious or biblical covenants was that of being "concluded [ratified] by some special religious sanction."[10]

Because of this religious element in the ancient covenants, they also carried an important sacrificial motif. Animals were sacrificed both to the gods and for the mutual consumption of the covenanting parties. The meal, therefore, was a religious act. One common practice was for an animal to be sacrificed and all its parts cut in half. The symbolism illustrated a grave consequence for the party who failed to uphold the terms of the covenant: "'Just as this [beast] is cut up, so may X [the party who failed] be cut up.' The recitation of such a formula was probably in the nature of a self-imprecation. The man who recited it thus declared his expectation of the fate that would befall him if he broke his treaty obligations."[11]

With this in mind, those who are familiar with the making of the Abrahamic covenant (Genesis 15) will immediately see the implications of the vision God gave to Abraham. After commanding him to sacrifice some animals and dividing their parts, the Lord dramatically walked between the halved animal parts. Normally, both consenting parties in a covenant or treaty were required to walk through the parts, but in this case, it was God alone. The message was loud and clear: God had made an unconditional covenant with Abraham. Abraham was totally passive. He had no obligation other than to receive this covenant by faith.

Moreover, since only the Lord went through the parts, He also consented by oath to keep His promises to Abraham. If He should fail to keep even one, the same thing that had happened to the sacrificed animals would happen to Him. Since it would be impossible for God to suffer the same fate as those slain, dismembered animals, we know that this was simply the strongest way possible for the Holy One to assure Abraham that He would keep those promises. The practice of cutting up an animal was also the basis of the common Hebrew expression "to cut a covenant" (לכרת ברית). Without the knowledge of the Ancient Near Eastern covenant-making procedure, this passage would be very difficult to interpret.

One other feature common to the Ancient Near Eastern covenants is the use of covenant signs. When an ancient covenant was made, an appropriate sign often accompanied the event. This generally took the form of an outward, visible symbol that served to remind the parties of the covenant and its terms.

The sign of the covenant with Noah, the rainbow, signified that mankind would never again be destroyed by rain from the heavens (Genesis 9:12–13). In addition, from God's perspective in the heavens, the bow was held backward, an ancient sign by which warriors often indicated that a battle was over.[12]

According to Genesis 17:11, circumcision was a very appropriate sign for the covenant God made with Abraham. The fact that it was performed on the male organ of reproduction signified that the covenant was to be passed on through Abraham's descendants, who would come through Sarah (not Hagar).

Exodus 31:12–13 indicates that the sign for the covenant made with Moses was the Shabbat. Just as circumcision was a perfect sign for the Abrahamic covenant, so is Shabbat a remarkably accurate sign for the Mosaic covenant. God instituted Shabbat before the covenant was made (Genesis 2:1–2). Thus, as a sign, Shabbat indicates that in order to be related properly to God we need to rest completely in Him and what He has done for us. This is the message of Hebrews 4, where the writer equates the concept of Shabbat with the Good News of Yeshua. However, after we have entered into that rest (eternal salvation from sin), Shabbat becomes the reminder of these truths, giving us the key to living the true blessings of that rest. This key is found by walking out the Torah in a continual Shabbat rest, knowing that we are the finished work of Messiah. Shabbat teaches us that as new creations in Messiah, we can now cease from our striving to become what we already are—the righteousness of God. Now we are free simply to live out that righteousness which He Himself has created us to be. Therefore, living the Torah is simply living consistently according to our new true identity. This is the essence of the Torah, the covenant with Moses. All of these truths are woven into a proper understanding of Shabbat, making it the perfect sign for this covenant.

We are not certain of the sign for the covenant with King David in 2 Samuel 7. It is our opinion that the sign may have been "the House." The Lord promised that He Himself would establish a house for King David, indicating that his dynasty would never be completely lost. (Of course, it would ultimately be fulfilled in Messiah, the royal Son of David.) This promise immediately followed the king's expression of a desire to build a house for the Lord, i.e., the Temple. Traditionally, the sages have referred to the Temple as *haBayit* (הבית), "the House." During the period of the first Temple, there was always a qualified descendant of David to rule Israel. Accordingly, when Messiah—the true heir to David's throne—returns, one of the first things He will do is build the House again. In the meantime, we, the holy community, are that House; and Messiah, Son of David, sits on the throne.

What about the sign for the New Covenant? We will deal with this later in the book beginning on page 33.

A last feature of the Ancient Near Eastern covenants that we will examine is that which characterized many international covenants, the type of covenant known as the *suzerainty treaty*. This was a national covenant between a nation and its vassal or dependent nation. Scholars have discovered that the format for many of the ancient suzerainty treaties, such as those from the 13th and 14th century BCE Hittites, very closely parallels the format in which the Torah was written, especially the Book of Deuteronomy.[13] By comparing the two formats, we can see clearly that the Torah given to Moses was, indeed, a treaty between the "Great King"—God—and His people Israel. Understanding this treaty/covenantal format will help us to grasp more fully the nature of the covenants in the Bible, especially the covenant with Moses and the New Covenant—the stipulations as well as the blessings and curses. We will return to the subject of suzerainty treaties later.

The Biblical Covenants

Bible scholars are divided on the question of how many covenants the Bible actually contains. The following list, compiled by Dr. Clarence E. Mason, includes every biblical text that could possibly be termed a covenant. While many scholars would find Dr. Mason's list representative of the traditionally defined Bible covenants, we take issue with some of his examples.[14] The first two entries—the "Edenic" and "Adamic" covenants, respectively—are not called covenants, nor do they contain many of the characteristics of covenants. In addition, Dr. Mason refers to a so-called "Palestinian Covenant" (land covenant) in Deuteronomy. We believe that if he were to take into account the characteristics of a suzerainty treaty, he would not list this as a separate covenant. The covenants as put forth by Dr. Mason (and others) are listed as:

- *Edenic*—Genesis 1:26–28; 2:15–17
- *Adamic*—Genesis 3:14–19
- *Noahic*—Genesis 8:21–9:17, 24–27
- *Abrahamic*—Genesis 12:1–3ff.
- *Mosaic*—Exodus 19:5–8ff.
- *Palestinian*—Deuteronomy 28:63–68; 30:1–9
- *Davidic*—2 Samuel 7:12–16
- *New*—Jeremiah 31:31–34, Hebrews 8:6–13

Of these, we will examine only the Abrahamic, Mosaic, Davidic, and New Covenant.

1. The Covenant of Promise: Abraham

Theologian Thomas McComiskey refers to God's covenant with Abraham as the "covenant of promise," that is, its contents consist exclusively of promises given by God to Abraham, and to his descendants Isaac and Jacob (Genesis 12:1–3, 7). These include the promise of great personal, family, and national blessing, the promise of many offspring, and the promise of land.

This is strictly a grace covenant; Abraham did not earn, merit or deserve these promises and blessings. The only expected covenantal response from Abraham was faith—taking God at His Word (chapter 15). This passage also records the covenant ratification ceremony. This is the nature of the blood sacrifice as discussed above.

This covenant of promise is also one of eternal blessing, not only for Abraham but for his sons Isaac and Jacob, and eventually even to the nations. All other covenants between God and Israel were built upon this primary covenant. "Its continuing validity is affirmed in a number of passages in both the Old and New Testaments,"[15] such as Exodus 2:24, Deuteronomy 4:31, Psalm 105:8, Luke 1:72–73 and Galatians 3:15–17.

The Abrahamic Covenant establishes the paradigm for all of God's relationships with people. God is the One who makes promises to undeserving sinners. The covenantal blessings can only be secured by faith in the God who makes those promises. Thus, the Brit Hadasha uses the covenant with Abraham as an example of the covenant of salvation made with all who believe. For example, we read in Romans 4:11 that before Abraham was circumcised—that is, before he could do anything he could use to claim merit before God—he was justified by faith. Thus, "he is the father of all who believe without being circumcised, that righteousness might be reckoned to them, and the father of circumcision to those who not only are of the circumcision, but who also follow in the steps of the faith of our father Abraham which he had while uncircumcised." (Romans 4:11–12)

2. The Covenant of Dwelling in the Promise: Moses

God's covenant with Moses can be studied in two complementary ways: as compared to God's covenant with Abraham, and on its own as an independent suzerainty treaty. (This covenant, while technically containing more than the five books of Moses, is nevertheless generally referred to as "the Torah.")

If the covenant with Abraham is considered the covenant of promise, the covenant with Moses may be considered the covenant of dwelling in the promise. Participation in the covenant of Sinai (a term used interchangeably with "the covenant of Moses") did not secure the promises given as a grace gift by God to Abraham and his descendants. Rather, the Torah (the covenant) was given "to protect the people for the promise, to aid them in the pursuit of their destiny, and to provide the legal standards so necessary to an orderly society." Again, "Not only did the [Torah] covenant define and amplify the promise, but it served to protect and secure the promise as well....The [Torah] was not the promise; it is a covenant distinct from the promise covenant. It establishes the conditions under which the terms of the promise could be maintained."[16]

Sha'ul (Paul) uses a similar comparison between the Torah and the Abrahamic covenant in Galatians 3:10-23. In verse 11 he says that clearly, "… no one is justified by the Torah before God." The text goes on to tell us why. Because, "The righteous man shall live by faith." In other words, the righteous will come into life by faith (the Abrahamic covenant) and, having done so, will live out that faith through obedience (see James 2:18) to the Word of God (the Mosaic covenant).

In the midst of this passage (verse 12), we find the rather enigmatic statement that, to translate literally from the Greek, "The law is not of faith." Often misunderstood, this phrase is critical to understanding the relationship between the two covenants. If we translate the Greek word *nomos* (νομος) as "Torah" instead of "law," we realize that Sha'ul is simply comparing the two covenants—just as we did above—to make the point that the Torah could never impart life to sinful man. The Torah, rather, is life for those already alive in God. One can only become alive in God through faith. We may conclude, therefore, that obedience would be the expected response in the covenant of Moses.

The last part of verse 12 also needs some clarification: "However, the Torah is not of faith; on the contrary, 'He who practices them shall live by them'." By adding these words, Sha'ul was saying that the way to live out the life which has been imparted to us through faith is to follow the Torah. In no way did he mean that faith is not involved when people embrace the Torah in order to live by it.

Sha'ul concludes in verse 21: "Is the Torah then contrary to the promises of God? May it never be!" Here the rabbi places the final touches on his masterful argument by restating one of his main points: both covenants are entirely complementary to one another, and the covenant of faith must always precede the covenant of the Torah. In other words, we must always trust in God for our righteousness, and then allow that imputed righteousness to live itself out as we follow God's Word.

The following chart (Figure 1) summarizes the comparisons of the covenants with Abraham and Moses.

Covenant with Abraham	Covenant with Moshe
Nature of the Covenant Promise	Nature of the Covenant Blessing, maintenance, and enjoyment of promises
Covenant response Faith	Covenant response Obedience

Figure 1

The Suzerainty Treaty

Ever since George Mendenhall conducted his studies in 1954, serious biblical scholars have been interpreting the covenant with Moses by comparing it to Hittite suzerainty treaties from the 13th and 14th centuries BCE. At first glance, one might be skeptical of such a comparison; after all, how could a wandering horde of ex-slaves (the Israelites) even know of such treaties? We must remember, however, that their former masters were Egyptians. During the period of the Exodus from Egypt, the Hittites, who dwelt just north of the Promised Land, vied for power with the Egyptians for control of the Promised Land. They often fought each other, and therefore would have had considerable diplomatic contact with each other. Moreover, having been raised and educated in Pharaoh's court,

Moses would have been familiar with the format of Hittite treaties. Thus, even if the average Israelite was not well versed with such treaties, the leadership of Israel most certainly was.

The ancient Hittite suzerainty treaties were a form of covenant. However, "Treaties such as these were not party treaties, treaties made between equals. They were called suzerainty treaties, treaties between a great king and a vassal nation. In these the vassal nation entered into an oath of loyalty and trust to the king out of gratitude for *benefits already received*."[17] (italics ours)

The covenant of Moses expresses the same theme. God Himself is the Great King. His "vassal" nation is Israel. He entered into a covenant/treaty with them, not as an equal, but as One to whom Israel owed their entire existence. God expected loyalty and obedience because He deserved it! He graciously delivered them from bondage and made them into a free nation. The expected loyalty was based on all He had done for them.

The outline below shows how the Book of Deuteronomy follows the well-defined format of a suzerainty treaty, making evident the special covenantal pattern of the Torah.

> **Preamble (Deuteronomy 1:1–5)**—introductory remarks concerning the nature of the great king. In the case of Deuteronomy, the preamble identifies Israel's God.
>
> **Historical prologue (Deuteronomy 1:6–4:49)**—a recounting of what the Great King (God) has done for His vassal people (Israel).
>
> **Stipulations (Deuteronomy 5:1–26:19)**—the covenant expectations and the covenant lifestyle, based on the graciousness of the great king. In Deuteronomy, this is the bulk of the book, commonly known to laymen as "law" but, more accurately, the stipulations given by God, the Great King, to Israel for the maintenance of this covenant.

Blessings and curses (Deuteronomy 27–30)—the consequences of unfaithfulness to the covenant and the great king. Biblically, these are the results of Israel's unfaithfulness to God and to the covenant He made with them.

Witnesses (Deuteronomy 30:19)—Usually the great king would call upon an appropriate witness to sign the treaty. In the case of God and Israel, God calls upon heaven and earth to witness this covenant.

Succession (Deuteronomy 31:1–8)—This section provides for the continuation of the covenant in the event of the king's death. God designates Joshua to succeed Moses when he dies.

Deposit/reading (Deuteronomy 31:9–13)—There were usually two copies of the treaty, one for each of the parties. The copies were usually kept in the temple of their gods. Likewise, God made two copies of the covenant in summary form—the Ten Commandments. This was accordingly stored in the Holy of Holies.

Unique Features

Several unique features of the suzerainty treaty may shed more light on the Mosaic covenant. First, the treaty made a distinction between those who were parties to the treaty and those who were not. "The covenant alone distinguished between people dealt with by force and those according to normal peaceful procedures…those under the covenant enjoyed peaceful interaction with the sovereign."[18] This thought takes us back to an earlier point about the relationship between the covenants with Abraham and Moses. Specifically, it reminds us that the covenant with Moses was designed to help the recipients enjoy the blessings promised under the Abrahamic covenant.

The historical pattern of the Near Eastern treaty shows that it was not obedience to the law which resulted in the covenant and a relationship with God....The covenant was made and a relationship was formalized, again at God's initiative....They [the stipulations] provided guidelines in maintaining the relationship and indicated what was expected of one in covenant relationship with God.[19]

To some, this may smack of "legalism"—man's attempts by his own efforts to earn or merit his righteousness. Let us assure you that this is not the case. Legalism has absolutely no place in a covenantal relationship with God. Remember that all must enter into such a relationship in the same way that Abraham did. He was chosen by the grace of God apart from any merit on his part. In fact, God did not even choose him because of any foreseen faith that Abraham might exercise in the future; He made a sovereign choice based on His own criteria, not on anything within man. After God chose Abraham, He enabled him simply to trust or believe in Him. When Abraham did so, the promises were his.

When an individual enters the Kingdom of God by faith, he also enters the Abrahamic covenant. The Scriptures are clear in their teachings on this truth: this is the only relationship necessary for salvation. However, in order to live out that salvation (that new life imparted) in a manner consistent with the nature of that life, the individual lives according to God's covenant with His redeemed. This, then, is where the Mosaic covenant comes in. "All that the Lord has spoken we will do, and we will be obedient!" (Exodus 24:7) The covenant with Moses, as we have already stated, was not one through which a person could begin a relationship with God. It was, rather, a covenant wherein the believer enjoyed his relationship with God through his obedience.

Another characteristic of the suzerainty treaties is that the treaty/covenant implies the existence of a community.

God did not make the Mosaic covenant with a single individual, but with a nation. This nation was bound together with a common purpose and will. Moreover, the purpose and will of this nation was to be in complete harmony with God's purpose and will. The covenant was meant to help facilitate that end. In order for it to function properly, the whole community of God's people had to be united in living that covenant.

The Torah, then, was designed as a covenant both between the individual members of that community, and between those members and God (the other party in the covenant). Remember that God's plan for this holy community was that it would be a light to the nations around them. This is abundantly clear in Deuteronomy 4:5–8. Why else would this passage appear in the Torah if it was not God's intention for Israel to become that light? According to God's plan, once the nations recognized the light that they would see in Israel and chose to embrace Israel's God, they would want to become part of that covenant community. They were not supposed to start their own covenant community. They were merely added to the divinely appointed one, Israel.

The third characteristic of the suzerainty treaty is love. In the secular treaties, the graciousness of the great king initiated the covenant and he agreed to enter into such a covenant with a people who were in many ways subservient to him. Likewise, in the biblical covenant, it was the graciousness of God that caused Him to institute all of His covenants.

This is a crucial aspect of a covenant relationship which, unfortunately, few have grasped in regard to the Torah. As Deuteronomy 7:7–11 and 10:15 make abundantly clear, love is what motivated God to make the covenant at Sinai. In turn, He desired love in return from His people—whom He, by virtue of regeneration, made capable of both receiving and returning such love. The stipulations, laws, and decrees that He taught them were not only descriptions of their identity as the people of God, but also the genuine expressions of the love of their new creation hearts for their Redeemer.

In Deuteronomy 6:4–9, God said, "And you shall love the Lord your God with all your heart and with all your soul and with all your might." Who? You, the redeemed people— the regenerated ones who, in reality, do love the Lord your God with all your heart, all your soul, and all your strength.

Yeshua spoke about such love in John 14:15: "If you love Me, you will keep My commandments." He was directing His teaching to the portion of the remnant of Israel whom He was training to reach their fellow Israelites—and the nations—for Him. This was a key and an insight which Sha'ul would later expound upon: the keeping of the commandments was a demonstration of the new creation person's love for Yeshua.

God is not setting up a standard, per se, to which we must attain in order to prove our love for Him. Rather, the words Yeshua speaks to us are a mirror in which He shows us our new creation selves. Remembering this will help set us free from our old pattern of reading the Word of God as a performance-based acceptance document. The natural expression of that love is to live out our new life in Him through the stipulations, laws, and decrees of the Torah.

Therefore, looking at Yeshua's words through our understanding of who we are as new creations, He was saying, in effect, "If you are one who loves Me, then you are one who is regenerated. And in that regeneration, you are a new creation who keeps My commandments." An unregenerate human being cannot love God. One who is regenerate is, by virtue of his or her new nature, one who does love God. We are to know ourselves as ones who do love God.

Remember that Yeshua did not make this statement in a vacuum. When His followers heard the word "commandments," they were naturally thinking of the Torah of Moses, as well as Yeshua's comments on it. Thus, Yeshua's statement was also calling forth covenant faithfulness from them based on the covenantal principle of love. To love God means to be covenantally faithful to Him. This fidelity is always expressed by living God's teaching, His Torah.

The same principle, therefore, also applies to non-Jewish believers in that they are also new creations in Messiah. Yeshua was not attempting to call forth some kind of nebulous, gushy feeling from His people; He was calling forth covenant faithfulness. Because He always relates to His people through a covenant, this applies to everyone whom He calls His own.

So far, there are at least two deductions that we can make. First, we may say that the Torah is not a law code, but rather a covenant. When we compare it to the ancient law codes, such as that of Hammurabi and that found at Ur Nammu, we can easily see that although some of the stipulations may be similar, "the explicit covenant formulation of Exodus [chapters 19–24] and Deuteronomy stands as strong, direct evidence that this is a treaty or covenant and not a code of law."[20] Second, "the concept of covenant shows that all of the Torah material must be understood as the grace of God."[21]

Let us examine one last characteristic of the Ancient Near Eastern suzerainty treaties: the provision for renewal. When the covenant makers died and new generations took over, covenants were often renewed. "When covenants were renewed, new documents were prepared which brought up to date the stipulations of the earlier documents."[22] We see evidence of this in the Tanakh. For example, when Moses and his generation died, there was a covenant renewal, such as the one recorded in Joshua 24:24ff. *When a covenant was renewed, the stipulations were sometimes altered to fit the needs of the generation that was renewing the covenant.* However, "one covenant does not set aside another; one does not invalidate another so as to nullify its stipulations. Rather, it renews, expands, adapts, updates."[23] This is the point Sha'ul makes in Galatians 3:17ff.

3. The New Covenant

(Before we begin this section we would like to suggest as background material the work that Messianic Jewish scholar and teacher Dr. John Fischer has done in relation to the concept of the New Covenant. It is the best treatment we have seen to date on this subject and can be found in his unpublished paper, as cited in our Bibliography.)

God made three covenants with the physical descendants of Abraham: the Abrahamic, Mosaic, and Davidic covenants. As the First Temple period was about to come to a close, the Holy One addressed the house of Israel once more to describe a future fourth covenant with them, now known as the New Covenant.

The English title for this covenant is quite misleading. Oftentimes, to English speakers, the word "new" implies something which never existed previously. However, in both Hebrew and Greek, it can also mean a *renewing*. For example, in the phrase "new moon," the Hebrew word *chadash* (חדש) indicates a renewing of the appearance of the moon, as opposed to a brand-new creation.

We are saying, therefore, "it seems quite possible that Jeremiah intended the New Covenant to be viewed as a *Renewed Covenant*."[24] In fact, the New Covenant promises in Jeremiah 31 are actually repetitions of promises that God had previously made to Israel. Let us look at them.

1. *God's Torah*—Jeremiah 31:33
2. *"I will be their God and they will be My people"*—Jeremiah 31:33 (cf. Exodus 6:7)
3. *"They will know the Lord."*—Jeremiah 31:34 (cf. Exodus 6:7)
4. *Forgiveness of sin*—Jeremiah 31:34 (cf. Exodus 34:6–7)

5. *Creation of a new heart*—see our point in chapter 14 about regeneration in the period of the Tanakh.

In what sense then, can the New Covenant be called new? Remember that covenants were renewed to adjust to the situation of the generation that does the renewing. This factor comes into play when we attempt to understand the references to the New Covenant in the Book of Hebrews. While keeping the same basic promises as the "older" covenants, Hebrews says that it was necessary to make some "adjustments" to the new situation in which the believers now found themselves. Hence, there were several reasons why a renewing of the covenant was necessary.

(**Publishers Note:** From this point forward, the covenant, often called the "New Covenant," will be referred to as the *as* the *Renewed Covenant*. The Scriptures commonly called the New Testament will be referred to as the *Brit Hadasha*. This is done in order to avoid confusion when distinguishing between the **covenant** and the **Scriptures**.)

1. The Needy People

One reason the covenant needed to be renewed is that there was a problem with the previous one, as expressed in Jeremiah 31:32 and Hebrews 8:7. The problem, however, could not be found in the contents or terms of the covenant; how can something which the Bible describes as "holy, righteous and good" (Romans 7:12) have problems? As Hebrews 8:8 says, God "(found) fault with them…." These "people" were those of Jeremiah's day, when the revelation of the Renewed Covenant was given. Thus, when Jeremiah spoke forth the Renewed Covenant prophecy to the people of Judah, he did so not only to encourage the remnant of the house of Jacob, but also to rebuke those of the nation in need of rebuke.

The spiritual realities described in Jeremiah 31:32ff. had, in fact, been available through the Abrahamic and Mosaic covenants; because of their sin, however, the people did not realize or embrace those truths. As Hebrews 4:2 says, "For indeed we have had good news preached to us, just as they also; but the word they heard did not profit them, because it was not united by faith in those who heard." In other words, those people whom Jeremiah was rebuking had the correct information, but they lacked trust in God.

Even now, during the age of the Renewed Covenant—blessed with the complete revelation of how we are regenerated—many experience the same spiritual difficulties. How often are we truly aware of ourselves as new creations in Messiah, knowing that it is no longer we who live but Messiah who lives in us? This is the clear message of the Good News, yet so often we fail to mix that message with faith.

In its context, the Renewed Covenant prediction was directed to two groups of people within the house of Israel. First were the saints, the godly believers, who grieved the imminent destruction of their nation because of its sin. God, through the prophet, sent words of encouragement telling them that He Himself would keep His covenant with their nation by renewing it.

The second group of recipients consisted of those who, although fully aware of the terms of the covenant with Moses, nonetheless persisted in spurning them. In doing so, they earned a sharp rebuke in the form of this Renewed Covenant prediction. If they would repent, the terms described in Jeremiah 31— ancient as they were—would be theirs as a gift from God, as it had been planned all along. The Renewed Covenant reflected that needy spiritual condition of the people with whom it would be renewed: the house of Israel and the house of Judah.

2. The Finished Work of Messiah

In the fullness of time, God sent forth His Son. This moment—

the pinnacle of human history, prepared before the creation of time—is one of the main reasons for the Renewed Covenant. In the period of the Tanakh, the saints believed in that which they had only seen through the eyes of faith. Now this promised Messiah had become a historical reality.

Messiah's sacrificial atonement required some adjustments to the covenant concerning the animal sacrifices. For example, Hebrews 9:12 tells us that Messiah did "…not (enter) through the blood of goats and calves, but through His own blood, He entered the holy place once for all, having obtained eternal redemption." Yeshua's death and resurrection required a significant change in the covenant with Moses. This change was in the area of sacrifices and everything involved in offering them. That is why Hebrews 8:13 tells us, "When He said, 'A new {covenant}' He has made the first obsolete. But whatever is becoming obsolete and growing old is ready to disappear." The writer was referring to the sacrificial system, which had completed its original purpose in the covenant. Since Hebrews was most likely written before the destruction of the Second Temple at the hands of the Roman legions in 70 CE, the Second Temple was still standing, and sacrifices were still being offered. However, they were all fulfilled by Messiah's sacrifice. Accordingly, although still standing, that Temple was on the verge of a literal passing away through physical devastation.

Messiah's completed atonement is the central element of the Renewed Covenant. Those who participated in the "older" covenant could only look forward to what Messiah would do. Participants in the Renewed Covenant can know in a new way the rich reality of Yeshua and His work. Thus, Messiah is appropriately called "the mediator of a Renewed Covenant" (Hebrews 9:15).

Moreover, it was Yeshua's blood—that which actually accomplished the atonement—which was stipulated to be the sign of the Renewed Covenant (Luke 22:20). The sign for the

Renewed Covenant is the blood of Messiah. For those who participate in the covenant, it is His shed blood through which all of its promises are made real; shed blood which ended the continual flow of blood from the animal sacrifices of the previous covenant; and His shed blood which cleanses us from sin, enabling the deep, spiritual promises of the Renewed Covenant to become a reality for the one who trusts in Yeshua.

3. The addition of the gentiles

There was one other change in the situation of God's people that necessitated a renewing of the covenant: the addition of multitudes from the nations who would be grafted into the house of Israel. Previously, the numbers from the nations who were grafted in had been a mere trickle compared to what God began to do after Yeshua's death and resurrection. Sha'ul says that before Messiah came into their lives, the gentiles were "excluded from the commonwealth of Israel, and strangers to the covenants of promise." (Ephesians 2:12) Now, however, "the gentiles are fellow heirs and fellow members of the body, and fellow partakers of the promise in Messiah Yeshua through the Gospel." (Ephesians 3:6) Again, Yeshua becomes central to the renewing of the covenant.

We can examine the Scriptures as closely as we desire, but—with the exception of Noah—we will never see a covenant made specifically with the gentiles. How, then, do non-Israelites fit in? Is there a covenant for them? Of course there is; God always relates to His people through a covenant. However, contrary to what some might believe, the Renewed Covenant was not made especially for the nations. Jeremiah is clear that this Renewed Covenant is with the descendants of Abraham, Isaac, and Jacob. What about the new believers from the nations? Surely they do fit in—or, should we say, they are grafted in!

God has made it clear that His people are to relate to Him through a covenantal relationship, and the non-Israelites are no exception. For example, Genesis 12:3 tells us that Abraham is to be a blessing for all nations. Referring to this covenantal provision in Romans 4:11, Sha'ul says that in addition to being the father of the Jewish people, Abraham is also "the father of all who believe without being circumcised." It is through faith in the greatest Son of Abraham, then, that gentiles can claim Abraham as their father. Moreover, is it any accident that, in Colossians 2:11, Sha'ul uses the word "circumcise" to describe what happens to the flesh when we become new creations? He could have used other words, such as "separated" or "split." Instead, he chose the word "circumcise" to show this primarily non-Israelite congregation that, indeed, they are circumcised! They bear the mark of Abraham's covenant.

Fitting Into the Covenants

Thus, the Renewed Covenant also indicates not only that Abraham would have physical descendants, but also that among these descendants would be future children of the promise. Born of faith, they would then be new creations in Messiah, and would therefore be circumcised. Moreover, he would have additional spiritual descendants not of his physical seed. Both groups of descendants would experience what is described in Colossians 2:11–12 where we read,

> ...in Him you were also circumcised with a circumcision made without hands, in the removal of the body of the flesh by the circumcision of Messiah; having been buried with Him in baptism, in which you were also raised up with Him through faith in the working of God, who raised Him from the dead.

By way of interest, notice that this spiritual circumcision was also a spiritual reality for people during the time of the Tanakh (see Deuteronomy 10:16 and 30:6).

Having established how the non-Israelites fit into the Renewed Covenant, what about the covenant with Moses? Can gentiles participate in that? Yes! We will see shortly that this was true according to Deuteronomy 4. Here we read how it was God's intention that those from the nations would desire both Him and His Torah. Moreover, we will also learn that Isaiah 56 explicitly indicates that many from the nations would be bound both to the Lord and to the Torah, demonstrating their covenant faithfulness by observing Shabbat as God intended. Furthermore, any non-Jewish believer following the teaching of the Brit Hadasha is, in reality, following Torah (God's teaching). Specifically, however, the teachings of the Brit Hadasha are a continuation of the Torah that Moses gave to Israel. The few exceptions are due to the renewing of the covenant of Moses.

There is even gentile participation in God's covenant with King David. The Scriptures indicate that all who believe in Yeshua—both Jews and non-Jews—are inseparably united with Him. In the Brit Hadasha, the phrase most often used to indicate this relationship is "in Messiah." Thus, we are in Him, and He in us. By virtue of this union with David's greatest Son, non-Jewish believers are therefore made part of David's royal family. Could this be the reason that, as prophesied in Revelation 20 and 22, all saints in Messiah will reign with Him?

Another indication that non-Jews are to participate in the Davidic covenant can be seen in the short phrase that King David uttered upon realizing the full impact of the covenant that the Holy One was making with him. Implying that the covenant had significance for all mankind, he said, "*V'zot torat ha'adam*" ("וזאת תורת האדם"): "And this is the Torah of the people." (2 Samuel 7:19) The New International Version of the Bible does not even translate this phrase. However, both the New American Standard and Jewish Publication Society translations attempt to render it into English as "May it be the law for the people," and "This is the custom of man," respectively. Thomas McComiskey sheds further light on the subject:

> Taken in its simplest and most literal sense, the phrase may denote that the promise that David's house would continue is the established body of teaching for all mankind. There is only one body of teaching that relates the concept of the offspring to the destiny of mankind, and that is the promise given to Abraham. This understanding of 2 Samuel 7:19 emphasizes the continuity between the offspring of the Abrahamic promise and the offspring of David. Both are viewed as mediating the divine blessing to all mankind (cf. Genesis 22:18).[25]

The gentiles are also connected to the Davidic promise of a king, in that it is to King Messiah that they will direct their worship when He returns. According to Zechariah 14, the remnant of believers from the nations will flow to Jerusalem to worship the King at the feast of Sukkot.

Summary

After examining some of the characteristics of both the Ancient Near Eastern covenants and the biblical covenants, we have seen that God intends all people to relate to Him on the basis of a covenant. The last covenant He made with the people of Israel is commonly called the New Covenant. That covenant could just as accurately be referred to as the Renewed Covenant because it was nothing more than a renewal of both the Abrahamic and Mosaic covenants made with the house of Israel, carrying on elements of both of those covenants. Yeshua the Messiah was/is the central feature of this covenant. It is through personal faith in Him that all—both Israel and gentiles—enter into the Renewed Covenant.

Thus, although non-Jewish believers are very intimately connected to the Renewed Covenant, we must not view it as having been made apart from Israel and only with gentiles;

neither should we see it as annulling those covenants that preceded it. The best way to interpret the New Covenant is to understand it as the *Renewed* Covenant—the renewal of the covenant with Moses, in which the Torah is written upon believers' hearts. (Jeremiah 31:33)

Hence, believers from the nations can rightfully call Abraham their father. Because they have been made citizens of Israel, they also may truthfully refer to David as their rightful King. They may fully participate in the Torah as their lifestyle because, through the blessings of the Renewed Covenant as mediated by Messiah Himself, they also have the Torah—the covenant with Moses—written upon their new creation hearts.

The chart (figure 2) on the following page will provide a good summary of the contents of the covenants. Across the top we have placed the names of the four covenants God made with the people of Israel. Descending on the left side are the five categories that we are comparing. One important thing to note is that each succeeding covenant presupposes the existence of the previous one and incorporates and builds on the previous ones.

Miscellaneous notes about the following chart:

1. Scripture

There are more Scripture passages than the ones listed that speak about each covenant. Those on the chart are merely the representative passages.

2. Type of Covenant

An argument can be made that each covenant has both a conditional and unconditional aspect to it. We are therefore, speaking here in general terms. Moreover, as Dr. David Friedman noted, "Every covenant is in reality a covenant of grace because, in the end, God is going to perform this promise." For example, the covenant with Moses can be called a conditional covenant. Deuteronomy 30 indicates that despite Israel's unfaithfulness, God will bring them back to the Land, to Himself and to the Covenant.

3. Sign

Some people think that Yeshua's followers, demonstrating love and unity with each other, may also constitute a covenantal sign. Sounds great to us! In addition, the Renewed Covenant may also contain the signs of the previous covenants. For example, participants in the Renewed Covenant have circumcised hearts, are placed in an eternal Shabbat rest by the Messiah, and constitute the Temple of God upon whose throne the King sits. In addition to all of that, the Brit Hadasha indicates in Luke chapter 22 that the blood of the Messiah is also a sign of the Renewed Covenant.

4. Davidic Covenant

We have said little about the Davidic Covenant because it is not germaine to our topic.

	Covenant made with **Abraham**	Covenant made with **Moses**	Covenant made with **David**	House of Israel **Renewed**
Scripture The predominant biblical references of the covenant	**Genesis 12, 15, 17**	**Exodus 19–24**	**2 Samuel 7**	**Jeremiah 31 Hebrews 7–10**
Provisions The basic tenets or promises God makes in the covenant	**Posterity, Inheritance, Land, Greatness and Blessing**	**Blessings or Cursings**	**A Kingdom and a dynasty**	**All of the provisions of the previous covenants.**
Type of Covenant "Conditional," "unconditional," or "both"	Unconditional	Conditional	Unconditional	**Both Conditional and Unconditional**
Expected Covenantal Response "Faith" or "obedience"	Faith	Obedience	Faith	**Both Faith and Obedience**
Sign The outward symbols God gives for the covenant	Circumcision	Shabbat	"A House?" or a King?	**The blood of Messiah** (assumes the continual validity of the previous conventional signs)

Figure 2

Chapter 2
Deuteronomy 4

Divine Attraction

Now let us turn our attention to a critical passage in the Torah that focuses on the relationship between Israel—the covenanted nation—and the other nations.

The children of Israel were camping on the plains of the Jordan Valley opposite Jericho and preparing to take possession of the Promised Land. The Lord had called this nation to be separate and holy unto Him. They were to live the Torah before the surrounding nations as a mighty witness of the true God: who He was and how His people may relate to Him. God equipped Israel for this task in a number of ways. For example, He chose to situate the nation physically at the crossroads of the world: the Promised Land was an ancient and natural land bridge between Japan, India and China in the Far East, Africa in the south, and Europe in the north. Accordingly, many of antiquity's most traveled trade routes traversed the land of Israel, affording the Israelites ample exposure to people from all nations of the then-known world.

Furthermore, the Holy One provided Israel with the Torah. This body of writing contained provisions and instructions for relating properly to Him, living peacefully with others, and finding prosperity in the Land. If Israel had made the Torah their national lifestyle as God intended, all nations of the earth could have discovered this life and flocked to Him. As we read in the Torah itself:

> See, I have taught you statutes and judgments just as the Lord my God commanded me, that you should do thus in the land where you are entering to possess it. So keep and do {them} for that is your wisdom and your understanding in the sight of the peoples who will hear all these statutes and say, 'Surely this great nation is a wise and understanding people.' For what great nation is there that has a god so near to it as is the Lord our God whenever we call on Him? Or what great nation is there that has statutes and judgments as righteous as this whole Torah which I am setting before you today? (Deuteronomy 4:5–8)

Let us suppose, for a moment, that it had worked as God had planned. Picture this: a caravan of idolatrous non-Israelites passes through the Promised Land while traveling the Via Maris from Damascus to Egypt. While resting overnight, they take time to visit a Torah study group in a Jewish city in the Galilee. As they listen, they are astonished to hear the manifold wisdom of the Torah as expounded by one of the local Levites. Their hearts are softened to learning more about the God who spoke these words. They decide to stay in that city for a time. The longer they remain, the more they are amazed at the quality of life in this community of Israelites, especially as they observe the depth and beauty of Shabbat. So impressed are they with this

God-centered, Torah-guided life that they eventually decide to become part of it. Would it not be incongruous for the community elders to admonish these seeking gentiles, "You may have and know our God, but His Torah is for the Israelites only"?

How is it that these gentiles came to know God? He was revealed to them, through both the teaching of the Torah and the Torah-oriented lives of that Israelite community. Indeed, the text in Deuteronomy clearly implies that to accept Israel's God also means to live by the revealed wisdom of all of His Word.

Chapter 3
The Mo'adim

There is another crucial passage in the Torah that has important relevance to our subject. We have seen that God relates to people through the establishment of a covenant. We have just examined how God's covenanted people were designed to attract others to them and to their covenant. Now, we will look at how the covenant community was instructed to worship.

Both corporate and private worship are essential elements in our relationship with God. As believers of previous generations have wisely stated, the chief end of man is to worship God and enjoy Him forever. A person may worship God at any time and anywhere he chooses, for to worship God is merely to praise Him for all that He is and all He has done—from a simple and sincere *Baruch haShem!* ("Praise the Name [Lord]!") to a lengthy recitation of specific praises, spoken or sung unto the Lord.

But what about corporate worship? How does the holy community gather together in praise and worship? Interestingly enough, it is not in the Brit Hadasha that we are given specific instructions about God's provision for corporate worship (although, in light of what we know about biblical continuity, this should not surprise us). God's provision is clearly outlined in the Torah, and this pattern continues through Yeshua's lifetime and beyond. If God had intended any changes, He would have defined them clearly in the Brit Hadasha. Since He did not, we can only conclude that His design for worship in the holy community during the period of the Tanakh continues to be the norm for today.

The Cycle

The cycle of worship laid out for us in Leviticus 23 specifies a number of occasions on which God's holy community is to gather for corporate worship. The Hebrew word for this cycle— mo'adim (מועדים), or "appointed times"[26]—conveys the idea that God, in a sense, has a calendar. There are certain fixed days, both annual and weekly, on which He promises to meet in a unique way with His people Israel. In effect, by referring to these days as mo'adim, God is instructing Israel to mark these times on their national calendar. It is noteworthy that the singular, mo'ed (מועד), is also used to refer to the place of community worship and meeting, the Mishkan (Tabernacle). It is called ohel mo'ed (אהל מועד), or "tent of meeting," because God met with His people there in an extraordinary way. What a remarkable thing—the eternal God, the Creator of the universe, so desires to meet with His people that He actually makes special plans to do so.

God called Israel to assemble on these days for two main reasons. The first was for each individual to remember something that the Holy One did for him/her and to render Him praise or thanks for it. (With the exception of Yom Kippur, a solemn occasion, the mo'adim are occasions of great joy.) The second was that Israel, as a corporate body, was to remember what God had done for them as a nation, both physically and spiritually. God designed the cycle of the mo'adim to proclaim in every generation, year by year, the Good News of the Messiah and His work of redemption in our lives (see also Hebrews 4:2). Accordingly, it should not surprise us that the Lord commanded these special days to be observed "throughout your generations wherever you live" (Leviticus 23:14, 21).

What about the non-Jewish members of God's family? Are they to be left out of the singing and the dancing, the celebrating of the Lord's redemptive work in their lives? Are they to be denied gathering for special meals, hearing the *shofar* (ram's horn) sound, or living for a week in a special *sukkah* (booth)? Yet these are the specified times of worship taught in the Torah and which Yeshua celebrated with His *talmidim* (disciples).

The history of redemption and the worship of the Redeemer were clearly intended to be celebrated by all of God's people through the mo'adim. This includes the believers from the nations, as they are part of that same redemptive history. Let us look briefly at just one way in which celebration of the mo'adim can benefit the entire body of Messiah.

A Teaching Schedule

How does the local believing fellowship teach all the essential doctrines of our faith during the course of the year? In some congregations, it is not easy: the tight preaching and teaching schedules of many pastors and leaders can make it difficult to find time for some of the Bible's most precious theological truths. This problem can be solved, however, by following the calendar of mo'adim in Leviticus 23. Let us see how this works.

Shabbat

On this day, including the *erev Shabbat* (Friday night) celebration, we have an opportunity to enjoy the reality of Messiah's atonement and to bask in the truths of Yeshua our Messiah, grace, and eternal life. When Shabbat is properly observed, all the fullness of Hebrews 4 and Isaiah 58 is reemphasized, and time is set aside to practice walking out who we are as a new creation holy community.

Passover

Teaching concepts for this mo'ed would include redemption, salvation, deliverance, freedom, slavery to sin and Messiah as our Savior and Passover Lamb. Moreover, the Passover *Seder* is the most appropriate time to observe the "Lord's Supper," since that, in fact, is what it originally was.

Feast of Unleavened Bread

This special time, considered part of Passover itself, begins on the first night and continues for a full seven days. The emphasis during this week is on the truths of 1 Corinthians 5:6–8 and Galatians 5:7–10, which stress the concept of sanctification. For believers, "all that detracts from their holy newness of life is an example of the leaven of sin…the real significance of leaven is shown in 1 Corinthians 5:7 as being destructive and typifying what does not belong originally and essentially to life, namely sin. It is sin disturbing and penetrating daily life."[27] This week is set apart that we may face the issues of sin. The skills practiced during this week carry over into our lives during the remainder of the year.

Waving of the First Fruits

These are the First Fruits spoken of during the week of Unleavened Bread. Many believe that it was on this day that Yeshua rose from the dead. Therefore, this is a good time to celebrate Yeshua's resurrection and our identification with Him in that resurrection (Romans 6:1–6). On this day, the Torah instructs us to wave a sheaf of barley grain before the Lord. In the Scriptures, the chaff of the grain is the symbol of our sinful flesh. As new creations in Messiah, we are like the pure kernel of grain covered over by the "chaff," that is, a veil of flesh.

Throughout the week of Passover, because we are dealing with that chaff, our all-knowing and wise *Abba* (Father) has ordained that in the midst of this particular week of having to focus on sin, we would celebrate this day of First Fruits. The theological teaching for this day consists of the truths and realities of our salvation, which teach us about God's unconditional love and acceptance. We, the pure grain with our chaff, are to know ourselves acceptable before the Lord. The process that He Himself has designed in our lives with which to confront our "chaff" is also acceptable before the Lord. This understanding, a crucial and healthy element of our freedom, enables us to confront our sin directly and honestly. This is the time that we teach the truths of Colossians 2:11–12 and are reminded of them ourselves.

Shavu'ot

Biblically, this is another First Fruits celebration. According to rabbinic thinking, this is also the time of year when the Torah was given on Mount Sinai. Moreover, it was also on the Shavu'ot following Yeshua's resurrection that the early believers were anointed and empowered with the Spirit of God so that they could take the Good News out to the entire world.

These three concepts combine to form an exciting picture. We can see that God would have us study the nature of written revelation (the Bible). In doing so, we will learn how God equipped the earliest followers of Yeshua with the power of the Word of God and the power of the Spirit of God to bear fruit for Him. Since it was a First Fruits mo'ed, we know historically that God indeed brought in a magnificent First

Fruits "offering" of new believers in Yeshua—about three thousand, we are told (Acts 2:41).

Accordingly, Shavu'ot is an ideal time for the holy community to study specific aspects of the Word of God, such as the nature and ministry of the Spirit of God, and the spreading of the Good News throughout the world (possibly including a discussion of the Book of Acts). It is also an opportune time for believers to explore their identity in Messiah and the relationship between Jewish and non-Jewish believers in God's holy community.

Yom Teruah (Rosh Hashanah)

This is the day when God instructed His people to assemble together to hear the blowing of the shofar. Judging from the biblical usages of the shofar, this is a most appropriate season for believers to be discussing spiritual warfare and the coming of Messiah.

Yom Kippur

The translation for this Hebrew phrase is "Day of Atonement." Yom Kippur is the best time to learn about the concepts of sin, atonement, sacrifice, substitutionary atonement, and forgiveness. A study of Hebrews 7–10 is also most appropriate. This day is specially set apart to celebrate the reality that all sins of the flesh that we will have to face this year have been fully paid for in Messiah's finished and complete atonement. The Day of Atonement also helps us address the issues of the flesh and to know ourselves separate from (Colossians 2:11–12) and free from "the sin that so easily besets us." (Hebrews 12:1)

Sukkot

This last of the mo'adim weaves together all the themes of the entire cycle. Of particular relevance are the concepts of harvest and God's provision, as well as the study of eschatology and the exodus motif.

Moreover, the week is specifically designated for joyous worship and celebration: building the family sukkah, singing and dancing inside it, seeing the glow on the children's faces as they sit cozily with those they love the most. It is a week set aside for living in our sukkah, talking about the Lord and what He has done, and allowing the Spirit of God to blend the whole community into close-knit fellowship with Him and with each other. As the holy community participates in this mo'ed, it will not be difficult to follow the Lord's commandment in Leviticus 23:40: "…and you shall rejoice before the Lord your God for seven days."

For the Children

In addition to providing a theological education for adults, observing the mo'adim affords creative avenues for the training of the children in the local fellowship. The Jewish community has known this secret for years! The rest of us would do well to follow such a God-ordained example.

Senses and Stories

As children experience the theological truths of the mo'adim, their celebration involves all five senses: they smell the challah on Shabbat, taste the special foods of Passover, feel the coarse texture of the barley sheaf, hear the sounds of the shofar, and see the sukkah being built. Each and every mo'ed is designed for the physical senses, through which knowledge of truth enters the heart.

Children often learn best through stories, and the cycle of mo'adim is just that: the story of Israel, retold year after year. It is the story of who God truly is and how He loves us; how He relates to us; and how He intervenes, rescues us, and sets us free—free to be who He Himself has made us to be. It is also the story of redemption.

Moreover, there are other stories that are also appropriate to tell during the mo'adim. These are stories about Israel, the Jewish people and how their lives were affected by each of the mo'adim. Some of these are true stories, some not. But they all help to enliven the child's experience of the mo'adim. The *Anthology Series* by Philip Goodman (Jewish Publication Society) is a great resource for stories that the gifted teacher can use to make learning an enjoyable and child-friendly experience.

The mo'adim have been brilliantly designed by Abba to bless His children (of all ages) with the perfect settings in which to participate in truth.

Come and Dance!

As we have been saying all along, the special days in Leviticus 23 form a cycle. If we were to draw this on a piece of paper, we would first draw a circle. Like a circle, the cycle of mo'adim has no beginning and no end; these times are always with us, year in and year out. And what do we do in circles? We dance! The cycle of mo'adim is like a dance circle. If you have never participated, the best place to begin is—anywhere!

We would like to issue a special invitation to those of you from among the nations who believe in Yeshua to join the dance circle. We feel a bit awkward inviting you because, in reality, this is your circle too. In the past, for a number of unbiblical reasons, you have been denied permission to participate in this dance. Still, it is not too late. Come experience the joy of the mo'adim with us. You can join the circle anywhere you like. What we know about the dance, we can share with you. In fact, we will all learn to dance better together—the way it was meant to be.

Thus, to all of you who love the Messiah and are not naturally born of the house of Israel, this circle is also for you. Come dance with us!

The Cycle of Sanctification

The use of the word "mo'adim" in Leviticus 23 indicates that these special days are not only God's appointed times and seasons for His people to gather and remember His gracious and mighty acts of the past, but also times to look forward to His sovereign works in the future. Moreover, they are appointed times and seasons in which we can experience His love and grace now—in our daily lives.

God's mo'adim are not only a cycle of redemptive history, but a cycle of spiritual growth as well, guiding the believer to new levels of spiritual maturity through their interaction with truth. When we participate in the yearly pattern of Holy Days as God intended, we will discover one of the least known secrets of the cycle: we will find that this participation is a major key toward growing in the grace and knowledge of our Messiah. These are uniquely appointed days in which the Lord our God will carry out His process of sanctification in our lives, setting us free to walk more fully in who we are as new creations in Messiah. To put it in more familiar terms, this cycle is not a mere repetition of Messianic prophecy, but a pattern for personal freedom: a cycle of sanctification. The one who chooses to live out this cycle, year after year, will discover the deep spiritual meanings inherent in the mo'adim.

Summary

Are these appointed times, which result in a life of worship, for the people of Israel alone? That is a difficult question to answer. Without a doubt, they have special relevance to the descendants of Abraham, Isaac, and Jacob. They are unique reminders of their historical relationship with God. As such, their observance could mean very little to those who are non-Jews.

The situation, however, changes when those disinterested non-Jews become believers in Yeshua. At once, they are placed into an entirely different relationship with Israel, and therefore with the celebrations of Israel's history, the mo'adim. Because of their union with the Messiah of Israel, all believers—whether they are aware of it or not—have come into a special relationship with His people, the people of Israel. When we read about how severe the Egyptians task masters were, how can we sit unmoved with compassion? Likewise, when we celebrate the mighty work of deliverance that God did for Israel, who is able to contain the joy? These are stories of Yeshua's people. These, therefore—because we have Messiah in us—become redemptive acts for which all believers in Yeshua can praise God.

In addition to the historical aspect of these special days, we should not forget that they are biblically referred to as mo'adim. Since they are specially appointed times when God promises to meet with His people, does it not make sense that God would never intend to exclude any one of His own children from these special meetings? If the Scripture is true that, in Messiah, Jews and gentiles are both equal and one with each other, then it would follow that when God designates a specific time at which to meet with His people, that would include all of His people—both Jewish and non-Jewish believers in Messiah.

There is one more aspect to this subject. There is no special revelation in the Brit Hadasha instructing the believers from the nations concerning the times when they were to gather for worship. One fair assumption is that there was no need for such instruction since that subject was already covered in Leviticus 23.

In light of that, we concur with Messianic leader Barney Kasdan, who writes about the relevance of these mo'adim to both Jewish and non-Jewish believers in Yeshua:

> It is, I believe, a tragedy that the Christian community has not understood, for the most part, the rich heritage on which its faith is built. Many believers, however, rediscovering these connections, are wondering just how they can understand the Jewishness of their faith in a practical way. The biblical holy days are a pragmatic way. These feasts were revealed by God for his own particular reasons, and through them all believers can be blessed, Jews and gentiles.[28]

Thus, through the cycle of mo'adim, we believe that God grants permission to all non-Jewish believers to take hold of their divine inheritance with Israel and to participate fully with their fellow Jewish believers in one unified and blessed celebration of His mighty acts of history.

Please allow us to take this point one step further. If we can agree that there is divine permission for non-Jewish believers to participate fully with their brothers and sisters from the remnant of Israel in celebrating the cycle of mo'adim, can it not also be said that there is divine permission for them to follow other teachings of the Torah as well? Why single out the mo'adim? Are not the other visible practices of the Torah designed for the benefit of those who believe in the one true God? Yes, they are. (Please refer to *Torah Rediscoverd* and other materials produced by First Fruits of Zion for more details on this subject.)

We are ready to move on to the next section of revelation—the Prophets. Let us summarize what we have established thus far upon examining the revelation in the Torah.

We have looked at three aspects from the Torah which all have one thing in common—they stress the fact that God was building a holy community. This community of called-out ones individually and corporately related to Him through covenants. These provided the pattern for all future relationships—all are to relate to God through a covenantal relationship.

We also examined Deuteronomy chapter 4. Here we saw that it was God's express intention to draw gentiles into the holy community as they learned and beheld the Torah lived out by the people of Israel. The Torah was meant to be God's book of wisdom and teaching of righteousness for the gentiles as much as for Israel.

Finally, we asked the question, how does the holy community worship? The Torah had a great deal to say on the matter. We explored Leviticus 23 and the cycle of mo'adim to see what implications they had on the subject of worship as it was practiced by God's people. Here we learned many of the fascinating ways that all of God's people—both Jewish and non-Jewish—can worship the Redeemer and pass on the message of redemption to the next generation.

Let us now move on to the Prophets in order to see what they have to say about how the believers from the nations of the world relate to Israel and Israel's Scriptures, the Torah.

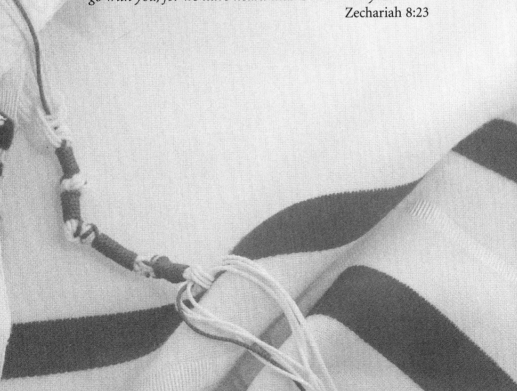

Unit Two

Taking Hold
According to the Prophets

Thus says the Lord of hosts, "In those days ten men from all the nations will grasp the garment of a Jew saying, 'Let us go with you, for we have heard that God is with you'."

Zechariah 8:23

Chapter 4

Isaiah 56

Participants in the Covenants

Let us examine God's revelation after the period of the Torah. Sometime between the late 600s and early 700s BCE, the Holy One raised up the prophet Isaiah, perhaps the greatest prophet of Israel/Judah. The words of Isaiah were given with the intention of admonishing Israel and Judah to forsake their sins and live by the covenant of the Torah. He also encouraged the faithful remnant of believers to continue in their faith in God and in the covenant.

However, Isaiah had a message for the nations as well. Part of his message consisted of words of rebuke and warning, as chapters 13–23 indicate. On the other hand, particularly in chapter 56, we also find words of encouragement for the remnant of gentiles who followed the God of Israel. Indeed, this remarkable passage merits our close attention.

Chapter 56 of Isaiah opens with an encouragement to the remnant of Israel to continue following the covenant of Torah. The prophet calls upon them to "maintain justice and do what is right" as well as to "keep the Shabbat." These are words that we might expect a prophet of Israel or Judah to speak to the Jewish people. Notice, however, whom Isaiah is addressing in verses 3 and 6. He speaks about "the foreigner"—but not just any foreigner. These foreigners have *bound themselves to the Lord.* In other words, the prophet has some important things to say to non-Jewish believers.[29]

First, Isaiah tells these non-Israelites (non-Jewish believers) that the Lord Himself will be certain to include them with the remnant of His people among Israel. This is the thrust of 56:3.

Second, because these non-Israelite believers share a portion with Israel, Isaiah reminds them that the Lord will grant them access to "My holy mountain." In addition, He will accept their offerings at the Temple, because "My house shall be called a house of prayer for all nations." (In the Hebrew, the word translated here as "nations" is *amim*—literally, "peoples.") In other words, God was doing all He could to assure these non-Israelite believers that they were on *equal footing* with Israel, the people of the covenant. Yet, He refers to them not as Israel, but as foreigners!

Third, notice how Isaiah describes the lifestyle of these believers from the nations. He characterizes them in verse 6 as people "who keep the Shabbat without desecrating it and who hold fast to My covenant." This is an utterly remarkable statement to make about believers not born physically into the nation of Israel. It implies that, although they cannot be called "Jews" because of their birth, yet, because of their relationship with the Lord they are entitled to follow the Torah—and even encouraged in their observance! In addition, they are described as participants in "the covenant." This could be either the covenant with Abraham or the covenant with

Moses made at Mount Sinai, or both. Since the context is a discussion of Shabbat, the sign of the covenant with Moses, perhaps we can assume that the reference is to the covenant with Moses.

Finally, in verse 8, Isaiah—looking beyond his present situation—prophesies concerning the generations to come. "The Sovereign Lord declares—He who gathers the exiles of Israel: 'I will gather still others to them besides those already gathered'." At the very least, the Lord was promising that many from among the nations would believe in Him, thereby becoming a part of Israel. This would include living by the Torah! When would this happen? Certainly, the fulfillment of this prophecy was beginning to happen during the period when the events recorded in Acts took place. But the ingathering of the gentiles has been taking place in increasing numbers ever since then. Perhaps this prophecy will be ultimately fulfilled when Messiah returns.

Chapter 5
Zechariah 8

Those Who Take Hold

There is a second main passage from the prophets which bears heavily on our theme. The prophet Zechariah ministered approximately 200 years after Isaiah. He spoke to the people of Judah after their exile in Babylon was over. "The temple was still unbuilt, the walls and city of Jerusalem lay in ruins; the people were constantly exposed to the hostility of their neighbors; there was no sign of the predicted prosperity of Israel; and Judah was still under a foreign yoke." Accordingly, "The visions and prophecies of the book of Zechariah concern themselves largely with the messages of *comfort* and *consultation* God gave in answer to the intercession of the angel of the Lord on behalf of the people of Jerusalem and Judah."[30]

In the midst of these messages of encouragement to Israel, Zechariah has some fascinating predictions for the remnant of believers from among the nations. Let us see how this unfolds.

Can you imagine a day when Jerusalem will be so characterized by correct teaching and sound doctrine that it will be called "the city of truth"? Can you also picture a time when the Lord Himself will dwell in Zion, seated on the throne of David? Can you envision an era when the land of Israel will produce abundant grain and wine in total peace and security, when farmers and merchants will not have to worry about thieves and cheats stealing their products and destroying their businesses? Finally, are you able to see a day when people from all over the world will have the ability to travel to the land of Israel without fear of terrorists or political hostilities?

Such a scene may sound impossibly perfect; however, if you read the predictions described in Zechariah 8, you will see that our description tells only half the story! This passage is replete with a description of an age of peace, security, blessing, and hope when Messiah will be King, reigning on planet earth from the city of Jerusalem. It is a time yet to come, to be enjoyed and experienced by countless numbers of people completely dependent on the finished work of the Messiah. These promises provide more than ample hope and encouragement for faithful followers to live in the present.

Let us focus, for a moment, on the last prediction of this remarkable chapter of biblical prophecy. Of that same period, the Millennial Kingdom, verse 23 says, "ten men from all the nations will grasp the garment of a Jew saying, 'Let us go with you, for we have heard that God is with you.'" Some unusual features of this prophecy deserve particular attention, as they carry critical implications for the body of Messiah today.

Ten to One

This passage foretells a time when many non-Jewish people, having heard that God is with the children of Israel in a unique way, will seek them out in order to receive a blessing. Although the word translated "people" is sometimes rendered "men," the Hebrew itself is not gender specific; women will also participate in this search. Furthermore, the words commonly translated .as "from all the nations" literally mean "from all the tongues of the *goyim* (gentiles)." Thus, the number of gentiles seeking Jewish people will not be limited to the nations that are in the world, but will include all languages, nations and tribes as well.

Finally, although it is not possible to be dogmatic on this point, the prophet can be understood to be speaking of a mathematical ratio of up to ten seeking gentiles for every Jewish believer! This is another indicator of the size of the multitude who will be called out from among the gentiles to seek the people of Israel.

Only Those Who Follow the Torah

These vast numbers of gentiles will not be satisfied with finding just any Israelite; they will be seeking those Jewish people who live according to the Torah.

Again, we must turn to the Hebrew for the full meaning of this point. The New American Standard Version reads, "In those days ten men from all of the nations will grasp the *garment* of a Jew...." (italics ours) The Hebrew tells us specifically what part of the garment the gentiles will grasp: it is called a *kanaf* (כנף). This word literally means *corner*. Why would someone want to grab the corner of another's garment unless there were something special about that part of the clothing? It is safe to assume that where the text mentions the corner of a Jewish person's garment, it is in reference to that person's fringes.

The people of Israel are instructed in Numbers 15:37–41 to attach a fringe to each of the four corners of their garments. These fringes are to serve as visible reminders to the person who wears them; to remind him/her to follow the Torah and, in doing so, to follow God alone (15:39). Those who wear them are motivated by a love for the Torah and a sincere desire to live it in their everyday lives. Thus, the gentiles who will seek after the Jewish people are described as taking hold of the *tzitzit*, or fringes, that are part of a Torah-practicing Israelite's clothing.

In other words, Zechariah foresees a time when gentiles from all over the world will desire to attach themselves to Jewish people—specifically, those Jewish people in whose lives the Torah occupies a place of special importance. Might we also say, therefore, that Zechariah is predicting a day when gentiles will have an insatiable desire to be identified with the Torah of God (signified by the tzitzit)? This will be a day when God Himself will reveal to His people (both Jewish and those grafted-in from the nations) the true nature of the Torah and its relationship to our identity in Messiah. And when, having received the revelation of their identity as new creations in Messiah, they will want to learn how it is that the Torah lifestyle is designed by God Himself to help us on a daily basis to live out our new identity in Messiah.

This prophecy makes it quite clear that when gentiles find such a Torah-observant Jewish person, the ensuing attachment will not be merely polite or casual. The word we translate as "take hold" has a root meaning of "strong," *chazak* (חזק). When used as a verb, as it is in this verse, it can be rendered "to grab hold of something very tightly, or with much strength." This represents real determination on the part of the gentiles to participate in the life that their Jewish brother is living and thus be included in the blessing that their Torah-observant Jewish counterparts are experiencing.

Individuals from among the nations of the world, then, will be seeking the Jewish person whose Torah observance is consistent with that of the Living Torah Himself. In other words, the gentiles will seek to be closely united with Torah-observant Jewish believers in Messiah Yeshua.

The context of these great promises includes other

unfathomable and glorious predictions that still await us. It is a millennial passage, finding its ultimate fulfillment in the next age—the age of Messiah's reign on earth. Having understood the contextual time of fulfillment, does this passage have any valid application for life in the body of Messiah in the here and now?

Two Kinds of Remnants

If the Messianic movement began with tens of thousands "…among the Jews of those who have believed, and they are all zealous for the Torah" (Acts 21:20), and if the same can be said—as Zechariah does—concerning the remnant of believing Jews in the future millennial age, can we not experience this same zeal in the present age? We are surrounded by two great legacies of Torah-observant Jewish believers in Yeshua, both past and future; it only makes sense that this is a valid position for today's Jewish believers as well.

What application does our passage have for the multitude of believers from among the gentiles? Again, we must look to the past—with an eye to the future—to determine how to live in the present.

According to Acts 15, the early Messianic community included a number of gentiles. In fact, the leaders in Jerusalem wrote a letter of encouragement to some of these, introducing them to those aspects of Torah observance most conducive to fellowship with Jewish believers. As true shepherds, these men knew the reality of Yeshua's words, "My sheep know My voice and they follow Me." They knew that the gentile believers would be present in the synagogue service every Shabbat; that, listening to the Torah, they would hear their Shepherd's voice and follow the Words of Life. Thus, these leaders merely reminded them, "For Moses from ancient generations has in every city those who preach him, since he is read in the synagogues every Sabbath." (Acts 15:21)

The holy community embraced the earliest believers from among the nations. As new believers in Messiah, they were born into a Torah-based and Messiah-centered community. There was simply no other expression for their community life. It was a community of Jewish and non-Jewish believers celebrating their inheritance together.

When we look at Zechariah's prophecy concerning the future of the Messianic community, we find a similar picture. The difference is that the Messiah Himself will physically live in the midst of the community, and the community will have perfect biblical understanding: it will be the millennial age.

Thus, in the past, non-Jews were welcomed into the Messiah-oriented Torah community as equal participants in the grace of God, encouraged to live by the Torah; the same will be true in the millennium. So why not now, in this day and age? The best way to think through this question is to practice simple biblical continuity.

Not only will there be a time in the future when gentiles of all nations will diligently seek out Jewish believers and hold tightly onto their Torah, but this has already begun to happen. Even as we write, scores of non-Jewish believers are seeking out the Torah God gave to Moses, asking, "Is there something here for me, too?" They are asking from within their own hearts a very insightful question: If the Torah of Moses was God's revelation of righteousness, teaching the redeemed community how to live, is it not the same for the redeemed community in every age?

Chapter 6
Ezekiel 47

A Place in the Land

It is relatively easy to see how the Torah and the prophets teach that believers from among the nations can have a meaningful relationship with the people and the Scriptures of Israel. Can they also have such a relationship with the physical land of Israel? We will study one more passage from the prophets in order to ascertain an answer to this question.

Lest there be any doubt about the new relationship between non-Jewish believers and the covenanted children of Israel, let us turn to Ezekiel 47. Here the prophet looks far ahead of his own time to the coming Messianic age, when Yeshua will be seated on the throne of David in Jerusalem. This will also be the time, according to Ezekiel, when the final land inheritance is divided among the people of Israel. However, as we see in verses 21–23, believers from among the remnant of the nations will desire to live among the people of Israel.

The Lord at that time will instruct Israel with the following word regarding the distribution of the inheritance:

> "So you shall divide this land among yourselves according to the tribes of Israel. And it will come about that you shall divide it by lot for an inheritance among yourselves and among the aliens who stay in your midst, who bring forth sons in your midst. And they shall be to you as the native-born among the sons of Israel; they shall be allotted an inheritance with you among the tribes of Israel. And it will come about that in the tribe with which the alien stays, there you shall give {him} his inheritance," declares the Lord God.

Do you see what God is teaching here? He is instructing the Israelites regarding their relationship with those who have come to live among them. They are so grafted in that they are to be considered native-born Israelites, with full rights of inheritance. If non-Jewish believers can be entitled a parcel of land (and all related responsibilities the Torah requires) among the people of Israel in the Messianic Kingdom, surely they may be permitted to enjoy the blessings of the Torah among the people of Israel right now!

In Summary

The prophets built upon what lay in seed form in the Torah. In their ministry of either rebuking or encouraging Israel, the great men of God also spoke of God's plan for the remnant of believers from among the nations. What they said was truly remarkable. They told how there would be such a remnant who would not only follow the Lord God, but would also seek to be meaningfully connected with the remnant of God's people, Israel, through participating in Israel's covenants.

Moreover, the prophets also predicted that in the last days there would indeed be great numbers of gentile believers who would take hold of Messianic Jews and want to walk beside them on an equal footing. Finally, we learned that the prophets also saw into the distant future to a time when the remnant of believers from among the nations would also desire to live in the land of Israel. Speaking on God's behalf, the prophets told the gentile believers that they had God's blessing to walk in all of those desires; they had divine permission to take hold of their inheritance with Israel and live in it.

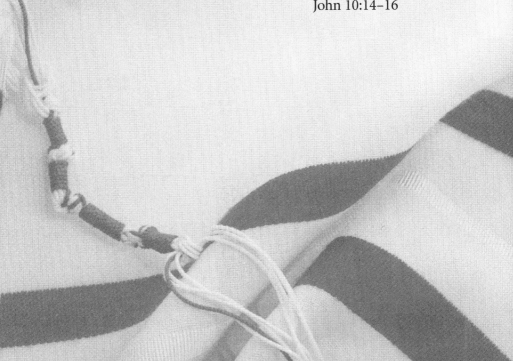

Unit Three

Taking Hold
in the Gospels and Acts

I am the good shepherd; and I know My own, and My own know Me, even as the Father knows Me and I know the Father; and I lay down My life for the sheep. And I have other sheep, which are not of this fold; I must bring them also, and they shall hear My voice; and they shall become one flock with one shepherd.

John 10:14–16

Chapter 7
Matthew 5 & 28

Training Torah Teachers

If we were to end our study right at this point, there would be very little argument about our thesis. The teaching and tenor of the entire Tanakh all point to the fact that God has—at the very least—given believers in the God of Israel who are from among the nations divine permission to be an intimate part of His remnant of believers from Israel. In doing so, He has also granted them His blessing to take hold of the Torah and to live their lives according to the Torah.

Having established what the Tanakh teaches, our next consideration will be the fact that all believers in Yeshua earnestly desire to follow the teachings of their Messiah. Therefore, we will examine what He has to say on the issue. Furthermore, how did His first followers understand the matter? The purpose of this next unit is to look into some of their teachings and actions to learn what they thought about the relationship between Jewish and non-Jewish believers in Yeshua to each other and to the Torah.

It is not surprising that Yeshua taught very little about this relationship. He Himself said that He was sent unto the lost sheep of the house of Israel (Matthew 15:24). However, two important passages have bearing on our topic. Both have to do with Yeshua's teaching which he instructed His students to pass on to others. We have decided to include these passages in one chapter, since they are related.

Yeshua's Torah Theology

The first passage we will study is Matthew 5:17–19. Undoubtedly, this chapter in the Gospel of Matthew is one of the most significant places in Scriptures that reveal Yeshua's thoughts about the Torah. In these verses, Yeshua had several points to make on the subject.

A Forever Torah

First, He taught us that His coming did not do away with the Torah. This is the simplest way to understand Him when He says, "Do not think that I came to abolish the Torah or the Prophets... not the smallest letter or stroke shall pass away from the Torah, until all is accomplished."

To gain a more accurate understanding of this passage, we must remember to translate the Greek word for "law" correctly. Yeshua was not teaching about a law. He was instructing about the Torah. Accordingly, the Greek word *nomos,* should be rendered "Torah."

The Proper Interpretation

There is a deeper sense in which we can understand these words. In fact, according to the Jewish background of the passage, there is a more accurate way of interpreting it. When Yeshua said that He did not come to abolish but to fulfil the Torah, He meant that He came to give the Torah its fullest meaning. In other words, Yeshua came to interpret the Torah properly.[31]

This understanding surely fits the context. If we were to read through the rest of this whole passage (Matthew 5–7) we would find an oft-repeated statement by Yeshua that runs something like this: "You have heard that it was said…but I say unto you…." With these words Yeshua was not introducing a greater or higher teaching than Moses, as is often claimed. Rather, He was in a continual debate with some of the Torah teachers of His day concerning their understanding of various instructions found in the Torah. When Yeshua said, "You have heard," He was citing the oral tradition that many Torah teachers had received and were passing on to the people. Then when He added, "But I say unto you," the Messiah was giving the people the proper, original, God-intended meaning of the particular Torah passage in question. Much of the oral tradition had interpreted the Torah erroneously. Yeshua was setting the matter straight, as the Torah teacher *par excellence*!

Blessings for Torah Teachers

There was a third important concept that Yeshua was conveying to His students in this passage. He said in verse 19, "Whoever then annuls one of the least of these commandments, and so teaches others, shall be called least in the Kingdom of heaven; but whoever keeps and teaches [them], he shall be called great in the Kingdom of heaven." The commandments in question would have to have been the *mitzvot*, (מצוות) or "commandments," which are found in the Torah, since that is the literature being discussed in the context.

There are two important concepts here: First, Yeshua rebukes those who do not practice the commandments and who teach others not to practice them as well. Conversely, Yeshua promises a reward for those who not only teach the commandments, but who also practice them. What else can these words mean but that Yeshua is teaching his students the importance of studying the Torah, living it out, and helping others to do the same?

Please pay careful attention to this next point. What Yeshua said in this passage takes on ever greater importance when we realize that this was, in essence, a teacher-training session. His students were the ones who would carry His teaching to the ends of the earth. They would therefore have, taught the Torah to other Jewish people. But it also implies that the Torah was to be the textbook of instruction for non-Jews as well. In addition, as verse 19 indicates, learning the Torah was not just to be an intellectual exercise, it was taught with the intention that its precepts would constitute the lifestyle of all who would receive its instruction.

The Disciple-Making Textbook for the Nations: Matthew 28:19–20

Closely connected with the teaching of Matthew 5:17–19 are the ideas found in Matthew 28:19–20. In the first passage, the Messiah laid out His Torah theology, so to speak. In this latter section, we learn how deeply He thought about the Torah and how much He desired all His followers to learn it.

Just before returning to His Father's throne, the Messiah gave careful instructions to his *talmidim* (disciples):

> Therefore, go and make people from all nations into talmidim, immersing them into the reality of the Father, the Son and the Ruach HaKodesh, and teaching them to obey everything that I have commanded you. (Matthew 28:19–20 JNT)

This passage, often referred to as the "great commission," contains points frequently overlooked by Bible teachers.

First of all, we need to remember that this passage was among the final instructions that Yeshua gave to His students. Accordingly, it represents some of the teachings that are most dear to His heart. Foremost among these is His concern for people other than Israel. In the companion teaching found in Acts 1:8 we have the same priority repeated again—the mandate to take the Good News of Yeshua into all parts of the world and to make disciples of all peoples.

Second, notice what Yeshua instructed His students to teach to all of their disciples—the Torah. Actually, the text indicates that Yeshua refers to these teachings as "My commandments." Bear in mind that Yeshua was most likely speaking either Hebrew or Aramaic (both closely related Semitic languages common in the late Second Temple period in Judea) to His followers.[32] In doing so, Yeshua would have used the word *mitzvot*, which we have translated "commandments." Most people would have understood the word "commandments" to refer to the directives given in the Torah. In other words, Yeshua was instructing His followers to teach the Torah (the teaching on God's righteousness) to those gentiles who would believe. This is perfectly consistent with the prophecy of Isaiah 56 that we examined in chapter 4.

Some may argue that Yeshua was telling his followers to teach their future disciples Yeshua's commandments, not the ones from Moses. In reality, however, they were one and the same! Even if it could be argued that Yeshua taught some things that Moses did not, whatever He taught would have been totally consistent with Moses's teaching. In addition, a good argument can be made to suggest that whatever "new" things Yeshua taught were nothing more than expansions and practical applications of Torah concepts.

Yeshua proves to be the most able Torah commentator who ever lived; moreover, simply because of who He is, He puts many of the implied and explicit Torah teachings into the form of commands. Hence, Yeshua's expression "My commandments" most likely refers to the Torah (which, in fact, consists of Yeshua's commandments given to and written down by Moses), as well as to Torah teachings which He now reformulated as commands. A good example of this is in Matthew 28:19–20. This passage is not a direct quotation from the Torah. Yet, it most certainly reflects the entire thrust of the purpose of the revelation of the Torah—to make Israel the light to the nations.

Summary

We have examined two important passages from the teaching of Yeshua that reveal His viewpoints concerning the Torah. What we have uncovered is that Yeshua declared that there is great reward for all of those who teach and live out the Torah of Moses. Moreover, among His final instructions to His students, He told them that the Torah was to be their primary textbook as they made disciples of all who would believe their message about Him.

We know from history, of course, that Yeshua's followers took their message not only to their fellow Jews who were scattered throughout the Roman world; but to non-Jews as well. How, in fact, did those believers from the nations relate to the teaching of the Torah? This is the thrust of the next chapter.

Chapter 8

Acts 15

Introducing the gentiles to the Torah

The next important passage relating to our subject is Acts 15. To be sure, this has not been an easy passage to interpret. It is, however, an important passage for us, as it contains a record of how the non-Jewish believers were received by the early Jewish followers of Yeshua. There is much we can learn from this passage about the relationship of non-Jewish believers to the Torah.

First of all, Acts 15 indicates that no one may follow the Torah—Jewish or gentile—in order to achieve justification. Concerning this salvation, the leaders confirmed that "He made no distinction between us and them, cleansing their hearts by faith." (verse 9) This council decided that no gentile had to be circumcised or follow the Torah in order to be considered part of God's family and held in good standing among the holy community. To demand such prerequisites would be to subscribe to legalism, encouraging the belief that a person may earn his eternal salvation through obedience to a set of standards that he/she performs.

The Torah, of course, does not teach legalism. In fact, the faith of the people of Israel itself began as a "grace" religion. The common teaching of first-century Judaism—although not always apparent in the letters of Sha'ul—was that

> "election and ultimately salvation are considered to be by God's mercy rather than human achievement." Pinchas Lapide, a Jewish scholar of Brit Hadasha studies, concurs: "The rabbinate has never considered the Torah as a way of salvation to God....[we Jews] regard salvation as God's exclusive prerogative, so we Jews are the advocates of 'pure grace.'" [33]

The problem with early Judaism, therefore, was not so much theological as practical. In everyday life, the Torah, rather than faith, was seen as the means of obtaining the promises of God. Even today, Judaism is, "on paper," a grace religion; yet its daily application appears most often to be quite legalistic.

So then, if there was a tendency even among Jewish people to misunderstand the purpose of the Torah, how could we expect greater discernment from those unfamiliar with the Torah itself? In the case of the new believers from the nations, while some believed they had to follow the Torah in order to be justified, others were convinced they had to follow it in order to maintain their justification before God. As Acts 15 makes clear, the leaders of the Jerusalem Council did not subscribe to either of these forms of legalism.

A History of Torah Seekers

That so many from the nations have desired such a relationship with Israel and the Torah should not surprise us. There was apparently much more "missionary" activity among the gentiles from the Jews during this period than most people realize.

The Scriptures refer to the Temple as the house of prayer for all nations. This is vividly illustrated for us when we examine the practice of many gentiles in the late Second Temple period. There is a great deal of evidence supporting the fact that many gentiles made pilgrimages to the Temple from outside of Israel. Neither the impurity, which Jews imputed to their heathenism, nor the injunction against their partaking of food deterred gentiles from making the pilgrimages to the Temple or from having sacrifices offered there. Tradition and practice rendered gentile sacrifices acceptable; often, particularly on feast days, gentiles could be seen at the Temple. They came to prostrate themselves before God, to hear the Torah, and to bring their offerings.[34]

Phoboumenoi and Seboumenoi

Doctoral candidate and Messianic educator Patrice Fischer has studied the relationship between Jews and non-Jews in the late Second Temple period.[35] From this study, she outlines at least three groups of gentiles. The first group could be classified as pagans with no visible interest in the God of Israel, the Scriptures of Israel, or the people of Israel. (Some, however, were most certainly interested in the land of Israel—to conquer it, that is!) The second class of gentiles, known as proselytes, were at the opposite end of the spectrum: so attracted were they to the God, the Scriptures, the people, and even the land of Israel that they wanted to become part of Israel in a formal way. Consequently, they were willing to embrace everything necessary to do so, even to the point of circumcision.

There was, however, a third group who loved Israel so much that for all practical purposes they became part of it. However, they stopped short of undergoing physical circumcision. Messianic Jewish scholar Dr. David Stern describes these gentiles, known in the Brit Hadasha as *phoboumenoi* (φοβουμενοι), or God-fearers. The appellation "God-fearer" did not simply refer to one's morality or ethics, rather

> A God-fearer is regarded by most scholars as a technical term describing a gentile who attached himself to Judaism but chose not to undergo formal conversion, which included circumcision and public immersion (proselyte baptism). This class of gentiles, known in Judaism as "proselytes of the gate," was quite large at this time [the late Second Temple period]. They were attracted to the nobility of Jewish worship and to the truth of the one God who had revealed himself in the Bible but for various reasons did not become Jews.[36]

In addition to observing that the word appears five times in the Book of Acts, Fischer counts six instances of an apparent synonym, *seboumenoi* (σεβομενοι)—sometimes paired with *theon* (θεον)— "to denote gentile adherents to the Jewish faith who were not proselytes."[37] The most famous example of such a God-fearer was Cornelius of Acts 10. Fischer continues:

> It cannot be emphasized too strongly that the first gentile believers mentioned in the Book of Acts are from this special and technical realm of God-fearers and are NOT gentiles who only felt warmth and attraction to the God of Israel. The God-fearers already had received considerable Jewish training and had made a considerable Jewish commitment.... These formergentile pagans who were now known as God-fearers were already practicing the Torah in their everyday lives.[38]

Hence, the God-fearers did not need to be introduced to the Torah, other than to learn how it speaks of Yeshua and other Messianic applications. The reason for this is that they already were studying the Torah. Moreover, the God-fearers formed a large share of the core of the congregations founded by Sha'ul. They were not, for the most part, pagans converted overnight.[39] Most important, the Scriptures give no indication that any of the God-fearers mentioned in the Book of Acts gave up their Torah observance after becoming believers in the Messiah of Israel.

The Leaders' Counsel

Part of the instruction that the Jerusalem leadership decided to lay down for the non-Jews who were believing in Yeshua consisted of a letter that they sent to those largely non-Jewish believing congregations. This letter is recorded in Acts 15:23–29, but is summarized in verses 20–21. In essence, they told the gentile believers that they were "to abstain from things contaminated by idols and from fornication and from what is strangled and from blood" (verse 20). All of these instructions were Torah-based, if not specific commands from the Torah of Moses. The question is, why did the leaders single out these specific commands and not others? Was this to be the extent of the Torah instruction the gentile believers were to receive from their Jewish brothers and sisters?

One possible answer is that these four instructions were just a version of the Noahide laws. This, in our opinion is not the best interpretation. The first reason is that the Noahide laws were formulated by the sages to be a means for gentiles to obtain righteousness. In other words, "Our rabbis taught, 'the sons of Noah [gentiles] were given seven commandments: practicing justice and abstaining from blasphemy, idolatry, bloodshed, robbery, and eating the flesh from a live animal.' Rabbi Hananiah ben Gamliel said, 'Also not to drink blood taken from a live animal'." (Sanhedrin 56a)[40]

We know that the leaders of the Jerusalem believers would never agree to this kind of theology. They lived and died for the doctrine of salvation by grace through faith.

There is a better way to understand the thrust of what the leaders were attempting to do. To understand this interpretation, we need to keep in mind the kind of gentile believer to whom these instructions were written. We know from our discussion about the relationship that both the proselytes and the God-fearers had to the Torah, that they were not the recipients of these requests. Their Torah knowledge was well beyond the elementary teachings of this letter sent by the Jerusalem leaders.

However, the third group of gentiles, the pagans, had no such Torah instruction. Accordingly, we are suggesting that it was to gentiles from a pagan background that Acts 15 was directed. The wise Messianic leadership wanted to introduce these new believers, who were ex-pagans, into the Torah slowly and carefully. The Jewish elders in Jerusalem were doing everything possible to demonstrate wisdom in discipling these Torah-illiterate, non-Jewish believers. The Jewish believers had grown up with the Torah; many had significant portions of it memorized. It was their life and breath, their joy and heartbeat (see Acts 21). To many from the outside, however, the Torah was a strange book. Many had never even been exposed to it before receiving the message of Messiah. The Jerusalem elders knew this. They also knew that the only existing body of teaching for believers, Jewish or non-Jewish, was the Tanakh.

Why were these specific Torah instructions chosen to be sent to the ex-pagans? We agree with the suggestion provided by Dr. David Stern,

> ...they were primarily practical social requirements for fellowship between Jewish and gentile believers. A gentile who did not immediately observe all four prohibitions would so offend his Jewish brothers in the faith that a spirit of community would never be able to develop.[41]

This understanding carries more weight when we realize how important "table fellowship" has been all throughout the history of the Near East, including this present day. The deepest and longest-lasting relationships were formed sitting around a table eating a common meal. That was, undoubtedly, when the best fellowship took place among the believers. Because of this, the Messianic leaders wanted to do all they could to foster the best possible fellowship between two groups of people who traditionally had been suspicious of and antagonistic toward each other.

Moreover, we also need to remember that historically Jewish people have not readily accepted gentile table fellowship. Peter Tompson, referring to scholars Strack and Billerbeck, states the issue succinctly when he writes:

> Social intercourse with non-Jews was practically impossible....Only reluctantly, one would enter a non-Jewish house; and a Jew would feel even more uncomfortable when having a Goy in his own home. Hence table fellowship of Jews and Goyim was hardly possible, whether the Israelite was host or guest.[42]

There is no reason to assume that Jewish sensitivities diminished after they became believers in Yeshua. Those who were Torah observant before coming to faith continued to be observant as believers—only now they practiced mitzvot without legalism.

Therefore, given the great difficulties that existed in establishing essential table fellowship between Jewish and gentile believers, it was necessary that some of the first Torah instructions given to the former pagans were those which were conducive to establishing fellowship with their new Jewish brothers and sisters.

Give Us More Torah!

The plan of the leaders in Jerusalem, however, may have been more than just to create table fellowship. There is a strong hint of this in 15:21. Following the teachings in verses 19–20, the elders made this rather cryptic statement to the gentiles: "For Moses has been preached in every city from the earliest times, and is read in the synagogues on every Shabbat." What is the meaning of this comment? It seems to make very little sense—unless we understand it as the elders' encouragement of those non-Jewish believers to continue in their study of the Torah. And since Torah instruction was available in the local synagogue of almost every city in the Diaspora, this would not have presented a problem.

In other words, the Jewish elders were telling the non-Jewish believers that, as they participated in the holy community and in the synagogue on a weekly basis, they would grow in their understanding of the Torah. Thus, in their wisdom, they knew the reality of Yeshua's teaching that "My sheep know My voice and follow Me." The Torah is the voice of Yeshua, and these young lambs would hear and follow.

If our understanding is correct, notice the kindness and wisdom of those great Messianic shepherds. The gentile believers who used to be pagans needed to be taught the Word of God, which at that time was only the Tanakh (including, of course, the Torah). But since the Scriptures were so foreign to these ex-pagans, the leaders' plan was to introduce the Torah to them slowly. First, they would give instruction that would facilitate table fellowship. Then, they directed these precious new believers to the place where they would have been able to learn the Torah to their hearts' content!

Let us state this in slightly different terms. By delineating the four Torah-based instructions for table fellowship in Acts 15:19–20, the wise and loving elders were saying to the non-Jewish believers: "You are our equals in the body of Messiah. Our teachings are your teachings. It will take some time, however, for you to begin to understand the Holy Book. For now, you need only concern yourselves with what will best facilitate fellowship between you and your Jewish brothers and sisters. You will gradually learn more of what it means to walk with God. We will send qualified men to teach you the Torah."

From this we conclude that, far from minimizing the role of Torah in the life of non-Jewish believers, Acts 15 provides ample encouragement for them to continue in the Torah and to learn it at their own pace.

Unit Four

Taking Hold
According to the Letters
of Sha'ul of Tarsus

So then you are no longer strangers and aliens, but you are
fellow citizens with the saints and, are of God's household...
                                                    Ephesians 2:19

Chapter 9
1 Corinthians

Former Pagans and the Torah

By many accounts, Corinth was one of the most pagan places to which the Good News of Yeshua was brought. It is often thought that the constitution of the Messianic community in Corinth also reflected that blatantly non-Jewish culture. Even a cursory reading of I Corinthians reveals problems—even among the believers—of incest, idol worship, and divorce.

The student of I Corinthians will observe yet another peculiarity in this letter from Sha'ul. Much to our surprise, I Corinthians reflects quite a Torah-educated community of believers. From a closer look at the rabbi's letter, we see that the Corinthian fellowship is "[a] good example of a congregation that failed even in these basic instructions"[43] sent by the leadership in Acts 15. The problem, therefore, was not that the Torah was never taught to them; they simply failed to obey it properly.

There is an important lesson in this for all believers, especially for those who sincerely desire to live out the Torah. As we will see, the Corinthians were not Torah ignorant. They probably even celebrated Passover, as well as following other teachings of the Torah. However, in their zealousness to follow the Torah as they were learning it, it seems that they lost track of other Torah teachings besides the outward ones. They failed to apply the Torah principles of justice, holiness, and integrity. These Torah teachings are every bit as important as the more visible ones such as wearing the fringes or celebrating a mo'ed. Yet the Corinthians were not consistent in letting these Torah qualities be the mark of their lives. Let us not follow their example. Rather, let us who express faith in Yeshua, the Living Torah, allow the written Torah to lead us to truth, justice, holiness, and integrity. In short, let us all make sure to let Yeshua live out His life in us and through us at all times. Embracing the Torah, then, means much more than simply beginning to celebrate Shabbat and the other mo'adim, wearing tzitzit, or eating kosher.

What Torah instruction did the Corinthian congregation receive? Judging from the material in I Corinthians, a fair amount—and from an excellent teacher. Consider, for example, Sha'ul's remarks on leaven, as well as his references to Yeshua as the Passover sacrifice and the Passover Lamb, in chapter 5. Furthermore, notice his observations (in chapter 10) on the important third cup of wine drunk during the ancient (and modern) Passover Seder, in which he calls it "the Cup of Blessing," the second and least known of its names. In addition, depending on one's interpretation, mark his references to the Passover Seder itself in his admonitions in chapter 11. Finally, Sha'ul not only refers to the exodus story in the beginning of chapter 10, but he does so in typical rabbinic fashion—by making a *midrash* out of it.

How can we account for so many references and allusions to the Passover story? The history of the Corinthian fellowship may provide us with some clues. According to Acts 18:8, the ruler of the synagogue and his family became believers. In addition, the man who lived next door to the synagogue, a gentile, was called "a worshiper of God" (18:7). The Greek word used here is *seboumenos* (σεβομενοs). A near synonym for God-fearer, this is a technical phrase indicating that he was a non-Jew who lived a Jewish lifestyle and worshiped the God of Israel.

Nowhere does the text indicate that these two people—a Jewish person and a gentile—were instructed to leave their Torah-centered lifestyles behind upon becoming believers. In fact, as verse 11 informs us, "Paul stayed for a year and a half [in Corinth], teaching them the Word of God." What was the "Word of God" that Rabbi Sha'ul knew, studied, memorized, lived, and taught? It was the Tanakh, including the Chumash (the five books of Moses). Thus, in light of the strong biblical influence in this congregation and the length of time that Sha'ul spent there, we can assume that they received much instruction from the Torah. But their instruction was not merely for the sake of head knowledge; we are suggesting that they were taught how to apply the Torah to their corporate and individual lives. Accordingly, Sha'ul most likely led them in at least one Passover celebration while he was with them.

In Acts 18:13 the unbelieving Jewish population accused Sha'ul saying, "This man persuades men to worship God contrary to the law." This statement can be interpreted in either of two ways. One is to interpret the word "law" (*nomos*) to mean Jewish or rabbinic law, as opposed to the Torah. It is true that the word "nomos" usually means Torah, but it can also encompass any legal system, such as rabbinic law. Indeed, Sha'ul was definitely teaching the people under his care to conduct their lives and worship in a manner different from that which the rabbis commonly accepted. He was not, however, teaching contrary to the Torah of God.

A second interpretation is that the rabbi's accusers were accusing him of breaking Roman law. It is for this reason that they accused him before the Roman proconsul, Gallio. While they may have been debating Jewish or even biblical law within the confines of the synagogue, if a case was brought before the Roman ruler, it undoubtedly must have involved a question of Roman law.

Gallio's response is quite enlightening for us. His decision was that Paul was not guilty of breaking Roman law. As he saw it, the case was merely a Jewish religious debate. "What Paul was preaching, in his view, was simply a variety of Judaism that did not happen to suit the leaders of the Jewish community at Corinth but which was not for that reason to be declared *religio illicita*."[44] Since the teaching of Sha'ul of Tarsus was regarded by the Roman legal authorities as a sect of Judaism, then it can be reasoned that Sha'ul was teaching like a Jew, instructing his listeners in Jewish ideas and themes. Of course, the foremost of these Jewish themes was the Torah.

In summary, we see in 1 Corinthians considerable evidence that the Torah was taught to a predominantly non-Jewish congregation of believers in Yeshua. We also believe it was taught in such a way as to include the celebration of Passover—an indication that the Corinthians had a biblically based lifestyle.

To be sure, the Torah that Sha'ul taught was applied in a unique way in order to meet the special halakhic needs of the Corinthians. Nonetheless, the Torah of Moses was the primary tool of instruction for their faith and practice.

Chapter 10

Romans 11

Grafted In

We have seen that the Torah itself made provision for the non-Israelites to relate to it. We have read Isaiah's magnificent prophecies to the remnant of believers from among the nations concerning their relationship to Torah and Israel's covenant. We have learned that Yeshua as well as Sha'ul of Tarsus instructed His followers to teach the Torah to the non-Jews; and we know that the elders of the young Jerusalem fellowship laid down a number of principles to help the non-Jewish believers in their pursuit of Torah.

Now we come to one of the most important passages concerning the relationship between non-Jewish and Jewish believers in Yeshua, Romans 11:11–21. To be sure, this passage does not speak of the Torah. However, it does teach that gentile believers have a significant relationship with Israel.

It is only a matter of reasoning that, since non-Jewish believers are closely connected to Israel, they may also have a close connection to the Torah—just as Deuteronomy 4 implies.

In Romans 11:11–21, Sha'ul provides one of the most exciting truths in the Brit Hadasha for non-Jewish believers. Elsewhere, he had described unbelieving gentiles as those who were uncircumcised, foreigners to the covenants of the promise, without hope, far away (Ephesians 2:11–13) and pagan idol-worshipers (1 Corinthians 12:2). In contrast, because of what Messiah Yeshua did for these countless numbers of non-Jewish people, they have now been brought near and "grafted in" to Israel.

There is some difference of opinion among scholars about into what exactly the gentiles are grafted. Some say that they, along with Jewish believers, are grafted into Yeshua. However, since Yeshua represents the nation of Israel, even as the High Priest represents the nation Israel on Yom Kippur, then, it would seem that by being grafted-in to Yeshua would also mean the same as being grafted-in to Israel. But biblical scholar Marvin Wilson takes issue with this interpretation when he states,

> But this view confuses the expression "root of Jesse"…or "root of David"…with "root of the olive tree." The flow of the context supports the conclusion that the root represents the patriarchs: Abraham, Isaac, and Jacob, the faithful Forefathers of the Jews.[45]

If it is correct, then this passage is telling us that non-Jewish believers in Yeshua have a significant relationship with Israel through being grafted into the olive tree of Israel. Again, let us permit Wilson to summarize this beautiful truth for us:

Thus the church, firmly planted in Hebraic soil, finds its true identity in connection with Israel. The church is fed, sustained, and supported by that relationship.[46]

On an Equal Footing

What are some of the implications of being grafted in? One of the lessons that the passage teaches us is that Jewish and gentile believers are now on an equal footing with each other. The text in Romans 11:17 says that gentile believers "have become a partaker with them [the Jewish believers] of the rich root of the olive tree." The word translated by the NASB as "partaker" is the Greek word *sugkoinonos,* (συγκοινωνος). The Greek root is a word that has been used to mean "to be connected with something...in the sense of actually taking part."[47]

Thus, "According to Romans 11:17, the gentiles who are like branches grafted into the olive tree of Israel now share in its election and promises."[48] Moreover, it is not just a casual sharing. Both groups are very intimately bound together in this relationship. This same Greek root has been used elsewhere to speak of the close intimate unity that the early believers shared with one another. For example, the root *koinonia,* (κοινωνια) is used in Acts 2:42 to denote the kind of intimate special fellowship that the believers shared on a regular basis with each other. It appears that the word used in Romans 11:17 is the same word, but with a preposition meaning "with" added as a prefix. This would stress the equality of their relationship; the Jewish and gentile believers share a deep mutual fellowship with one another.

Mutual Benefit

Romans 11:11–21 carries a second important implication. F. F. Bruce notes that it has been the custom of olive farmers "to invigorate an olive tree which is ceasing to bear fruit, by grafting it with a shoot of the wild olive, so that the sap of the tree ennobles this wild shoot and the tree now again begins to bear fruit."[49] This grafting helped both trees. The wild olive tree produced poor olives. Its ingrafting enabled it to bear wonderful fruit. On the other hand, the cultivated olive tree sometimes needed to have new vigor put into it. This was accomplished by the grafting in of a new shoot. The process was beneficial to both. "In such an unusual grafting, we are told, both the graft and the stock on which it is grafted are affected; the old stock is reinvigorated by the new graft, and the new graft in turn, fed by the sap of the olive stock, is able to bear such fruit as the wild-olive could never produce."[50]

No Arrogance

Based on the above information, there is yet a third implication for us in these verses. Notice that it is the gentile believers who are grafted into the olive tree of Israel (specifically the believing remnant of Israel) and not the other way around. The grafted-in branches, therefore, find their fullest meaning and fruitfulness by being part of the olive tree of Israel. "The gentile believers must not yield to the temptation to look down upon the Jews….Israel owed no debt to them; they are indebted to Israel."[51]

It is for this reason that the passage itself advises the grafted-in ones not to fall prey to arrogance. Marvin Wilson aptly points out that it is the root that supports the grafted-in branches. He observes that the Greek word translated "support" carries with it the idea of nourishment, life support, and submission. "This nuance, then, suggests the proper attitude required of the gentile believer in regard to his place in the family of God. Firmly supported by the fatness of the olive root, Israel, gentiles have no room for a spirit of arrogance, pride, or self-sufficiency (Romans 11:20)."[52]

Olives, Not Peaches!

The fourth implication from these verses is that the branches were grafted into the olive tree in order to bear olives, not peaches, oranges, or any other kind of fruit. The produce from an olive tree bears all of the characteristics of an olive tree. That is only natural. That would, therefore, imply that gentile believers would be permitted to do the things that would naturally be applicable for Israel. However, it is not the non-Jewish believers who determine what Israel looks like, but the standard for "Israeliteness" is solely determined by the Scriptures of Israel, specifically the Torah.

It is important to note that when the gentiles are grafted in, they do not eliminate Israel nor change Israel into something other than Israel. The tree remains an olive tree! Other branches are merely added on to it, not replacing any of the natural ones.

As we can see, these are incredible truths that the rabbi from Tarsus taught to the fellowship of Jews and gentiles in Rome. And they can lead us to draw an incredible conclusion: The fact that the believing gentiles have been grafted into Israel and share equality with the believing remnant is a fulfillment of Isaiah's prophecy. gentiles can now benefit from the covenants. They can inherit a living and active relationship with the Land, the People, and the Scriptures of Israel. Because of Messiah, they are "no longer foreigners and aliens, but fellow citizens with God's people and members of God's household...." They have been made part of the commonwealth of the children of Israel. This idea will now be expanded in the next chapter. As we study this, we need to remember that being grafted into Israel does not mean that the gentiles have become Jewish. Jewishness is a term which is both a cultural and a genealogical title reserved only for the physical family of Abraham, Isaac, and Jacob. It is a matter of physical descent.

Chapter 11

Ephesians 2–3

We move on now to study one of the most powerful passages in the Scriptures that discusses the relationship between Jewish and non-Jewish believers, and in turn, reveals significant truths concerning the issue of divine permission. In fact, in our opinion, the details of this passage and their implications for our study are quite astonishing. We are speaking of Ephesians 2:11–3:12

Context

Ephesians is a book that provides an abundance of teaching concerning the believer's new identity in Messiah. For example, chapter 1 describes how all believers were chosen by God, adopted into His divine family, redeemed by the blood of His Son, forgiven of all their sins, and granted the assurance of eternal life by means of His Spirit as a seal on their lives. Such "theological" words as "chosen," "adopted," "forgiven" and "redeemed" are used to accurately describe our identity in Messiah. Chapter 2 of Ephesians continues with the same theological theme. This chapter begins by describing what we were all like before we became believers in Yeshua. Sha'ul then details what Yeshua did for us (saved us by His grace) and how we can now describe our new identity in Him. This leads us to our critical passage, Ephesians 2:11–3:12. This section hones in on gentile identity *after* they believe in Yeshua.

One of the main themes for this passage (2:12–3:12) is unity, unity between the two main people groups of the world—Jew and gentile. Unity between these two groups is close to the heart of God. This passage describes four aspects of that unity.

Aspect One—The Need for Unity

Sha'ul explains that without Messiah, the gentiles could not be unified with the ancient people of Israel. He outlines several ways in which gentile unity with the people of God was hindered.

First, apart from Messiah, the gentiles were "separate from Messiah" (2:12). Messiah is the essential element necessary for bringing any two or more people together in a deep and harmonious union. That is why Sha'ul mentions Messiah first. It goes without saying that if a person is separated from Messiah, he is, in reality, separated from God Himself. In the previous section of Ephesians (2:1) Sha'ul says that the reason for the separation from God was sin. The gentiles, just like the Jews, were dead in their trespasses and sins. God has to redeem people from both of these groups before He can bring them together.

The second reason that gentile were not at one with the people of God is that they lacked union with Israel. Why was it of such consequence to be separate from Israel? The answer is because unity with Israel meant that the gentiles would be in a direct relationship with the ongoing stream of the people of God. That stream is called *Israel*.

We see, then, that this passage posits Israel as the normal stream of the continuous flow of the people of God through the centuries. Of course, we understand this to be speaking of the Remnant of Israel, the true spiritual representatives of their nation. Every description of the new identity of non-Jewish believers in Messiah is given as a comparison, and in reference, to this Remnant of Israel. When God reveals what the believing non-Jews now possess in Messiah, it is in relationship to Israel, the people of God. For instance, before Messiah, gentiles were excluded from *citizenship* in and with Israel. In addition, they were considered aliens to the *covenants* of Israel. However, when Messiah connected them to God's people, they became *fellow heirs* with Israel.

Notice that the text says that the gentiles were "excluded from the commonwealth of Israel." The word, commonwealth, may not be the best translation. The Greek word in question is the word, *politeis* from *politeia*—πολιτεια. A good portion of the uses of this word, especially in secular literature, point to the fact that "citizenship" is the best translation.[53] Furthermore, we need to realize that a commonwealth back in the Roman world (if, indeed, there was one) may not necessarily carry the same characteristics as it does today. Therefore we prefer "citizenship" as a translation of politeis.

One of the essential elements that the gentiles lacked for them to be at complete unity with the Remnant of Israel— the Jewish believers in Yeshua—was that they were simply citizens of a different nation. They were not Israelites, that is, members of a redeemed nation. Furthermore, if they were not one with the Messiah of Israel, they were, in reality, not connected to the people of Israel. If, on the other hand, they were one with the Messiah, they would have been also connected to the people of Israel through Him.

The third problem confronting the gentiles and their lack of unity with Israel is that they were not connected with the covenants of Israel, specifically the "covenants of promise." The covenants of promise are those legally binding agreements that define what it means to be united in a relationship both with God and with His people. By referring to them in the plural, Sha'ul probably meant all of the covenants which are associated with Israel: Abrahamic, Mosaic, Davidic, and Renewed. In reality, all of them were dependent upon the first, the Abrahamic covenant, wherein God gave the promises of blessing to His people.

We read that the gentiles were "strangers" to these covenants. The Greek word for "stranger," xenos—ξενοσ, is a word that denotes one from a "foreign country."[54] The use of this word, therefore, is quite appropriate. Since they were separate from Israel, they were excluded from those agreements that defined Israel, i.e., the covenants. They, indeed, were foreigners.

We can easily link together the last two elements necessary for unity found in 2:12. The text says that the gentiles lacked hope and were without God. They were lacking hope because they had no union with God. They could only be united with God if their sin was taken away, since sin was the factor that separated them from God. Yet without Messiah, they did not have atonement for their sin. Since they did not have atonement for sin, they could not be a part of the people of God. They were still dead in their sins, whereas the people of God were alive unto God. It all amounted to the fact that they were people without hope of being united with God and/or God's people, unless there was a drastic intervention. This intervention was the work of salvation and redemption in their lives.

Aspect Two—The Hindrance to Unity

While 2:11–14 discusses the need that the gentiles had for unity with God and His people, verses 15–16 hone in on the specific problem that hindered gentiles from taking hold of the provisions that God gave to them for unity. Verse 16 spells it out clearly. We are told that when Yeshua died, He put to death the *enmity,* or deep-seated hostility and hatred, that has kept the people of Israel and the gentiles from getting along and relating in a peaceful and amicable way. That strong malice was crucified with Yeshua. That is why it is only through Him that true unity can be accomplished.

In addition to specifying enmity as the main culprit to God's unity between Jewish people and gentiles, the text also states the outward expression of that enmity. Thus, in 2:14–15, we read, that when Yeshua died, He "broke down the barrier of the dividing wall, by abolishing in His flesh the enmity, [which is] the Law of commandments [contained] in ordinances." However, at this point, there are two difficult problems in these phrases that have stumped commentators. The first difficulty is what is "the dividing wall" which was broken down? The second problem is what is meant by the words, "the Law of commandments?"

"The Law of Commandments"

Let us first attempt to ascertain the meaning of the words "Law of commandments." By far, the most common understanding of these words is that they are a reference to the written Torah of Moshe. The very fact that the New American Standard Bible capitalized the initial letter of law ("Law") is an indication of how widespread this interpretation is among evangelicals. Indeed, such eminent commentators as Westcott, Hendrickson, Meyer, and Abbot "all interpret the passage to mean that either some or all of the Mosaic Law is abolished by the cross of [Messiah], and that some or all of the Mosaic Law created enmity between Jew and non-Jew."[55] On the surface, it would appear that the written Torah is, in fact, what is meant. However, we suggest that this is a good example of where commentators have succumbed to the tradition of anti-Torah interpretation which has plagued God's people for centuries.

In fact, there are several problems with the traditional evangelical understanding of these words. First, it contradicts Yeshua's own statement in Matthew 5:17 that He did not abolish the Torah. Second, it would contradict what we know of the person who penned these words, Sha'ul of Tarsus. As we have seen, he would never suggest that Yeshua did away with the Torah by His death. Last, we should note that "the written Torah never demanded a wall between Jew and Gentile."[56] This point was brought out quite effectively by Tim Hegg in a presentation to a meeting of the prestigious Evangelical Theological Society. Hegg points out that the Torah "gives very clear instructions against erecting barriers to separate Israel from the nations."[57] Some examples of his evidence include Exodus 22:21; 23:9, and Leviticus 19:33 to show that the same respect and treatment was to be afforded to both native-born Israelites and foreigners. In addition, Hegg cites Exodus 23:12 and the Sabbath as examples where both the Israelites[58] and the foreigners were to share participation in matters of Torah and life.

Therefore, because of these difficulties it is safe to rule out the traditional evangelical interpretation, even though doing so may run against the grain of many well-known and respected Bible teachers and commentators. If, however, Sha'ul was not referring to the written Torah in this passage, then what is specifically meant by the "law of commandments and ordinances" that served to separate Jew from gentile? It seems that the best way to understand these words is to interpret them to mean the rabbinic oral tradition, not the written teachings of Moshe. Please permit us to us elucidate.

On the one hand, the Torah of Moshe *did* legislate separations between Israel and the nations. These separations served several purposes. First, they attempted to guide Israel to live out her divine calling to act as a beacon nation, shining the light of God to the nations of the world. Second, these separations served to help keep sin and unrighteousness from contaminating this called-out nation. Third, these distinctions were intended to separate the believing Remnant from the unbelieving nations. Israel was instructed to eat differently, dress differently, believe differently, and act differently from the pagan nations. However, when one from among the nations believed in Israel's God, they were, then, to be granted equal status within the congregation of the righteous. The separations were no longer valid. This was the way of the Torah. In other words, the Torah did not create a distinction between Israel and gentiles *per se*. Rather, it created a distinction between the redeemed Remnant and those who were not part of the redeemed.

God made His will clear in the Torah concerning separations and restrictions between people. It is not wisdom to go beyond the simple instructions of the Torah and erect additional barriers or separations between Israel and the nations. Yet, when we read parts of ancient rabbinic literature, a different viewpoint emerges. A host of examples can be given from ancient rabbinic literature which indicates that "the practical outworking of the rabbinic laws of purity raised a strong wall of separation between the observant Jew and the non-Jew. According to oral Torah mere contact with non-Jews could render a person unclean, as well as contact with the residence of a non-Jew or with land outside the land of Israel. Clearly the oral Torah of the 1st Century functioned to separate Jew and Gentile in a dramatic way."[59] Therefore, we understand that it was the application of the oral Torah as it was understood in the 1st century by many Jewish religious teachers that was a chief expression of the growing enmity that existed between Jews and gentiles.

"The Barrier"[60]

This leads us to the second difficult phrase in 2:14, "the barrier of the dividing wall." What is meant by this expression? There have been at least three suggested interpretations of this phrase.

The first suggestion sees this phrase as expressing the results of the written Torah. Practicing it, according to this view, creates a barrier, a wall that divides people, especially Jews and gentiles, from each other. However, as we have just observed, since the "law" in question in this context is clearly not the Torah, then the barrier in question cannot be practicing the Torah, the teaching of Moshe.

There is a second popular understanding of this passage in Ephesians. This suggestion sees the words, "the barrier of the dividing wall" in verse 14 as a reference to the barrier wall that was erected in the Temple courtyard during the Second Temple period. The phrase "law of commandments contained in ordinances" in verse 15 according to this view, is not the written Torah of Moshe, but rather rabbinic law that legislated this barrier that separated the Court of the Gentiles with the Court of the Israelites.

This is the view that we espoused in our first edition of *Take Hold*. However, since then new evidence has surfaced that has slightly modified our viewpoint. This evidence is a research paper written by Tim Hegg (see above), who skillfully shows the need to adjust such an interpretation. One of Hegg's main lines of argumentation is that the Greek words in our text translated "barrier of the dividing wall," was not the usual way of referring to that barrier in the Temple. If Sha'ul had meant specifically, and only, that wall which separated the Court of the Gentiles from the Court of the Israelites, he would have used the common Greek way of referring to that wall. Moreover, notes Hegg, this barrier in the Temple was still standing at the time when Sha'ul wrote Ephesians, it was not broken down, as we read in Ephesians 2:14.

Thus, although it appears that the barrier wall in the Second Temple is not the primary subject of the text in

Ephesians, nevertheless, its existence in fact, serves to illustrate our point. It was erected, at first, to protect the Temple from people who were not biblically permitted to enter its courts because of a condition of ritual uncleanness. Since many from the nations who came there either did not know about the instructions for ritual purity or chose not to honor them, the Temple had to be protected from such.

However over a period of time, the barrier became symbolic of an attitude of hatred and enmity that grew between Jews and gentiles. The rules and regulations that governed the use of this wall—including the death penalty for any gentile who trespassed beyond it—were inventions of a late Second Temple period rabbinic mindset that was (for the most part) filled with enmity against gentiles as a whole. In fact, as recorded by Josephus, signs were posted in the Second Temple courtyard—written in both Latin and Greek—warning gentiles of the death penalty for entering further into the Temple area. Two of these signs have been recovered. [61] They did not take the time to distinguish between those gentiles who were part of God's Kingdom or not. The wall, therefore, was in a real way, the product of oral tradition influenced by enmity.

Consequently, over the years, considerable animosity had arisen between Jews and gentiles. It began when sincere Jewish people attempted to protect the Temple, as discussed above; it grew worse as, due to abuse from foreign armies and the nations, the Jewish population began to look upon gentiles with suspicion and fear. Furthermore, because the gentiles did not keep kosher dietary standards, observant Jews were not permitted by Jewish law to eat with them, purchase their food, or drink their wine.

Given the attitude of many rabbis toward gentiles, it is easy to see how enmity could have arisen among the gentiles toward the Jews, for contempt for Jews was notoriously widespread in the ancient gentile world. "In the Greek and Roman literature of the time, the judgments about Jews are in general very derogatory. Passages from writers of the time—Josephus, Juvenal, and Tertullian—give us the impression that the Greco-Roman culture saw Jewishness as quite ridiculous." [62] Moreover, the ancient military and political powerhouses of Assyria, Babylon, Medo-Persia, Greece and Rome treated the Israelite nation ruthlessly, especially in terms of their religious practices.

We can see, therefore, how the barrier separating the Court of the Gentiles from the Court of the Jews provides a good illustration for the kind of enmity of which the text in Ephesians speaks. However, as evidenced by Hegg, it itself is not the "dividing wall." Hegg provides important linguistic and literary evidence to suggest that "the dividing wall which was abolished by [Messiah] was none other than those Rabbinic laws which had enforced a separation between Jew and Gentile in opposition to the written Torah." [63] Part of that evidence consists of the Greek verb that Sha'ul uses in 2:14 to identify this "dividing wall." The word in question is *phragmos*—φραγμοσ. A cognate of this word (*peirphrassein*—πειρφρασσειν) is found in rabbinic literature to speak of the *oral Torah*. *Peirphrassein* means to "fence about." There is an important use of this word in the *Letter of Aristeas* (written sometime during the Second Temple period before Yeshua) to refer to the oral tradition as a fence around the written Torah, which has the effect of separating Jews from non-Jews in ways in which God's Word was never intended to be understood. The Letter states, "our lawgiver...fenced us about with impenetrable palisades and with walls of iron to the end that we should mingle in no way with any of the other nations." [64]

We repeat the above phrase, "*that we should mingle in no way.*" This phrase shows clearly the point that we have been trying to make. God and His Torah, though teaching us to be holy and, therefore, separate from the pagan nations around us, never intended "*that we should mingle in no way with any of the other nations*" (italics ours). In our opinion, this is diametrically opposed to our divine and eternal calling to be a light to the nations teaching them of our God and of His ways.

Putting It Together

Let us tie all of this together. It is clear that Sha'ul indicates that the problem that separated Jews from non-Jews was severe enmity between them. One of the major expressions of, and contributors to, this enmity, according to the text is the rabbinic law, or oral tradition, which had developed during the Second Temple period. The main result of the oral Torah was that it "enforced a separation between Jew and Gentile in opposition to the written Torah." [65] Thus, when Ephesians tells us that Messiah "abolished in His flesh the enmity," it refers to the inward hatred that took the form of outward hostility between Jews and gentiles. Yeshua took care of this hatred through His atoning death and life-giving resurrection. He made us both "clean" and in Him we are one!

Aspect Three—The Accomplishment of Unity

We have already alluded to the work of Yeshua in removing the hindrance to uniting Israel and the gentiles. Now let us state it more explicitly. It is clear from 2:13–14 that unity between Israel and the nations is only accomplished by and through the Messiah. In verse 13, we are told that gentiles can be made one with Israel by being" in Messiah." That means being united with Him through faith in Him. Moreover, the verse concludes by saying that it is through Messiah's blood that the gentiles are "brought near." This speaks of the atoning sacrifice of Yeshua that is so essential to forgiving and removing the sin, which contributed to the enmity that separated the two groups. As a result, in verse 14, Sha'ul says that "He Himself [the Messiah] is our peace and made both groups into one." Thus, it is only when an Israelite and a gentile come to faith in Yeshua that unity between these estranged two people groups is accomplished.

Aspect Four—The Results of Unity

We have looked at the *need* for unity, the *hindrance* to unity, and the *accomplishment* of unity. Let us now examine the results that the establishment of unity have for the relationship between Jewish and non-Jewish believers in Messiah. They are found in 2:14, 19–22 and 3:6. Sha'ul's means of expressing this new unity between the Remnant of Israel and the Remnant from among the gentiles is by using four Greek verbs that begin with a prefix which means "with" (sum—συμ), or its grammatical variations. These verbs are: *sumpolitai—συμπολιται, sugkleironoma—συγκλερονομα, sussoma—συσσομα,* and *summetoxa—συμμετοχα.* They are translated respectively as fellow citizens, fellow heirs, fellow members, and fellow partakers.

Fellow Citizens (*sumpolitai—sumpolitai*) 2:19

The first element of this new unity is that it gives the gentiles a new citizenship. They have become honorary, grafted-in, citizens with Israel. Thus, we read in verse 19, "you are no longer strangers and aliens, but *fellow citizens* with the saints and are of God's household" (italics ours). Let us not ignore the simple meaning of the text. Whatever the Torah meant by referring to non-Israelites as foreigners and strangers does not apply to the gentiles who have trusted in Messiah. Through union with the Messiah of Israel, God made them a complete part of the Remnant of Israel.

It is important to note one qualifying point. Being part of the Remnant of Israel does not make a gentile into a Jewish person. Likewise, adopting Jewish cultural habits and/or customs is not what being fellow-citizens with Israel means. Taking this one step further, living according to Jewish traditions is not necessarily synonymous with living a Torah-based lifestyle. The Torah was meant to include people from all different cultures, and is able to instruct gentiles from all nations in godliness and righteousness. It is always a tragedy when non-Jewish believers, in their zealousness to take hold of their inheritance with Israel, begin to look like, act like, and talk like Jewish sages from 18th century Eastern Europe or 20th century New York. This can be greatly offensive to those Jewish people whom they are imitating, and it is not what being part of Israel and Israel's covenants are all about!

Fellow Heirs (*sugkleironoma—sugkleronoma*) 3:6

The second result of the new unity between the Remnant of Israel and the gentiles is that God made the believing gentiles fellow heirs with Israel. When we think of Israel's inheritance, we immediately think of the blessings that God promised to the Patriarchs. What Sha'ul seems to be indicating here is that through the Messiah, non-Israelites are made partakers of these same blessings, not to mention the inheritance of eternal life! This thought is perfectly consistent with what Sha'ul taught the Galatians (3:6–9) about gentiles as children of Abraham by faith. This also would qualify them as fellow heirs with the Remnant of Israel.

One may object at this point and assert that the promises of land to the people of Israel through Abraham, Isaac, and Jacob do not apply to the gentile believers. However, remember that we are only contending a position of "divine permission." This means that if the gentile believers so chose, when Messiah returns they also can have an inheritance of land with their Jewish counterparts. That is the thrust of Ezekiel 47, which we have examined earlier in this book.

Fellow Members (*sussoma—sussoma*) 3:6

This word was not known to have been used in Greek before Sha'ul used it.[66] Perhaps he himself coined it to express the truth that there is one body of believers. The Greek word can be rendered literally (though awkwardly!) as "one body with." This body consists of the chosen Remnant of Israel and the chosen Remnant of the gentiles. However, the use of this word implies that part of the body has already existed. It is the gentiles that are added into that body of believers, which has always been referred to as "Israel." Sha'ul is not expressing that there is a creation of an entirely new entity. He is merely describing the *addition* of the gentiles to an already existing body. Moreover, these believing gentiles are on a completely equal footing with the Remnant from among Israel.

Fellow Partakers (*summetoxa—summetoca*) 3:6

Sha'ul expresses in verse 6 that the gentiles are, in Messiah, fellow *partakers* in "the promise." This phrase is reminiscent of Ephesians 2:12 which indicates that outside of Messiah, gentiles are strangers to the covenants of *promise*. Therefore, when we are told that in Messiah, non-Jews are fellow partakers of the promise, it seems that Sha'ul is teaching us that they are equal participants in the covenants of promise. This, of course, would include all of the four covenants that God made with Israel. If this is true (and it is!) then, it seems that this truth is a fulfillment of what Isaiah was preaching as recorded in chapter 56—that the remnant from among the gentiles can equally participate in Israel's covenants.

Parting Thoughts

There are several thoughts that we need to share as we conclude our study of this monumental passage.

Family!

First, from this text we learn that because of the work of Yeshua there is a deep-seated unity between Jewish believers and gentile believers. It is almost as if the Scriptures are saying that we are, for all intents and purposes, family. Indeed, Ephesians 2:13 says that "you who formerly were far off have been brought near by the blood of Messiah." This phrase, "brought near," is the key phrase. It can have at least two meanings, one building on the other. Using the words "brought near" in conjunction with "blood" points directly to the image of a sacrifice. Remember that Sha'ul, though he is writing in Greek, is nonetheless a Jewish man who thinks in a Semitic thought pattern. The word for sacrifice in Hebrew is *korban* (קרבן). It is from the Hebrew root *karov*—קרב, which means "to bring near." Thus, when one offered a sacrifice, he was brought near to God.

In addition, the Hebrew word for "relative" is also derived from the same root (*karov*). This root is sometimes rendered "relative" (according to the context) both in biblical Hebrew (see Leviticus 21:2-3, for example) as well as modern Hebrew. It makes sense since relatives are family, people that are near and dear to us.

Hence, based on the use of the phrase "brought near" in 2:13, there seems to be two implications. First, when God established unity between Jewish and gentile believers, He also brought the gentiles near to Him, just as near to Him as believer from Israel had ever been. Second, it is quite possible to say that this new unity is such that Jewish and gentile believers are actually now relatives in the family of God. That does not make the latter Jewish—just grafted-in adopted family members.

One New Creation

The second concluding thought is a point in the text that we think needs some clarification. We are referring to a frequently misunderstood expression from 2:15, "one new man." This is often taken to mean that, in the body of Messiah, there are no more Jews and no more gentiles. Therefore, since we are now "one new man," we need no longer concern ourselves with the Torah, because Yeshua has put an end to it.

Such a reading misses the point of both the text and the Brit Hadasha as a whole. We are all new people in Messiah: each of us received the gift of new life when we put our trust in Him. We are not who we once were, but truly new creations in Messiah. Yeshua, therefore, through His atoning sacrifice, brought together both groups of new creatures in Messiah and unified them. He did not abolish Jewishness and non-Jewishness; nor did He abolish the Torah. He simply abolished the interpersonal enmity that separated both groups of humanity—Jews and gentiles—and for the first time made peace a possibility.

Moreover, God did not do away with Israel, particularly the righteous Remnant; the covenant people of God have always been and always will be Israel. Nor did He do away with gentiles. It is important to note that when Sha'ul was addressing the non-Jewish believers in Yeshua in Romans 11:13 he called them "gentiles," even after they believed in Yeshua. They can never change their physical line of birth, just like Jewish people can never cease to be physical descendants of Jacob. The word "gentile" is not a dirty word!

The "one new man," therefore, is not a new stream of the people of God. Rather, it consists of both the righteous Remnant of Israel and the righteous Remnant from among the gentiles who have been grafted into Israel and who are each individually a "new man," a new creation. They are *one* new man on whose heart is written one righteousness, the Torah itself!

Yeshua Himself dramatically illustrated this point for us in John 10:14–16. Addressing an audience of descendants of Jacob, He illustrates His identity as their Shepherd by saying,

> I am the good Shepherd; and I know My own, and My own know Me, even as the Father knows Me and I know the Father; and I lay down My life for the sheep. I have other sheep, which are not of this fold; I must bring them also, and they shall hear My voice; and they shall become one flock with one Shepherd.

Notice He taught them that while there might be two folds, a remnant from both will be united into one flock with Him as the Shepherd. Furthermore, He indicates that He must bring the sheep from the other fold to the sheep of the household of Israel—and not the other way around. The "new man" is the individual believer—regenerated by God and constituted the righteousness of God (Romans 5:19). When a sheep from either sheepfold comes to faith, each one is a new creation. In becoming the righteousness of God in Messiah, the sheep from both folds are united as one—one body and one flock. The righteousness that they have become is one righteousness, the same for both. Moreover, that righteousness is revealed, described, and portrayed in both the Living Torah (Yeshua) and the written Torah—the whole of the Scriptures, including the first five books.

The Mystery

A third concluding thought centers on the word "mystery" that Sha'ul uses in 3:2–3. Sha'ul describes this wonderful unity between these once estranged groups as a "mystery." Biblically, a mystery is not something like a Sherlock Holmes episode, where we have to guess the missing elements to solve the plot. Nor is it something known only by a few select individuals, as for example, in gnosticism. Rather, the Greek word translated "mystery" or "secret" is the word *mysterion—μυστηριον*. "Practically wherever it occurs in the [Brit Hadasha], *mysterion* is found with verbs denoting revelation or proclamation, i.e., *mysterion* is, that which is revealed. It is a present-day secret—not some isolated fact from the past which merely needs to be noted, but something dynamic and compelling."[67] In other words, a biblical mystery is something that was kept secret in the past, but is now being revealed.

Based on this definition of mysterion, we can learn two things about unity from Ephesians 3:2–3. First, by calling it a mystery, Sha'ul implies that the unity which he was describing has always been a reality for those who knew God. From the beginning, this was the way God designed for believing gentiles and believing Jews to relate to each other. However, the Scriptures did not necessarily describe this unity with the theological terminology available to us through the Brit Hadasha. It provides for us another example of the importance of knowing about progressive revelation.

Second, we can now rejoice that God has finally revealed the details of this mystery to us. The reason why the people in the Tanakh period did not know these details is because the finished work of Messiah is central to this unity. It served God's eternal purposes to reveal this mystery in the days after the Messiah had come to accomplish the redemption of all whom the Father had placed in Him.

What, specifically, is the mystery that is now being revealed? According to 3:6, the mystery is "that the gentiles are fellow heirs and fellow members of the body, and fellow partakers of the promise in Messiah Yeshua through the Gospel." When the text says "the body," it means that they are now fellow members of the already existing community of believers, i.e., the Remnant of Israel. They are also equal partakers of the promise in Messiah Yeshua through the Gospel. We have already seen in Hebrews 4 that the Gospel revealed in the Brit

Hadasha is the same one that was preached to Israel in the wilderness after leaving Egypt. Thus, what we have here is biblical continuity from the period of the Tanakh to the present period. What was hinted at in the Tanakh is made explicit in the revelation of the Brit Hadasha. What is this mystery now being revealed? It is the fact that because of Messiah, Jewish and gentile believers are united together in one body—the Body of Messiah.

Summary

Does all this sound too good to be true? But it *is* true! The inclusion of the gentiles together with the Jews as participants in the covenants of promise was done, as Sha'ul tells us in Ephesians 3:11, "in accordance with the eternal purpose which He carried out in Messiah Yeshua our Lord." This being the case, then, it seems that at the very least, non-Jewish believers have divine permission to participate fully in every aspect associated with the Land, the People, and the Scriptures of Israel—as long as it is consistent with the Scriptures. Have gentile believers not been granted citizenship with Israel? Have they not been made partakers of the covenants? And is it not true that now, because of the blood of Messiah, we are all one family?

If non-Jews who are believers can biblically claim their citizenship with the remnant of Israel, it only makes sense that this new relationship to Israel would change their previous status as "strangers to the covenants of promise" (Ephesians 2:12). Having been brought near through their union with Messiah, they may now participate fully in those covenants—including, of course, the Torah.

Words of Caution

Two words of caution are necessary at this point. The first word is directed to those from among the nations who have been grafted into the holy community. For those in the body of

Messiah to whom this rendering of biblical continuity is a new concept, there could be a deeply felt objection rising up within them. They could feel that to recognize that they are fellow citizens with the real Israel, and that the church does not replace Israel, would then mean that all believers would have to embrace "Jewishness"—that is, to take upon themselves Jewish culture.

Allow us to state clearly that anyone embracing their inheritance with Israel is not therefore obligated to embrace Jewish culture. Jewish culture varies as to the countries in which Israel as been dispersed. European Jewish cultures and American Jewish cultures are in many ways different from modern-day Israeli culture, and that Jewish culture is very different from the Moroccan Jewish culture, or that which comes from India, or even Ethiopia. In other words, there is much diversity in Jewish culture. There is no one Jewish culture for gentile believers to embrace as their own. Even if there were, it would not be incumbent upon non-Jewish believers to live according to that culture.

What there is to embrace, however, is all that is written. The written Word of God delineates for us all the aspects of righteousness in this earth, and that is what we are now free to embrace! In order, then, to walk in our full inheritance, we now embrace a biblical lifestyle and not just a cultural lifestyle. Any cultural traditions which do not change what is written and are creative in their application of what is written are available for us to enjoy. Any tradition which detracts from or changes that which is actually written is not part of who we are as new creations in Messiah. For that reason and that reason alone, we do not embrace cultural traditions that are not true to the written Word of God. For "that which is written" includes that which is written on our new creation hearts (Jeremiah 31:33), and everything that stems from the mystery of Yeshua in us.

Remember that He is the same yesterday, today, and tomorrow. He is the righteousness of God as revealed in the written Word—all the written Word—and it is His life in us that we are now free to embrace.

And now a word to our fellow Jewish believers in Yeshua: There are some of our number who might object to the aforementioned unity. They may think that to espouse such a unity would detract in some way from the unique calling of the Jewish people. Allow us to emphasize that nothing could be further from the truth! The unity that the Scriptures describe in no way changes the unique calling of Israel and the unique calling of the nations. Individuals from the nations being grafted in to Israel as full citizens in no way replace Israel, nor does this unity diminish Israel's significance. In every way, it is only to her glory that she receives with open arms all those whom the God of Israel draws unto Himself. How can the fulfillment of Israel's calling to be a light to the nations be anything but her glory?

A Different Kind of Expression of the Faith

There is one last application which may be drawn from our study of this passage in Ephesians. Sincere Bible teachers have interpreted this text in a most unfortunate way. Over the centuries, they have asserted that there is a new movement of the people of God, called "the Church." In doing so, and by calling it "the Church," many have unwittingly contributed to the centuries-old disunity which has been so characteristic of the body of Messiah. Many have taught that the Church has replaced Israel as God's covenant people. This is error. Still others maintain that God in this age is dealing with the Church, and when He raptures them out of this world, He will again deal with Israel. We believe this teaching to be equally incorrect as it contradicts the second and third chapters of Ephesians.

One of the visible results of this disunity is the rise in the number of denominations over the years. In many cases, new groups arose from movements of believers who were striving for purer doctrinal expressions than were found in their current denomination. Thus we have the Methodists, Presbyterians, Baptists, Pentecostals, and countless others— each group with its own doctrines and practices which differ markedly from those of the others.

What would have happened to these different and disunifying expressions of faith if all of them had been keenly aware of their intimate connection to Israel, the continual stream of the people of God? What would have happened to the Protestant denominational movements if believers everywhere had decided to let the Torah (as well as the Brit Hadasha) be their guide to faith and practice instead of their particular religious traditions?

Why not introduce a biblical continuity into our expression of the faith? Why not worship, dress, think, do business, and live in the manner described by the Torah (as did the ancient holy community) and simply let the Brit Hadasha be its God-inspired interpreter? Would this not be the natural outcome of believing in the God of Israel and the Messiah of Israel, benefiting in the covenants He made with Israel, and sharing in citizenship with the people of Israel?

If only the "Church" had been keenly aware of its true biblical identity! Since the nature of God's people can best be understood if we consider the biblical terminology that describes that identity, in this next unit we will examine how an understanding of our identity, both individual and corporate, will help us accept the divine permission granted to us to take hold of our inheritance with Israel.

Unit Five

Taking Hold
Through a Knowledge of the
Believer's Identity

This one will say, "I am the Lord's"; and that one will call on the name of Jacob; and another will write on his hand, "Belonging to the Lord," and will name Israel's name with honor.

Isaiah 44:5

Therefore if any man is in Messiah he is a new creation; the old things passed away; behold, new things have come.

2 Corinthians 5:17

Chapter 12
Progressive Revelation

Thus far, we have been examining portions of Scripture from almost each section of the Bible to build the case that non-Jewish believers in Yeshua have complete divine permission and freedom to take hold of their divine inheritance with the Land, the People, and the Scriptures of Israel.

There is yet one more piece of biblical evidence—the identity of the believers in Yeshua. We have already examined some aspects of that identity in our study of the passages in Romans and Ephesians. But there is more. Let us delve into other passages that are also relevant and discover how a knowledge of the believer's identity can help us to think through the matter of divine permission.

A Lesson in Biblical Continuity

We will comprehend the believer's identity more fully if we see the continuity of that identity throughout all of Scripture. The similarity in identity between believers of the Tanakh and Brit Hadasha periods is amazing.

As we launch into this aspect of our study, we must first discuss the concept known in theology as "progressive revelation." Recently we attended a lecture sponsored by one of the most prominent Jewish educational institutions here in Jerusalem. A non-Jewish theologian who professed faith in Yeshua was given an unprecedented opportunity to speak on his view of the nature of God. Specifically, he was sharing how his understanding of the doctrine of the trinity is perfectly consistent with the unity of God, that is, trinitarianism does not contradict monotheism. After the lecture, a religious Jewish man asked a question from the floor. Though this was his own question—nonetheless his question is typical of how most Jewish people feel about some Christian doctrines. He asked, "If the trinity is true, then how could the Son contradict the Father—that is, how could what the Father spoke at Sinai later be annulled by the Son and His followers?"

This man's sincere question provides for us an important glimpse into the need for those of us who believe in Yeshua to apply the principle of progressive revelation consistently in all aspects of our understanding of the Scriptures. If church people had applied these principles centuries ago, not only would this Jewish man—and countless other like him—have had less difficulty in accepting the biblical doctrine of the Godhead, but he also would not have been led astray into thinking that Yeshua and His followers annulled the Torah that was given at Sinai.

This story illustrates for us the need to discuss the concept of progressive revelation. After all, the docrine of progressive revelation is in many ways the heart of the issue of this man's question. Our approach will be first to define our interpretation of the term, then present several examples of it. After that, we will devote a whole new chapter to the discussion of the biblical continuity of our identity as believers.

Progressive revelation is the concept that God discloses His truths in a gradual and deliberate manner. Dr. Clarence E. Mason Jr. defines this concept as follows: "It was not God's purpose to reveal all the truth concerning any one doctrine at one given time. Rather His method has been to unfold progressively the doctrine through successive writers.... In light of this fact, later books may be expected to elaborate upon and elucidate the teachings of the earlier."[68] Let us look at a few examples of this principle.

1. Prophecy

The biblical prophecies and their fulfillment in the Brit Hadasha provide a vivid illustration of progressive revelation. "Some of the most important prophecies are first couched in general terms, but in the course of God's progressive revelation increase in definiteness and particularity...they remind one of a bud that gradually opens into a flower."[69] Indeed, it is wonderful to study the Messianic prophecies from Genesis to Malachi and learn both what they meant to the people who heard them (the "bud") and to see how they were wonderfully fulfilled in the person and work of Yeshua (the "flower").

2. Holiness

The same bud/flower analogy can also be applied to the gradually unfolding teaching of holiness. Indeed, "The organic progress is from seed-form to the attainment of full growth; yet we do not say that in the qualitative sense the seed is less perfect than the tree."[70] Some believers sincerely ask, "We have the New Testament now. That is our standard for holiness, and if we follow those teachings we will be separate unto the Lord. Why do we still need the Torah?" There is some merit to this objection. The Brit Hadasha does indeed admonish us that we, like ancient Israel, are called to be holy unto the Lord, "who has saved us, and called us with a holy calling." (2 Timothy 1:9) What does the Brit Hadasha, in fact, teach on the matter?

Rabbi Sha'ul of Tarsus, a staunch follower of the Torah, reminds us that, "[There is] one body and one Spirit, just as also you were called in one hope of your calling; one Lord, one faith, one baptism, one God and Father of all…." (Ephesians 4:4–6) What does this unity mean if it does not speak of one standard for holiness and the continuity of God's Word? There is complete biblical continuity between the Brit Hadasha and the Torah concerning biblical holiness and our righteousness in Messiah. As this same teacher wrote in Romans 7:12, "So then, the Torah is holy, and the commandment is holy and righteous and good." Sha'ul always taught that to be holy was to live by the Torah.

Those are but two of the manifold examples that can be furnished to illustrate progressive revelation. But from just these illustrations, we have ample evidence to see that God did not choose to reveal all of that which He intended to make known to us at once. During this process, one concept is built upon another. Nothing is contradictory, and there is complete continuity between what is revealed in the Tanakh and what is made known at a later time.

It is imperative to see the biblical continuity between the theology and lifestyle of the people of God from Genesis to Revelation. This leads us, therefore, to a discussion of the continuity of God's people, the body of believers that is called "the Church." If we can establish the existence of such a continuity, then that will be of great relevance to the thesis of this book.

Chapter 13

To Be or Not To Be

The Continuity of the Believer's Identity

In essence, this chapter is a continuation of the previous one. There we provided some brief examples of the concept of progressive revelation. Here we will examine four illustrations of progressive revelation that have particular relevance to the overall theme of this book. We will attempt to see the continuity of the believer's spiritual identity between the period of the Tanakh and the revelation of it in the Brit Hadasha. First, a short note on the concept of "identity."

The Importance of Knowing Our Identity

There is a considerable amount of emphasis in today's world placed on people finding out who they are. This is one of the major workings of the present version of the New Age movement. Because the subject of one's identity is a major focus of the New Age movement, we hesitate to approach it here, lest we begin to sound "New Age" ourselves.

However, there is a kernel of truth behind all of Satan's counterfeits; otherwise they would not be considered counterfeits. The truth of the matter is that it really is important for people to know who they are. The problem with Satan's counterfeits is that they are lies. He tells people that they are all acceptable without a personal relationship with God. On the other hand, there is an abundance of information found in the Word of God concerning the true identity of believers in Yeshua. Again, Satan has managed to lie to people in this area. He has distorted many people's Bible teaching so that many believers have failed to realize the complete truth of what Messiah did for them and how it applies practically to their lives.

A good example of this is the expression, "I am just a saved sinner." On the surface, it gives an air of humility. After all, since we still sin as believers (the thinking goes), sin must, therefore, be at the heart of our identity; hence we are still sinners although we are somehow saved ones. The biblical reality, however, is that we are no longer sinners. Repeatedly, the Scripture refers to believers in Yeshua as "saints," or those who are called-out and set apart for God. We are, then, saints who sin, not sinners who sometimes act saintly.[71] Permit us to let Dr. David C. Needham summarize this truth for us:

> Contrary to much popular teaching, regeneration (being born again) is more than having something taken away (sins forgiven) or having something added to you (a new nature with the assistance of the Holy Spirit); it is becoming something you had never been before. This new identity is not on the flesh level, but the spirit level—one's deepest self. This miracle is more than a "judicial" act of God. It is an act so REAL that it is right to say that a Christian's [believer's] essential nature is righteous rather than sinful. All other lesser identities each of us has can only be understood and appreciated by our acceptance [of] and response to this fact.[72]

It is simply a theological truism that we think and behave in accordance with what we believe about God and ourselves. That is one reason why the Bible is so important. It is the revelation from God about Himself and it also tells us who we are both before and after we become believers in the Messiah.

People will take hold of their divine permission only if they believe that they have a God-given right to do so. We have attempted to show from several separate biblical passages that there is, indeed, divine permission. But it is also important to know that by taking hold of our unity with the Land, the People, and Scriptures of Israel, we are being true to what the Bible declares our identity to be.

It is in this light that we will examine several aspects of our identity as it is revealed from the Torah to the Book of Revelation. If it can be established that believers of every age share the same spiritual identity, then there is, indeed, all the divine permission necessary for all believers everywhere to take hold of their inheritance with Israel. We have chosen four examples of biblical continuity concerning the identity of the believer. We could have studied many more, but these four will be sufficient for our purposes. Let us look closer at each of these in order to see how the Tanakh presents the seed form of our identity that flowers so beautifully in the Brit Hadasha. In the process of this study, we will get another glimpse of the divine permission for non-Jewish believers spoken of in this book.

These four illustrations are four important concepts that are introduced in the Torah. They have to do with the nature of the community of God's people and how it operates.

The Kehilah

This treatment on the nature of the community of God's people will not be an exhaustive study. Many respected authors have described the functions, appearance, and purposes of the body of believers.[73] Overall, however, they have not explained the body in Torah terms—with a few notable exceptions, such as works written by Messianic Jewish scholars Dr. Daniel Juster (*Jewish Roots* and *Growing to Maturity*) and Dr. David H. Stern (*Messianic Jewish Manifesto*). Our purposes here will be somewhat different from theirs. We intend to demonstrate how the body of believers described in the Brit Hadasha is actually a continuation of that which God began in the Torah.

Called-Out Ones

One of the most common ways in the Torah of referring to the community of Israel was to use the Hebrew word *kehilah* (קהלה). The Messianic community is described in the Brit Hadasha as "the Church." The Greek word most commonly translated "church" is *ekklesia* (εκκλησια)— literally, "called-out ones." According to the *Dictionary of New Testament Theology*, the term "represents exclusively the Hebrew *qahal* [קהל]...[which is] probably related to *qol* (voice), [and] means a summons to an assembly and the act of assembling...."[74] Qahal is from the same root as kehilah. Hence, by referring to His people in this way, the Lord is saying that He has called them out to assemble in order that they might hear, worship, and serve Him. Moreover, by this linguistic connection, it is easy to see how the Church is connected to the kehilah of the Torah. Thus, both linguistically and conceptually, the identity of God's people is the same in the period of the Tanakh and the period of the Renewed Covenant: they are both God's chosen and called-out people, separated unto God in order to serve Him.

This concept of being summoned by God to a sacred assembly is dramatically demonstrated in the account of the exodus of the children of Israel. Throughout his encounters with Pharaoh, Moses persistently appeals: "Thus says the Lord, 'Let My people go, so that they might worship Me'." (Exodus 7:16, 8:1, etc.) At Mount Sinai, God again calls out His people to serve Him. Here, as He gives the Torah to His people, the Holy One commands them to sanctify themselves; that is, to set themselves apart to serve Him alone by faithfully living out the terms of the covenant He was making with them (Exodus chapters 19–24).

Dr. James M. Boice aptly summarizes what we have been saying concerning the nature of the Church when he writes,

> ...the church has its roots in the Old Testament and cannot be understood well without that background. This is true theologically because the idea of a called-out "people of God" obviously existed in the Old Testament period, just as in the New. It is also true linguistically since the Greek word for church (ekklesia) occurs frequently in relation to Israel in the Greek translation of the Old Testament (the Septuagint) and was therefore known to the New Testament writers.[75]

Closely related to the concept of being called out is that of sanctification. Those undergoing this process are referred to in the Bible as "saints." The Greek word—from the root *hagiois* ($\alpha\gamma\iota o\iota\varsigma$)—corresponds to the Hebrew word whose root is *kodesh* (קֹדֶשׁ). Both carry the idea of being set apart for a particular purpose.

Interestingly, the same root is found in Ugaritic, an ancient Canaanite dialect which is closely related to biblical Hebrew. Archaeologists have found that at Ugarit, "these 'holy ones' were homosexual priests and priestesses who acted as prostitutes."[76] This indicates that the emphasis on this word, *kodesh*, is on the idea of being set apart—rather than on any particular innate moral goodness, as our common usage often suggests. Hence, just as the ancient Canaanite priests and priestesses were set apart from the rest of their world to serve their gods, the holy ones of the true God are set apart from the world of ungodliness in order to serve Him completely.

Thus, both the Torah and the Brit Hadasha refer to God's people collectively as the kehilah and ekklesia, meaning called-out ones. The Scriptures also refer to us with the terms "holy ones" or "saints." Combining these two concepts, then, we may say that believers in Yeshua—like the remnant of ancient Israel—have been called out of darkness in order to live for, serve, and worship the Holy One. Together, they form the *holy community*: those whom God has made holy to live a set-apart lifestyle that is delineated for us in the Torah and all the Word of God that follows.

Regenerated Ones

There are yet more similarities between the called-out community in the period of the Tanakh and the one described in the Brit Hadasha. One of the most important similarities is that both communities consisted of believers who were regenerated and indwelt by the Spirit of God.

In *The Holy Spirit in the Old Testament*, evangelical Bible scholar Dr. Leon J. Wood develops this point by first establishing that the saints of the Tanakh period were regenerated. He writes:

> The evidence that spiritual renewal, or regeneration, was true of such Old Testament people lies mainly in two directions. One is that these people lived in a way possible only for those who had experienced regeneration, and the other is the avenue of logical deduction that argues back from New Testament truth.[77]

Here is an example of that "logical deduction." Ephesians 2 states that although we were born dead in our trespasses and sins, God has made us alive through Messiah. From this we may infer that one is either spiritually dead or spiritually alive; there is no third state of being. Further, Romans 5:12–21 speaks of two spiritual domains: the kingdom of sin and death, and that of life and righteousness.

Again, we find only two options—citizenship in Satan's kingdom or in God's. If a person in the period of the Tanakh was not dead in his trespasses and sins, where did that leave him? If alive, he was alive unto God. And one can only become alive unto God through regeneration. It is doubtful whether all the saints of that period *understood* their spiritual condition, but that is precisely why the study of progressive revelation is so important. Whereas the saint living during the period of the Tanakh did not have the advantage of additional revelatory light, those living after the revelation of the Brit Hadasha have been given the full understanding of theirspiritual state. However, it is axiomatic that the saints of both periods have been regenerated. There is simply no other way to know God, to love God, and to live God's Word.

Wood goes on to note that, since the saints in the period of the Tanakh were indeed regenerated, they must have lived their lives through the indwelling Spirit of God, as do all those who are regenerated. Whenever a king or prophet has been called for a special task, he always received a special anointing of God's Spirit to carry out that task. However, these special anointings were distinct from the normal working of God's Spirit in their lives. Wood continues:

> Their [the believers mentioned in the Tanakh] lives were outstanding in faithfulness and dedication, and they are set forth in the Old Testament as examples to follow. Did they achieve such commendable lives by their own efforts? Did they have some resource in their own nature on which they could draw that people of Renewed Covenant time did not? The answer, of course, is that they did not. But, if not, they must have experienced an impartation of new life, just as saints of the Renewed Covenant, and this means regeneration...a strong argument that Old Testament saints were indwelt may be built on the fact that they were regenerated as shown above.[78]

Two Examples

What would a regenerated saint from the period of history before the revelation of the Brit Hadasha look like and sound like? There are many examples from which we can draw. But let us look at the following two individuals in order to see the similarities between the believers from among the remnant in the period of the Tanakh and believers today. Pay close attention as you read the statements of these two regenerated people. First, a male example:

> And behold, there was a man in Jerusalem whose name was Simeon; and this man was righteous and devout, looking for the consolation of Israel; and the Holy Spirit was upon him. And it had been revealed to him by the Holy Spirit that he would not see death before he had seen the Lord's Messiah. And he came in the Spirit into the Temple, and when the parents brought in the child Yeshua to carry out for Him the custom of the Torah, then he took Him into his arms, and blessed God and said, "Now, Lord, let your bondservant depart in peace, according to Your Word. For my eyes have seen Your salvation, which You have prepared in the presence of all the peoples, a light of revelation to the gentiles, and the glory of Your people Israel."

And now, the female:

> And there was a prophetess, Anna, the daughter of Penuel of the tribe of Asher. She was advanced in years, having lived with her husband seven years after her marriage, and then as a widow to the age of eighty-four. And she never left the Temple, serving night and day with fastings and prayers. And at that very moment she came up and began giving thanks to God, and continued to speak of Him to all those who were looking for the redemption of Jerusalem.[79]

There are many similarities between these godly individuals and the godly saints of today's believing world. First, note their soteriology (doctrine of salvation). Simeon understood that when he saw Yeshua, he was beholding God's salvation. Of course, this was true in a most literal sense because the name Yeshua means salvation. But the text implies more than just that. Simeon said that Yeshua was God's salvation. He understood that Yeshua was the Promised One of whom the prophets spoke. In addition, the text says that Simeon was waiting for the Messiah. We know he was a devout man and, therefore, knew and believed the Scriptures. Consequently, we can rightly assume that Simeon believed this long-awaited Messiah to be both the suffering servant of Isaiah 53 as well as the glorious king of Isaiah chapters 2, 9, and 11.

Anna also had a sense of that promised redemption. She stood in the Temple courts and proclaimed the news of His arrival to others who, like her, were expecting the redemption of Jerusalem (spoken of in the Tanakh).

Second, notice their reputations. It is said of Simeon that he was a "righteous" man. We know that all are born dead in their trespasses and sins. Moreover, the Scripture says that there is no one who is righteous, not even one (Romans 3:10). In order for Simeon to be considered a righteous man, there had to have been a fundamental change that occurred in his life. In other words, he had to have been regenerated. His old man would have had to die and new life—life from God—had to have been birthed in him.

As far as Anna is concerned, she too is described in terms that can only apply to a regenerated individual. For instance, "she never left the Temple, serving night and day with fasting and prayer." In addition, when she saw Yeshua, she could not keep quiet about Him and "continued to speak of Him to all those who were looking for the redemption of Jerusalem." Notice how vocal she became about Yeshua—even before His ministry, teaching, atoning death, and miraculous resurrection!

Finally, observe their doctrine of the Holy Spirit. For Simeon, the Holy Spirit was one who empowered him in a special way for special tasks, i.e., he "came upon him." In addition, the text describes Simeon as one who walked "in the Spirit." Moreover, the Holy Spirit was Simeon's teacher.

There are probably other details that could be mentioned. But these are sufficient to demonstrate that, in truth, the saints among the remnant of God's people in the period of the Tanakh shared the same spiritual realities as those following the revelation of the Brit Hadasha. Because of progressive revelation, we know more details about our spiritual reality than the saints of the Tanakh did. The Brit Hadasha provides us with an appropriate theological vocabulary to describe who we are in Messiah that the previous saints did not possess.

Some at this point may ask, "But what about the coming of the Holy Spirit on the day of Pentecost, recorded in Acts chapter 2? I always thought that was when the Spirit of God came for the first time to indwell believers." That is a fair question, and we will address it shortly.

The Redeemed Community

Another way of referring to God's collective people is by calling them the "redeemed community." Just as ancient Israel was redeemed from slavery to Egypt by the blood of the Passover lamb, so also are the people of God redeemed from slavery to sin by the blood of the Passover Lamb, Yeshua the Messiah.

It is important to note that not all of the people of Israel were spiritually redeemed. The nation as a whole was redeemed from physical slavery, thus providing a Torah picture of what it means to be spiritually redeemed. But there was and always has been a minority within that nation who constituted "the remnant." They were those who were both physically and spiritually redeemed.

We can illustrate the concept of "The Remnant" by using the following three circles (figure 3). The circle of the top represents all of the physical descendants of Abraham, Isaac, and Jacob. The circle on the bottom represents the world of the gentiles. The smaller circle in the middle represents the Remnant—both the Remnant from among Israel and the Remnant from among the gentiles. Notice that the small remnant remains apart of the two respective people groups. The Remnant from the gentiles is still considered gentile. Likewise, the Remnant from Israel still considered to be a part of the larger people of Israel.

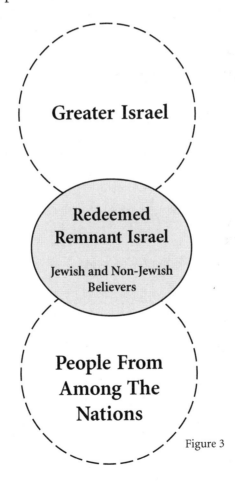

Greater Israel

**Redeemed
Remnant Israel**

**Jewish and Non-Jewish
Believers**

**People From
Among The
Nations**

Figure 3

The Torah was not given to Israel while they were still in bondage. Rather, God set them free and delivered them before He gave them the Torah. This fact is critical to our understanding of the Torah's relationship to salvation. If God had given the Torah before Israel was redeemed, it might be suggested that redemption could be achieved through obedience to the Torah. However, that is clearly not so. The Torah was provided after the exodus, after the slavery had ended, after they were called out of darkness. Its purpose was not to provide salvation through obedience, but to teach the children of Israel how to enjoy their freedom, their deliverance, and their new life with God. Torah is the teaching of the Redeemer to the redeemed on how to live as the redeemed community.

The Torah, as well as the rest of the Scriptures, tells us what the redeemed community looks like—how it relates to God, to one another, and to the rest of the world. In the Torah we see, for example, instructions covering all facets of life within the redeemed community. There are teachings concerning how the redeemed community conducts justice, how it worships and celebrates, how it does business, and so on. The Brit Hadasha provides specific commentary on the Torah's instructions for daily living, designed to meet the particular needs of new congregations who needed to know how to apply the Torah's instructions to their situations, especially now as the Torah community would be going out from Israel to the whole world. Because of the nature of the relationship of the Torah to the redeemed community, all the instructions of the Word of God, from the first book to the last, are divinely inspired and given for the regenerate remnant of all generations.

It was in God's plans that the holy community would no longer live only within the land of Israel. Yeshua announced this as one of His final instructions before He returned to His

Father's throne. He said, "and you shall be My witnesses both in Jerusalem, and in all Judea and Samaria, and even to the remotest part of the earth." (Acts 1:8) Because the redeemed community was now to go out among the nations bearing the Good News, special empowerment and instructions would be needed. Those joining the redeemed community living outside of the Land would need special instructions concerning how to live their new lives in the Torah. The textbook for spiritual instruction was still the same Torah they had always had. Now that they would be part of the holy priesthood and living stones (of the living temple), they would also need teaching which would enable them to minister in their new roles. These instructions, which we now read and study from the Brit Hadasha, are for the regenerate remnant living among the nations in every generation, just as they had always been for the remnant living in the Land.

Community

Whether we call it the holy community or the redeemed community, the common denominator is the word "community." This is a crucial concept for those who desire to identify with the Land, the People, and the Scriptures of Israel—especially those from a non-Jewish background.

We note, first of all, that when God gave the Torah at Mount Sinai, He gave it to the whole community of Israel. True, God spoke the words specifically to Moses, but he was merely the representative of the community. Just after the first part of the revelation of the Torah was given, it was the people of Israel—as a group—that responded in the plural, "All that the Lord has spoken we will do, and we will be obedient!" (Exodus 24:7) Immediately before these words, the text says that the people responded "with one voice." Thus, the Torah was given to the community, and the community agreed in united consent to live by it.

Second, many commands found in the Torah use the second person plural pronoun "you." However, Numbers 6:24–26 (the Aaronic Benediction) uses the second person singular pronoun. In these words, Moses instructs the Kohanim to "bless the Israelites." (*Israelites*—literally, "the sons of Israel"—is in the plural.) The fact that this blessing is stated in the singular signifies that, while it is directed to all of Israel, God has the individual in mind. Yet, the individual is intimately connected to the whole, the community; in God's eyes, the two are inseparable.

Let us consider one last crucial point concerning the concept of the community of Israel. The passage which instructs Israel about the cycle of divinely commanded worship and meeting times specifically instructs Israel to meet on certain occasions *as a group*, calling these meetings "sacred assemblies." For this cycle to work, the whole community had to participate. In fact, for the whole of Torah to work properly, the whole community had to participate. How, for instance, could all debts be released every fifty years, as the Torah commands, without the cooperation of the entire community? How could sacrifices be brought if the Levites went on strike? How would idolatry be eliminated from the nation if only a few contributed to its demise?

The Torah was never meant to be followed on a strictly individual basis. To be sure, there is a limited amount of blessing one can derive in the absence of community; nevertheless, the greater the community participation in the Torah, the greater the blessings—both to the community and, in turn, to the individual participant in that community.

The body of believers described in the Brit Hadasha is the same holy community. We find an equal amount of instruction designed for the whole community. For example, God gives revelation in the Brit Hadasha concerning the spiritual gifts that are part of who we are as a new creation in Messiah. We are taught that these spiritual gifts are given "for the building up of the body." Moreover, just as God gave a governing format to the people of Israel based on an elder system, so He also set up a similar governing system for the redeemed remnant that would now also live among the nations.

There is an equal amount of emphasis placed both in the Tanakh and the Brit Hadasha on the functioning of God's holy people as a community. Therefore, part of the believer's identity is that he can truly say that he is not an island unto himself. Rather, he is one of a vast and innumerable body of called-out and redeemed ones, regenerated by the Spirit of God and called together with all the others to lift up the head of the community, Messiah. He is lifted up before the nations and seen in His Glory as we all dwell together according to the instructions of the Book. We are the living stones being built into the spiritual Temple wherein dwells the *Shekhinah*—the Glory of the Living God!

The Bride

The Brit Hadasha uses another term to refer to the community of believers in Yeshua: "the bride of Messiah." At first glance, this appears problematic. On the one hand, it is clear from the Tanakh that Israel is God's bride. As we pointed out in *Torah Rediscovered*, a sacred wedding took place on Mount Sinai between God and Israel. In this context, the Torah assumed the function of a marriage contract, or *ketubah*, between God and Israel, specifying the conditions for that divine marriage. Furthermore, the fact that Israel is the bride of God is quite adequately affirmed in the rest of the Tanakh (see, for example, the prophecy of Hosea). Yet, on the other hand, Ephesians 5:21–33 uses the term "bride of Messiah" to refer to the community of believers in Yeshua.

What is the situation here? Does God have two brides? Is He a polygamist? Of course not! Neither is it possible that, as some have suggested, God divorced one bride, Israel, to marry another, the Church. Jeremiah speaks of this when he affirms God's everlasting covenant with the physical children of Israel in chapter 31:35–37. Sha'ul of Tarsus also affirms the continual existence of the physical people of Israel in Romans 9–11.

The best solution to this problem is to suggest that God has always had one bride: His chosen people. His bride has always been Israel. Since God has one bride, it would follow that the same *ketubah* (marriage covenant) the Torah, still defines this divine marriage. And because God has always made provision for gentile believers to be grafted-in to Israel, we may deduce that He cherishes these believers from among the nations every bit as much as He loves His people Israel. Together, remnant Israel and the remnant from among the nations constitute His dearly beloved bride.

Our non-Jewish brethren must begin to see themselves in this light, to know and believe that just as Israel is God's *segulah*—His especially treasured possession (Exodus 19:5)—so also are those from among the nations.

The Safe Place

The Torah describes certain boundaries, both geopolitical and spiritual, which God fixed for the ancient Israelites. These boundaries are an important physical reality for the nation of Israel. By God's deliberate design, they also serve as the Torah picture of the actual spiritual reality of God's Kingdom. Inside the boundaries is the Kingdom of God, and outside of those boundaries is another kingdom. The Torah is that instruction which identifies exactly where those spiritual boundaries lie—identifying that which is holy and that which is not holy; that which is clean and that which is not; that which is life and that which is death. Those who have crossed over from the kingdom of darkness into the Kingdom of light have been given everything they need to know in order to remain within the boundaries of their new reality.

In other words, a line is crossed when a member of the holy community ceases to dwell with others from that community. We are not referring to losing one's salvation, or becoming legally "kicked out" of one's spiritual position as a child of God; we believe this to be an impossibility as we understand the nature of grace and the full accomplishment of Messiah's atonement. However, in defining the limits of the holy community, the Torah speaks of itself as a guardian or protector of the redeemed. When followed, it provides spiritual, emotional, and even physical protection for the children of God. The realities of this truth are woven throughout the whole of the Tanakh, and are further delineated in the Brit Hadasha.

Figure 4 on the following page illustrates how the Torah works as a protector for the holy community. Shown is a picture of the Kingdom of light in the shape of Israel. It is bordered by the actual words of the Torah. Outside those borders is the kingdom of darkness. This diagram is not meant to imply that the nations outside of Israel constitute the kingdom of darkness; it is simply an illustration of the Torah's intended function as a protector. If we remain within the borders established by the teachings of Torah, we will enjoy our God-given inheritance, safe from the influences of the idolatrous peoples around us. We will also serve as a light to those nations.

This is also the reason for the commands of the Torah regarding those living in Israel who violate the Torah and must be put out of the community. One of the purposes of Israel was to be a place of safety, blessing and teaching. When a person violated this sacred place, he had to be removed from it for the sake of the rest of the holy community, until he either repented or was judged by God. Furthermore, this is also the reason that the "alien"—the non-Jewish person living among the inhabitants of the Holy Land—must live according to the Torah. For the sake of all those called to live in the Land, no act of rebellion can be allowed to compromise its holiness.

In Figure 5, we see that the teachings of the Torah establish *haMakom* (ha-ma-KOME, הַמָּקוֹם)—"the place" where believers can partake of and enjoy the blessings established by these teachings. The statutes that God laid down for us "are more desirable than gold, yes, than much fine gold; sweeter also than honey and the drippings of the honeycomb. Moreover, by them Thy servant is warned; in keeping them there is great reward." (Psalm 19:10–11)

The written Torah cannot and does not impart life (Galatians 3:21). The Torah community, created by obedience to the Torah, is the place where life reigns instead of death. It is the place of safety and teaching. "The statutes You have laid down are righteous, they are fully trustworthy" (Psalm 119:138, NIV) to "close up, hem in, and close within a place" (Galatians 3:23, translation ours). What place? *HaMakom*, the place of blessing! By so doing, then, the Torah "hits the mark" (the meaning of the Hebrew "Torah") of defining the place of blessing and life. This is true both for the remnant among Israel and the remnant from among the nations who are grafted-in to them.

Differences

We have just cited many of the similarities that exist between the called-out community that existed in the period of the Tanakh and that of the present age. Because of the principles of biblical continuity and progressive revelation, we would expect such similarities to exist, albeit all too often ignored. Is there a difference between the two?

Figure 4

Figure 5

The chart (Figure 6) on the following page lists some of the important factors to take note of when we attempt to answer this question. Please keep in mind that it is not an exhaustive list. There are more similarities. You may want to add some yourself. Note, however, the "callings." Let the chart speak for itself when we compare the two callings.

The difference between the two groups lies in the fact that there are physical descendants of Abraham who have been given the unique calling by God to be just that—the physical descendants of Abraham. The Scripture teaches that they always would survive as a nation. If this nation were to be lost, then we would have sufficient grounds for questioning our own security as believers.

This truth is evidenced in at least two passages. The first is Jeremiah 31:35–36, wherein the continuity of the existence of Israel as a nation is promised. In these verses, the continuity and perpetuity of the existence of the nation is compared to that of the entire creation of God! The second passage is really an extended passage. In Romans chapters 9–11, Sha'ul uses the nation of Israel as an example of what it is like to be justified by faith. God demonstrated His righteousness by calling Israel by grace, saving her as a nation by His grace, and keeping her as a nation by His grace. In this same way He relates to all individual people whom He has saved by grace in Yeshua the Messiah. Therefore, Israel always has been designed to be a teaching picture of the Good News to the nations.

The Mishkan/Temple

In addition to observing the biblical continuity between the kehilah and the ekklesia (Church), there is a second area for us to consider. Let us examine some of the progressive revelation concerning the Mishkan (Temple) and its counterpart in the Brit Hadasha.

The differences in identity between believing Jews and non-Jews	
Jewish Believers	**non-Jewish Believers**
Saved by grace through faith	Saved by grace through faith
Regenerated	Regenerated
Indwelt by Messiah	Indwelt by Messiah
New Creations	New Creations
Torah Written on Hearts	Torah Written on Hearts
Circumcised	Circumcised (in the Heart)
Sealed by the Spirit	Sealed by the Spirit
Indwelt by the Spirit	Indwelt by the Spirit
Anointed for specific tasks	Anointed for specific tasks
The Bride of Messiah	The Bride of Messiah
Physical Descendants of Abraham	Spiritual Descendants of Abraham

The differences in calling between believing Jews and Non-Jews	
Jewish Believers	**non-Jewish Believers**
Called to Display Unity	Called to Display Unity
Called to Display Love	Called to Display Love
Called to Testify for Messiah	Called to Testify for Messiah
Called to Be Holy	Called to Be Holy
Called to the Covenants	Called to the Covenants
Called to Live by Faith	Called to Live by Faith
A National Calling	Called to be "the Nations"
To Be a Teaching Picture	To Be the Benefactor of the Teaching Picture

Figure 6

Beginning in Exodus chapter 25, Moses gave the children of Israel instructions for building what we called a *Mishkan* (מִשְׁכָּן) or *ohel mo'ed* (אֹהֶל מוֹעֵד). The word Mishkan is translated as "tabernacle." The term ohel mo'ed is rendered "tent of meeting." This tent-like structure was to become the center of worship and instruction for the Israelites. Wherever God led them to move, they were to take the tent with them.

As its names suggest, this movable tent was to be the place where the manifested glory of God dwelt. In fact, the Hebrew name, Mishkan, is from the root שׁכן which means "to dwell." Moreover, as the place which hosted God's special presence, the Mishkan was also the ohel mo'ed, the tent of meeting, where man met with God in a special and unique way.

After the children of Israel settled in their land, the Mishkan eventually became a permanent edifice. King Solomon had the ark and all of the other biblical furniture housed in one of the most beautiful buildings in the entire Ancient Near East. At its core, however, the Temple served the exact same functions as the original Mishkan, with the addition of being the center of royal activity. Thus,

> Since the Exodus, when the Israelites built the Tabernacle in the wilderness, the Temple has been the center of prophetic revelation, the royal authority of the Davidic and Hasmonean dynasties. It was the high point of all religious ceremony and the seat of the High Priest.[80]

Besides being the place where sacrifices were offered and the holy ark of the covenant was housed, one of the outstanding features of the Mishkan was the visible presence of the glory of God which resided there. In rabbinic literature, this was called the Shekhinah, from the same Hebrew root as Mishkan. The Shekhinah took up residence there when the Mishkan was completed, as Exodus chapter 40 records. Because of thisspecial presence of God amid the children of Israel, the rabbis say, "Though the presence of God is everywhere, the Shekhinah rests pre-eminently on Israel rather than on the gentiles (Ber.7a; Shab. 22b; Num. R 7:8). For Israel is a people chosen and sanctified by God to be carriers of His will to the world."[81]

Unfortunately, Israel sinned as a nation. Israel's idolatry and ungodliness led to the First Temple's destruction. The prophet Ezekiel records for us one of the saddest moments in Israel's history. In chapters 10 and 11 we read the account of the departure of the Shekinah just before the Temple was destroyed and the people were taken into captivity in Babylon. Although another Temple was built after their return from exile, "the Second Temple was thought to have been devoid of the Divine Presence; cf. Toma9b."[82]

The First Temple was destroyed by the Babylonians in 586 BCE. The Second Temple was also destroyed—by the Romans in 70 CE. According to rabbinical sages, both Temples were destroyed on the exact same date (656 years apart). But even before its destruction, God stripped the Second Temple of most of its theological relevance when the Messiah Yeshua made His once-for-all atonement. This is the clear teaching of Hebrews chapters 8–10. Messiah's atoning sacrifice rendered the whole sacrificial system redundant. This also included the priests, and the entire function of the Temple as a place of atoning sacrifices and worship. Having made the above statement, we must keep two things in mind, however. The fact that the Temple was rendered obsolete does not mean that God did not accept worship there. Indeed, the Messianic believers worshipped there until its destruction. In addition, Ezekiel predicts a time during the Messianic age when God will have another Temple standing. There, the prophet says, sacrifices for sin and fellowship will again be offered and accepted by God.

In what way can we see a biblical continuity between the Mishkan of old and the body of Messiah? God Himself says that there is a connection. Whereas once the people worshipped and sacrificed in the setting of a particular building, the community itself is now the "building." In fact, He declares to the body of Messiah (consisting of Jewish and non-Jewish members), "Do you not know that your body is a Temple of the Holy Spirit?" (1 Corinthians 6:19). Moreover, Ephesians 2 alludes to the fact that the body of Messiah is a Temple, a living building, when it declares,

> ...you...are of God's household, having been built upon the foundation of the apostles (*sh'lichim*) and prophets (*nevi'im*), Messiah Yeshua Himself being the cornerstone, in whom the whole building being fitted together is growing into a holy temple in the Lord; in whom you also are being built together into a dwelling of God in the Spirit. (Ephesians 2:20–22)

Furthermore, in the quotation above, the writer said that the ancient "Temple has been the center of prophetic revelation, the royal authority of the Davidic and Hasmonean dynasties. It was the high point of all religious ceremony and the seat of the High Priest."[83] The same can also be said of the body of Messiah, the spiritual temple. God gave the body spiritual gifts enabling people to speak forth His Word (prophecy). Moreover, the body of Messiah is most certainly the center of royal authority since it has both King Messiah dwelling in each member, and the authority from the King to govern itself (Matthew 18). Finally, we have a new High Priest, Yeshua. This means that the spiritual temple is also the seat of the High Priest, just as was suggested above.

From all of this we can see that the concept of the Mishkan was not eliminated when God formed the body of Messiah. Rather, the same concepts which were in bud form in the Tanakh now bloom in full color in the Brit Hadasha.

That Fateful Shavu'ot

Moreover, there is one more important point of comparison between the Temple of the Tanakh and the temple of the Brit Hadasha. If we can understand and accept the concept of progressive revelation, we will be better equipped to have a clearer understanding of what happened in Acts chapter 2 on that fateful Pentecost.

Evangelical scholars generally agree that "The Word teaches that the Church was founded on the Day of Pentecost (Acts 2)."[84] We think that there might be another explanation for what happened in Acts chapter 2.

What we are about to say is merely a *suggestion*! We do not mean to propagate the following as if it is absolute truth. It is difficult to be a theological fish and attempt to swim upstream against the current fashions of biblical interpretation. In a sense, that is what we are about to do in presenting our theory below. What you are about to read is our attempt to practice the principle of progressive revelation and apply it to biblical teaching concerning the nature of the body of Messiah. Please grant us the grace to be wrong, if necessary! At the same time, please give the following ideas a chance.

Having written the above preface, here is our thinking regarding what happened in Acts 2 and how it demonstrates a biblical continuity between the Mishkan of the Tanakh and that of the Brit Hadasha.

We do not necessarily agree with Dr. Thiessen and a host of other fine Bible teachers who suggest that the church was born on Pentecost in Acts chapter 2. Yes, we do agree that something special *did* happen when the Ruach haKodesh (Holy Spirit) visited God's people on that fateful Shavu'ot. Yet, we do not think that this event was the beginning of a movement which would divorce itself from the Land, the People, and the Scriptures of Israel.

At the outset, we should note that the group of Messianic believers who were worshiping God on this holy day were Jewish believers. They were wondering when God would "restore the kingdom to Israel" (Acts 1:6). Messianic Jews in the Book of Acts never departed from the Torah in lifestyle or worship; they simply knew Yeshua to be the focal point of the community in which the Torah was the basis of life and instruction. Furthermore, they expected this same type of community to exist among the new believers from among the nations; this became especially evident when they encouraged the God-fearers to continue following the Torah.

Another Movable "Mishkan"

In our opinion, the events which occurred on this occasion represent a shift from that which was a covenant reality in the period of the Tanakh to a change under the Renewed Covenant. The major change lay in the form in which the Temple was now to exist. In the Torah, God commanded that a *Mishkan* (Tabernacle) be built, where He would manifest Himself and where the people would worship Him via offerings and sacrifices. Later, this movable Mishkan was made permanent and named *Beit haMikdash*, the Temple. Now, from the time of the events of Acts 2, this Temple would again become a movable Mishkan. However, the materials for this new Temple would be what the Brit Hadasha calls "living stones"—the lives of all who are called by God's grace to be a part of the body of Messiah.

To understand our viewpoint, one must realize that the meeting of believers recorded at the opening of chapter 2 took place in *the Temple*. The fact that the "blowing of a violent wind came from heaven and filled the *whole house where they were sitting*" (italics ours) leads many to believe that the disciples were meeting in the "upper room." However, scholar Danny Litvin rightly observes:

Such an interpretation is fraught with difficulties. It is impossible to imagine a crowd of three thousand people or more gathered with the disciples (verse 6) if they were in a small upper room. Even if the room had a balcony and the disciples were all standing on it speaking in tongues, the narrow streets of Jerusalem would not allow three thousand people to hear voices emanating from one small balcony.[85]

In addition, "the house" does not necessarily refer to a person's private home. Rather, this phrase was commonly used during the Second Temple period to denote the Temple itself. Litvin states:

> There is no need to assume that they were sitting together having a meal or discussing things around a table or on the floor. If one were to say in Hebrew, "He is in the house," [one] would say, "He is sitting in the house." This is a Hebrew idiom used to indicate location. Second, the Hebrew word for house (*bayit*) can either mean an everyday house in which people live or the Temple which stood on Mount Moriah….Even today, in Israel, if you were to take a taxi and ask the driver to take you to the Temple Mount, you would ask him to take you to "Har HaBayit," which translated literally means "Mountain of the House."[86]

Where would these Torah-observant Jews have been on the morning of Shavu'ot? It seems clear that the disciples were meeting on the Temple Mount, celebrating Shavu'ot as was their custom every year of their lives, as did the rest of their Torah-observant countrymen.

Indeed, this location is a central part of our argument. In Acts chapter 2, because of what He did on that day, it seems that God was making a clear statement about the new Temple. It appears that He was saying that the new and the visible Temple in the world would now be one in which living stones would be built into a spiritual house "...upon the foundation of the apostles and prophets, Messiah Yeshua Himself being the corner {stone} in whom the whole building, being fitted together is growing into a holy temple in the Lord; in whom you also are being built together into a dwelling of God in the Spirit." (Ephesians 2:21–22)

We believe this for two reasons. First, the Brit Hadasha clearly speaks of the chosen remnant of God as the Temple. 1 Corinthians 3:16–17, 1 Corinthians 6:19–20 and Ephesians 2:19–20 all describe the called-out holy community which was living the Torah—and which, in so doing, functioned as the Temple of the living God.

We know that within a few years after the Shavu'ot of Acts 2, the Temple in Jerusalem was destroyed, thus completing the shift of emphasis from a Temple made of stones to a house made of living stones. Consequently, the Shavu'ot of that year became the day in which God made a public proclamation before the nation of Israel: the holy community of believers in Yeshua would now be His Temple. This was not necessarily understood on that day; rather, we are able to discern it now in light of the completed revelation of the Brit Hadasha. (However, we would not be surprised to find out that many on that day had their eyes opened by the Spirit of God to exactly this message!)

The second reason for our interpretation of Acts chapter 2 is our understanding of the flames of fire which alighted on the heads of Yeshua's disciples. What were these flames? The Torah states in Leviticus 9:23 that when the priests and Levites were consecrated for their ministry, they came out "blessed the people, and the glory of the Lord appeared to all the people. Fire came out from the presence of the Lord and consumed the burnt offering and the fat portions on the altar." A Talmudic tradition based on this passage in Leviticus holds that this fire, while in context coming from the Holy of Holies, actually emanated from the heavens.[87] In other words, God sent fire from heaven for the altar of sacrifice.

On the Shavu'ot of Acts 2, just as God had sent the fire from heaven (from the presence of the Lord) to alight upon the altar of sacrifices, so also did He send this fire from heaven upon His new altar—the body of believers. The text in verse 3 indicates that the fire divided into tongues that touched each of the disciples, thus identifying them as the living stones which now would make up His Temple.

Accordingly, the Brit Hadasha instructs believers, "I urge you therefore, brethren, by the mercies of God, to present your bodies a living and holy sacrifice, acceptable to God, [which is] your spiritual service of worship." (Romans 12:1) The flames of fire upon the altar of sacrifice in the Tabernacle consumed the burnt offerings, enabling the savor of that sacrifice to rise up to God as a pleasing aroma. In the same way, God smells the sweet aroma of our lives as we daily offer ourselves in service to Him as living sacrifices. When we offer our bodies as instruments of God's righteousness on the earth, rather than walking carelessly in our flesh, the sweet aroma of our sacrifice brings Him great pleasure.

In addition to the Talmudic tradition about the fire from heaven coming down to set the altar of sacrifice ablaze, another rabbinic tradition says that a portion of that same flame was carried into the Holy Place and used for the fire upon the altar of incense.[88] As indicated in the Book of Revelation, the incense represents the prayers of the saints (5:8); hence, just as the incense was to burn continually in the Temple, we as believers are instructed to pray without ceasing.

Essentially, then, in our view, the true meaning of that defining moment in Acts 2 hinges on two concepts. First, God used the flames of fire to identify the new Temple. This Temple would be like the movable Mishkan of old: rather than standing in a fixed spot, it would move with believers wherever they were sent with the Good News of Yeshua. Up to this point, it had been the norm for the nations to come up to Jerusalem. Now the Temple would go out *from* Jerusalem—unto the uttermost parts of the earth. In the millennial age, the Temple will once again stand in the midst of Jerusalem. And again, the nations will come up to worship the King in Jerusalem.

Second, it was at this moment that He gave us the essential gifts and empowerment we would need to accomplish the task of taking the Good News to all nations of the earth. All that was needed for us to be the true "movable Mishkan" was provided for. Yeshua emphasized this necessary empowerment when He predicted the events recorded in Acts 2. Just before returning to His Father's throne in Acts 1:6–8, He told His students to wait in Jerusalem, presumably because Shavu'ot was approaching. Then He declared to them, "But you shall receive power when the Holy Spirit has come upon you; and you shall be My witnesses both in Jerusalem, and in all Judea and Samaria, and even to the remotest part of the earth." Notice the connection between the giving of the Spirit of God to Yeshua's followers, their empowerment, and their mission. As far as He was concerned, it was a simple sequence: the Spirit coming upon them to empower them for their new task, and the sending forth of His followers with that task.

There *is* biblical continuity between Israel—the people of God in the times of the Tanakh—and this present age. Admittedly, some differences may exist, such as the addition of multitudes to the continuing stream of the remnant people of God. Yet whatever characterized the believing community before Pentecost is that which would also characterize them afterward. Non-Jews together with the remnant of Israel are God's called-out people, designed to function most consistently in their identities as new creations and as a holy community when the Torah is lived out in their midst.

For, in addition to being that which established and defined the holy community in the past, the Torah is the basis for further instruction on the nature of that community in this present age. The epistles of the Brit Hadasha merely expound on its principles, while speaking to the specific needs of the local communities to whom they were sent.

There has been a long history of stressing perceived differences between those called out before and after the events of Acts 2. If we continue in this manner of interpretation, we will remain a fractured body of Messiah—one in which the Church and Israel (represented by the believing remnant) are seen as two distinct spiritual entities, two different flows of the stream of God's covenanted people. This is neither necessary nor true to our reality as believers in the same Messiah!

It is frequently stated that pictures speak a thousand words. Martha Stern, wife of Messianic Jewish scholar, Dr. David Stern painted a beautiful picture nearly ten years ago which depicts those earth-shaking events that took place in Acts chapter 2. She has graciously allowed us to place a black and white version of her brilliantly colored original in our book (Figure 7, following page). We feel that, better than anyone else, she has captured in visual form, what we have been attempting to describe in words.

The picture shows the biblical continuity between the Torah given on Shavu'ot at Mount Sinai and the Spirit of God equipping the believers in Yeshua as described in Acts chapter 2. In both cases, God was equipping His people so that they could serve Him. What power there is when the Spirit of God is combined with the Word of God! The inevitable result is always spiritual fruit.

Notice another detail in Martha's art: The Spirit of God is coming upon each individual standing in front of the Temple. This shows how people, believers in Yeshua, become the living and movable Temple, taking the glory of God with them wherever the Holy One sends them.

Figure 7

Those Who Have Crossed Over

Thus far, in our study of progressive revelation, we have seen that believers in Yeshua, both Jewish and non-Jewish, can be identified as God's holy community, God's redeemed ones, and God's temple. There is yet another descriptive word that might be used in reference to the people of God. This is the word "Hebrew."

To understand our point here, we need to refer back to our discussion about the two kingdoms. We need to remember that when someone becomes a believer in Yeshua, he is transferred from one spiritual kingdom to another, from Satan's kingdom to God's Kingdom. There is a point when that person has actually crossed over, as if there is a river that separates the two kingdoms. Once he becomes a believer, he is forever separated from that other kingdom.

The words "crossed over" are the key words for our discussion. These words are the best way to render the Hebrew word for "Hebrew," *'ivri,* which is from the root *avar* (עבר). Scholars have noted that in ancient Ugaritic, a sister language to Hebrew, similar words existed. Transliterated, they are *'apiru* or *habiru.* Ancient Near Eastern scholar Jack Finegan says that "phonetically the word Hebrew ('ivri) corresponds very closely with 'Apiru or Habiru…"[89]

Biblically, the word "Hebrew" was first applied to Abraham. Finegan says that "since the root *'br* means 'to cross a boundary,' the name can be explained as meaning 'those who have crossed a boundary,' that is, 'immigrants'." Thus, according to Finegan, Abraham was called a Hebrew because he crossed over from Mesopotamia and was an immigrant to Canaan.[90] Furthermore, we should also note that to bolster this view, the Septuagint uses the word *ho perateis* (ο περατης) to translate the word "Hebrew" in Genesis 14:13. This Greek word means "the one who passes through…" Many scholars concur and suggest that *avar,* therefore, means "to cross over."

What does all of this word study on the term "Hebrew" have to do with our subject? It means simply this: Just as a Hebrew was one who crosses over from one place to another, so also are all of those who have become believers in Yeshua. To be one of the people of God, one has to "cross over" from the kingdom of sin and death to the Kingdom of light and life. How does one "cross over"? He does so only by trusting in the Redeemer and in His mighty acts. Yeshua, our Redeemer, is the One who is able to accomplish this miracle for us.

According to this concept of "Hebrew," then anyone—Jewish or gentile—who has "crossed over" may rightfully be called a Hebrew![91]

Please note that we are not saying that such a person is Jewish. We are merely using the concept depicted by the word "Hebrew" to describe what it is that has happened to all—both Jewish and gentile—who have trusted in Yeshua. Before anyone is born again, he is of the kingdom of darkness—no exceptions! When anyone is identified in the death, burial, and resurrection of the Messiah, he has been translated out of the kingdom of sin and death and placed into the Kingdom of God's beloved Son. This is fact! This is reality. In this, there is no difference between gentile and Jew. In this we are "one new man," new creations hidden in Messiah, and among those who have "crossed over."

In this sense, therefore, we who are in Messiah are all "Hebrews." Like our father Abraham who is the father of all those who are now Hebrew (one who has crossed over through faith), we who are redeemed have all crossed over from the realm of sin and death to God's eternal Kingdom. It is only in this sense, then, that non-Jewish believers in Messiah can be called by their new identity—Hebrews.

A Torah Picture

Before leaving this discussion, we would like to share a Torah picture that we discovered one Shavu'ot. We present this picture just for your consideration and edification. It illustrates how the concept of "crossing over" is deeply seated in the fabric of Scripture.

We were studying Joshua chapter 3 when we noticed some hidden gems from the Hebrew of this passage. We will quote significant portions of the passage. It reads like this:

> "Then Joshua rose early in the morning; and he and all the sons of Israel set out from Shittim and came *to the Jordan*, and they lodged there before they *crossed (over)*. And it came about at the *end of three days* that the officers went through the midst of the camp; and they commanded the people, saying, "When you see the ark of the covenant of the Lord your God with the Levitical priests carrying it, then you shall set out from your place and go after it...that you *may know the way* by which you shall go, for you *have not passed this way* before. ...And Joshua spoke to the priests, saying, 'Take up the ark of the covenant and cross over ahead of the people.'...You shall, moreover, command the priests who are carrying the ark of the covenant, saying, 'When you come to the edge of the waters of the Jordan, you shall stand {still} in the Jordan.'"...So it came about when the people set out from their tents to cross the Jordan with the priests carrying the ark of the covenant before the people, and when those who carried the ark *came into the Jordan*, and the feet of the priests carrying the ark were dipped in the edge of the water (for the Jordan overflows all its banks *all the days of harvest*), that the waters which were flowing down from above stood {and} rose up in one heap, a great distance away at Adam, the city that is beside Zarethan; and those which were flowing down toward the sea of the Arabah, the Salt Sea, were completely cut off. So the people crossed.... (italics ours)

Biblical geography was carefully designed by the God of Israel to illustrate spiritual truths. If we combine the knowledge of biblical geography and the use of the concept of "Hebrew," i.e., "crossing over," we can see a beautiful and powerful Torah picture emerging. There are two phases of this Torah picture. The first phase pictures salvation and the second phase illustrates enjoying our inheritance. Both of these steps involve "crossing over" something.

The first "crossing over" was when God delivered the Israelites from Egyptian slavery at Passover. Through the blood of the Passover lamb, He redeemed them. But that was only half of the picture. God also saved them when He brought them face to face with death at the shores of the Sea. It was here that the Holy One told them "Stand still and see the salvation of the Lord!" They, indeed, could have done nothing else; they were utterly hopeless and helpless. God called upon them to simply trust Him and He would deliver them. What kind of faith was God requiring? It was the kind of faith that evidenced itself in obedience. Hence, to show that they truly trusted Him, God had the Israelites cross over the Sea. When they began to do so, He performed a miracle and they crossed over on dry ground (see Exodus 14:15). The act of crossing over did not save them. It was their trust in His Word that effected the deliverance. By crossing over, they crossed over from the pursuing kingdom of Egypt and into God's realm of safety.

The second "crossing over" was just as important, yet for different reasons. After 40 years of wandering in the wilderness, the children of Israel were finally on the verge of entering into their inheritance. It was already their inheritance through God's covenant with Abraham. But because of their disobedience, they had not entered into it. Now, after the 40 years, they were on the east bank of the Jordan River and about to cross over into their inheritance. It is at this point that a second beautiful Torah picture emerges. Salvation means "crossing over" from one kingdom to another. But enjoying their salvation/inheritance also meant they had to cross over

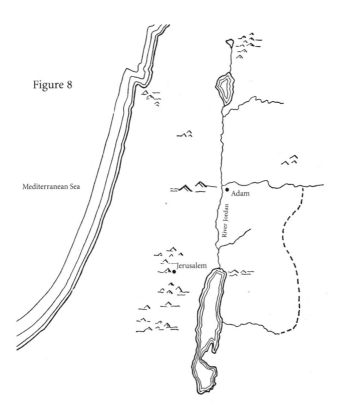

Figure 8

Mediterranean Sea

River Jordan

Adam

Jerusalem

into a place where only taking God at His Word and acting upon it could bring them the benefits of everything promised.

There are two Hebrew words that are critical to this Torah picture that we are about to paint: "Jordan" and "Joshua." In addition to understanding the meaning of these Hebrew words, we also need to know a little about Israel's geography to comprehend this Torah picture more fully.

First, let us examine the meaning of the Hebrew words. The name "Jordan" comes from the Hebrew word, *yarden* (ירדן). It has been accepted by some that the addition of the final *nun* (ן) brings into the word the concept of "judgment," *dan* (דן).[92] This point could be debated. But the possibility that it creates is interesting. If this is true, then this possible compound word can read, "down from judgment." We would suggest, then, that the river represents that which flows "down from judgment." Geographically, the Jordan River also flows down from "Dan," because, the tribe of Dan was originally in the north of Israel. It was near one of the headwaters for the Jordan River that flowed down from the melting snow on Mount Hermon. From the vicinity of Tel Dan, in modern Israel's panhandle, the river flows due south into the Kinneret (Sea of Galilee). It then leaves the Kinneret at its southern point and continues its flow south finishing in the Salt Sea, *Yam haMelach*, known today as the Dead Sea. (figure 8)

The Hebrew word "Joshua," the second key word in our Torah picture, is the same root from which we get the name Yeshua (ישוע). Its root means "salvation."[93] Hence, Joshua represented salvation to the people. They were to follow Him wherever they went in their inheritance. In Joshua, they conquered. In Joshua, they also rested in their inheritance.

Let us now combine all of these facts and attempt to discover the beautiful Torah picture that this passage is painting for us.

Since the word "Jordan" can mean "down from judgment," then the flow of the river would illustrate all the consequences that flow to people from being under the just judgment of God, our righteous Judge. Just as they were about to enter into their inheritance, the people had to cross over one more seeming barrier. They were already saved and redeemed from Egypt. But they were not enjoying their inheritance. God was about to teach them how to do so.

As they were about to enter the Promised Land, they realized that the Jordan River hindered them. What did God do? Miraculously, He stopped the flow of the river. The text makes a special point to tell us exactly where the flow was stopped: it reads, "afar off at a place called Adam." In modern

Israel, one can still visit the place called Adam located on the Jordan River about one third of the way from Jericho to the Kinneret. It is no accident that God picked a spot called Adam to be the place where the flow of the water stopped. If the Jordan pictures God's flow of judgment, then we realize that the judgment flowing since Adam because of his sin has been stopped for those who are the inheritors of salvation.

The critical lesson here is that in order for the people to enjoy their inheritance they must realize that they are people for whom the flow of God's judgment has ceased. Actually, it stopped at the Second Adam, at Yeshua. Did they believe that? Did they really believe that God stopped the river's flow? If so, then they merely had to take a step into the riverbed to see it. They had to cross over and actually enter into their inheritance in order to enjoy it. Crossing over meant trusting that what God said concerning their salvation was true. The way had clearly been opened before them. All there was for them to do was just to walk in it.

It was a vivid lesson of great importance for them—and for us today. It is impossible to enjoy the inheritance that is ours by faith unless we walk in that faith. It is a walk that continually remembers that God's flow of judgment from Adam upon us has ceased.

There is a second part to this picture. There was a definite order to their crossing over the Jordan. God instructed that the priests were to bring the Ark of the Covenant to the edge of that which was the barrier. Then it says, "When you *see* the Ark of the Covenant of the Lord your God...you are to follow it." (italics ours) In so doing, they thus entered the promised inheritance.

This can picture the fact that following the teachings of God (Torah) opens the way to the fullest blessings of the inheritance. We are not speaking of a works salvation at this point. Remember that they were already "redeemed," so to speak. Blessing comes, however, through obedience. Enjoyment of our salvation comes only through taking God at His Word. The covenant makes the passage (dry ground) so that the people can cross over and enjoy it.

Finally, there was Joshua. Because of his name, he pictures salvation for us. They were to follow Joshua everywhere in the Promised Land. In a sense, therefore, they were to follow "salvation"—or Yeshua—everywhere in the inheritance. It is critical to keep salvation at the forefront of our minds at all times. Otherwise, we may begin to attempt to live out the inheritance through our flesh. This eventually happened to Israel when the people lost sight of their salvation. The subsequent years of the Israelites' history became one of toil, strife, oppression, sin, and idolatry. The obedience God requires is one that is accomplished only through resting completely in the finished work of Yeshua. Sha'ul pointed us to this truth when he reminded the believers in Colossae, "As you therefore have received Messiah Yeshua the Lord, so walk in Him." (Colossians 2:6)

All of this was illustrated for us in the episode of the Israelites crossing over the Jordan River to follow Joshua in to possess the Promised Land.

The Torah

As we noted in our previous book, *Torah Rediscovered*, the writers of the Brit Hadasha had several things in mind concerning the Torah. First, they made it clear that for those who do not believe in Messiah, the Torah reveals their sinfulness and points them to the Messiah. Concerning God's people, however, the Torah delineates the specifics of the life of the holy community, and in doing so describes the lifestyle for the redeemed. In turn, the Brit Hadasha provides the best commentary on the Torah, even as it makes a more specific application to the holy community (which is comprised of those from among the nations as well as physical descendants of Jacob). In no way does the Brit Hadasha negate the Torah, replace it, or cause it to be rendered inoperable; on the contrary, the Brit Hadasha builds upon the foundation of the previous one, as is borne out by our discussion of progressive revelation. There remains, therefore, complete biblical continuity from Genesis to Revelation concerning the nature of the Torah, the saints of God, and the holy community.

The Scriptures themselves testify to this continuity. The Torah was given to Israel at the inception of their nation. As we have already stated, it defined what it meant for them to be God's protected covenant community. A thousand years later, just before the revelation of the Brit Hadasha, God still admonished His covenant community to abide by that covenant, the Torah. Thus we read in Malachi 4:4, "Remember the Torah of Moses My servant, {even the} statutes and ordinances which I commanded him in Horeb for all Israel."

The last of the Tanakh prophets, writing during the period of Israel's history when the First Temple was just a sad memory and the Second a mere dream, Malachi encourages the people of God to keep the Torah in the forefront of their minds. There is no hint whatever that the Lord intended to change that which gave them definition as a people. The next prophet of God to arrive on the scene is Yochanan the Immerser, calling the people to repent and live by that covenant. Then Yeshua the Messiah appears, powerfully teaching that very same Torah. Again, there is biblical continuity—the Torah remains intact. Finally, Sha'ul is sent to reach the nations for Messiah. What is he teaching? Torah. Indeed, the testimony of that period stands in these words: "You see, brother, how many thousands there are among the Jews of those who have believed, and they are all zealous for the Torah." (Acts 21:20)

We would like to comment at this point on the major difference between the Tanakh and the Brit Hadasha. The Tanakh is written both to physically redeemed Israel and to its remnant of regenerated believers. The Brit Hadasha is that body of revelation designed only for the *regenerate* remnant of Israel—including, of course, those grafted in.

Caution!

Before we conclude, there is one word of caution that we need to mention. The Torah can be both misunderstood and misused, especially by those who, in their zealousness to live by it, approach it without a clear understanding of what kind of document it is. This, of course, can cause problems.

One of the problems is confusing the Torah of God with the teachings of rabbinic Judaism. Many fall into this trap. Messianic Torah commentator Moshe (ben Shaya) Morrison has stated the problem like this: "What bothers me is people using (sometimes abusing) and selectively choosing traditional rabbinic sancta which suits their fancy and then calling it 'Torah Observance'."

This, indeed, is a problem that deserves serious attention. There is often a world of difference between what many rabbis teach and what the first five books of the Bible teach. Moreover, their expression and view of Torah is not always that which the Giver of the Torah intended.

There is a second part of this problem. Morrison summarizes by saying that these same proponents of rabbinic Judaism often criticize churches for having their own sancta and traditions which were originally intended to replace the faith and practice of the Old Testament. However, for the most part, these Christians are sincere in their efforts to express faithfulness to God's entire Word as they have been taught it.[94]

We would all do well to heed Morrison's warning. There is nothing inherently wrong with tradition, except when it expressly contradicts the written Word of God. We must be, careful not to let tradition, however time-honored it might be to become confused with the Word of God. On the other hand, it is not God's way for a believer to assume that he/she is called to criticize the understanding and the traditions of other believers. The key word is "criticize." Every tradition needs to come under the scrutiny of the Scriptures. However, God's way in correcting believers' misrepresentations of Scripture is to lovingly teach and minister His truths in His timing to those who need correction. We are to minister grace at all times in all of our dealings with one another.

Summary

God has always had a community of called-out ones who have embraced the Torah as that which defines their identity in Messiah and therefore also their way of life. Various names and designations throughout the Scriptures identify this community. It was never God's intention for two separate holy communities of covenant people to exist independently; Israel has always been and always will be God's holy community, specifically the remnant of Israel who believe in the Messiah. The Tanakh and the Brit Hadasha are consistent in revealing how non-Jews are added to that community.

If this is true, then it is the Torah which has historically defined the community of Israel. Since there is no biblical precedent for a change in that definition, the Torah continues to define the united redeemed community of Jewish and non-Jewish believers in Yeshua.

Believing Israel in the first century was a mighty light to the nations. As a result, many from those nations came to faith and were "grafted in" to the holy community (the Torah community). May the holy community of this present generation continue being that light to the nations, bringing many into "the Way, the Truth and the Life"—Yeshua Himself!

Is the Torah for me? Yes! For you? Are you grafted in? Are you a fellow-citizen with Israel? Then, yes! The Torah is for the holy community! As we all grow in our understanding of the consistent message of the Scriptures on the subject of the holy community, may we—like that ancient holy community standing at Mount Sinai—answer with one voice, "We will do and we will obey everything the Lord has said (ונשמע נעשה)." If this happens, the pagan and lost world of our day "will again distinguish between the righteous and the wicked, between one who serves God and one who does not serve Him." (Malachi 3:18) May we be encouraged by the assurance that the prophecy of Malachi 3:17–18 will, indeed, be fulfilled!

Conclusion

The idea of writing a book about the Jewish roots of our faith in Yeshua is not a new one. In fact, there are already several excellent works on the subject. Our approach, however, is unique. We intended to demonstrate that non-Jewish believers in Yeshua not only have their spiritual roots in the Land, the People, and the Scriptures of Israel, but also possess divine permission to take hold of and embrace in a visible and practical way their inheritance with Israel. Included in this, of course, is the divine permission to participate in the covenants of Israel, especially the covenant with Moses—the Torah.

We think we have done just that. Beginning with the revelation found in the Torah, continuing through the prophets, Yeshua's teaching and finishing with the writings of Sha'ul of Tarsus, we have demonstrated that the Scriptures provide ample evidence of the deep unity that exists between Jewish and non-Jewish believers in Yeshua. Indeed, the words "deep unity" do not even tell the complete story. The Word of God amply describes the special relationship that exists between the remnant of believers from among the nations (a people once so far away from the stream of the remnant of believers of God's people Israel) and the remnant from among Israel. Indeed, through the finished work of Messiah, gentile believers are now fellow citizens of Israel and fellow participants in the covenants of Israel. We believe, therefore, that they have divine permission to fully participate in the Torah oriented lifestyle that the Holy One designed for the people of Israel—and all who call upon the name of the Lord.

Your Responses

Some of the issues discussed in this book may seem rather radical in comparison to traditional Bible teaching. It is not our desire to be controversial; rather, our goal is to be true to the Scriptures. Again, there may be a temptation to brand the authors as Judaizers (proponents of the belief that non-Jewish believers must follow the Torah and live a Jewish lifestyle to be in good standing among God and His people). We have pointed out, however, that the ingrafting of non-Jewish believers to Israel does not make them Jews, but merely grants them "citizenship in Israel," to use Sha'ul's terminology. Moreover, we have never suggested that one must convert to Judaism in order to be justified before God.

Another form of this objection would be the charge of legalism. Such labeling would betray a complete misunderstanding of what we have attempted to communicate. Legalism is man's attempt to earn or keep his eternal salvation by the works he performs or by adherence to a legal code, whereas we have stated unequivocally that salvation is completely dependent upon one's personal faith in the person and atoning work of Messiah Yeshua. Moreover, we have clearly indicated that the Torah is not a legal code, but a covenant. In addition, we have taught that the Torah was never given to God's people in order for them to earn, merit, or keep the grace gift of His salvation. God's acceptance of us is not performance-based, but unconditional.

The Middle Wall

We dealt with the subject of the "middle wall of partition" in chapter 2. For those who believe that we are attempting to restore this wall, we would like to present the following thoughts.

Both the Jewish and evangelical communities have instituted their own codes of law—codes which, having little to do with God's teachings, serve mainly to alienate people from one another. For example, in Jerusalem's ultra-Orthodox neighborhood of Me'ah She'arim, everyone follows the rabbinic laws for keeping a kosher kitchen. However, because of variations in what is considered truly "kosher," many feel they cannot eat in their neighbors' homes. In the evangelical world, joining a local fellowship often involves conforming to a list of do's and don'ts, such as "You cannot go to movies," "You cannot dance," "You cannot drink any alcoholic beverage," ad infinitum. Granted, the original intent of these rules may have been good; nevertheless, their message is clearly one of performance-based acceptance. As a result, such rules have also created division among brothers and sisters in Messiah.

It is the sinful enmity between brothers, reflected so tellingly in their rules and regulations, which builds the so-called middle wall of partition. If people would embrace the Torah as their only true standard for righteousness, they could drop all the man-made standards that have separated brother from brother for generations. Thus, we must always remember that God's Torah is not that middle wall, nor did Yeshua's sacrifice take away the Torah. Yeshua's atonement, rather, dealt with man's sinful tendency to alienate himself from others by building his own middle walls with his own man-made regulations.

Preconceived Ideas

For the average believer, preconditioned by years of anti-Torah teaching and replacement theology, the mere mention of the word "Torah" conjures up all sorts of legalistic notions. This conditioned, negative reaction is not unlike the phenomenon experienced by many evangelicals whenever hands are raised in worship: while they will readily agree that the practice is rooted in biblical teaching, yet—because of misunderstandings concerning the Charismatic segment of the body of Messiah—they are emotionally conditioned to shun the practice.

Brothers and sisters in Messiah, let us give the Torah a second look. Some, to be sure, are guilty of approaching it in a legalistic manner; however, we would caution against "throwing out the baby with the bath water."[95] When we take a different look at the Torah and the Brit Hadasha through the eyes of the Torah we will emerge with a much clearer perception of the continuity between the people of God in the Tanakh and the people of God in all succeeding generations.

The Zealots

We believe that, by the grace of God, there will be many positive responses to what we have written, and that many will find great encouragement and assurance therein. Unfortunately, in the midst of their enthusiasm, some may unwittingly exercise poor judgment. For example, we might find some misguided believer, flush with the desire to follow the Torah, standing on the street in a white shirt, black coat and trousers, and a black *kippah* and hat, like an observant *chasid* from Me'ah She'arim in Jerusalem or Williamsburg in New York City!

That, of course, would be unfortunate. Living like an Orthodox Jewish person is neither desirable nor undesirable, *per se*; however, taking hold of our divine permission to live out our inheritance with Israel does not require that we look, act, or even think like Orthodox Jews. God has called us to live by His Torah within the culture in which He has sovereignly placed us; to embrace the Bible, but not necessarily to adopt every tradition that has grown up around it. Furthermore, if we are to maintain integrity, we must understand that Orthodox Jewish expressions of faith belong to Orthodox Jews. It would offend them to see non-Jewish believers dressed in their garb.

Equally disturbing is the specter of novice zealots taking up their Torahs and using them to judge, rebuke, and condemn all who disagree with their views. While it is wonderful to be excited about living the life described in the Torah, it is quite another matter to insist that others do likewise. Think about how long it has taken you to come to your position, and let the graciousness of God permeate all your discussions on the subject. Remember that each and every person is in the hands of a sovereign God who opens people's eyes in His timing alone.

There is another serious matter which we who embrace the whole of the Scriptures and desire to live our inheritance with remnant Israel must consider: it is sometimes our own behavior that is responsible for the rejection of our message. Because our detractors are watching so closely, we must take very seriously the stewardship of our attitudes and behavior. While this applies to every aspect of our lives, we are referring specifically to those attitudes and behaviors that concern the Torah (as well as the rest of the Scriptures). The way we think and act reflects our understanding of what the Torah truly is and the role it plays in our lives. This is why our beliefs in regard to the Torah are so crucial. If we attempt to live by the Torah, but not through the Spirit of God, then it is merely a flesh activity and, therefore, no longer Torah. Why? It is because the Torah is Yeshua's life being lived out in us. Hence, if we are walking (behaving) in the flesh, then it is not Yeshua's life in us; it is therefore also not Torah.

Needless to say, all these negative and misguided positive reactions reflect misunderstandings of our message. We espouse none of these ideas or lifestyles. We have avoided the idea that people should, must, or have to follow the Torah, as these sentiments have no place in a discussion of new creation human beings and the role of the Torah in their lives.

Our identity as believers in Yeshua, then, is many-faceted. We are new creations, with the Torah written on our hearts. We are also equal partakers of God's covenants with His chosen people, Israel. Living by the Torah, therefore, is not really a matter of "you should," "we must," or "I have to." It is merely a matter of letting the Living Torah who indwells us live His life in and through us.

Epilogue

"Happy the Day"

Did Israel deserve the inheritance? No! The blessings of the covenants were given purely from God's grace. This gift, however, can be a source of incredible happiness to all who embrace it properly. What about non-Jewish believers in Yeshua? Can living consistently with the covenant also bring them joy? The rabbis have some encouragement for them. In his comments on a Talmudic passage, Rabbi Abraham Cohen shares some very pertinent comments about the Torah and the people of the nations:

> It is therefore evident that, in the opinion of the Rabbis, their people [the people of Israel] possessed no exceptional inherent superiority for which they inherited the distinction conferred on them by God, and the special status would come to an end immediately on the abandonment of the Torah. Furthermore, they did not look upon the Torah as their exclusive possession. *On the contrary, it was destined for all mankind, and happy the day when all nations accepted it.*[96] (italics ours)

Indeed, blessed is Israel when they live the Torah. And happy is the day when all nations accept it! Are you ready? Then simply "take hold" of our tzitzit as we walk together in our mutual pursuit of the joyous life which the Torah opens up for us. We will walk together in the delight of our Messiah. After all, you have divine permission to do so!

Restoration

God has always intended the body of Messiah to live in true unity. For too long, divisions in the Body have hampered God's work from being performed in this world. We are not promoting an unbiblical form of ecumenism, that is, "The organized attempt to bring about the cooperation and unity of all believers in Messiah"[97] at the expense of compromising essential biblical doctrines. The integrity of biblical doctrine must be preserved. However, it is time for these rifts to be healed.

We hope you now have a clear picture of the precious unity between Jewish and non-Jewish believers that God has desired for Messiah's body from the beginning. The Holy One, blessed be He, designed this unity to help bring the message of the Good News to all peoples of the earth. Unfortunately, history is filled with ugly incidents which have conspired to oppose such a unity. As a result, today's body of Messiah is fractured and weakened. Jewish believers desiring to live by the covenant find only a spark of acceptance; any non-Jewish believer who shares that desire is strongly discouraged from acting on it.

Of all the passages of Scripture describing the magnificent future revival among the people of Israel, one of the most exciting is found in Romans 11. Verse 25 speaks of a time when the Spirit of God will have so worked among the Jewish people that eventually "all Israel will be saved." Lest we be sidetracked by the question of exactly what "all

Israel" means, let us focus on what, contextually speaking, appears to be one of the primary reasons for this amazing revival. Sha'ul tells us that, until this time, there will be a partial hardening upon the people of Israel—"until the fullness of the gentiles has come in." What does this phrase mean?

C. E. B. Cranfield suggests that "the fullness of the gentiles" most likely denotes the full number of the elect from among the gentiles.[98] However, this is by no means the only interpretation of the phrase.[99] Professor Mark Nanos believes it refers not to a number but a "completion." He also suggests that the phrases "come into something," or "share in something" may accurately render the Greek. Moreover, Nanos sees something of a time aspect here, citing the fact that the Greek word often rendered "come in" can be translated as "enter into" or simply "begin." Thus, says Nanos, "It is what will occur after the hardening of part of Israel has completed its function, signaling that it is time for the fullness of the gentiles to *begin*."[100] Specifically, Nanos concludes, Sha'ul has in mind the future "incoming of the gentiles to Zion."[101]

What might this mean in practical terms? Perhaps the gentiles will come into a fullness they never realized was theirs: a common heritage and a shared place of blessing with Israel. Synthesizing the views of Cranfield and Nanos, the phrase "when the fullness of the gentiles comes in" may signify a time when believers from the nations will apprehend their intimate connection with Israel. Perhaps they will do so to such an extent that they will live out Israel's Torah/Covenant—which, indeed, turns out to be theirs as well.

The text implies that the beginning of this gentile fullness will somehow contribute to the salvation of Israel. We can only speculate how this would occur, but the scenario is not too difficult to imagine. For centuries, the body of Messiah has been so divorced from its heritage with Israel that most

Jewish people have concluded—understandably—that Yeshua is not the Jewish Messiah. One of the chief stumbling blocks has been the attitude[102] of non-Jewish believers toward the very document that defines Israel: the Torah. The disparaging of it by many believers has been extremely offensive to the people of Israel, and is largely responsible for their belief that the Good News of Yeshua would, in fact, be *bad* news for them.

Imagine what would happen if the Jewish people were to see a major change in the attitudes of non-Jewish believers in Yeshua toward the Torah and the covenants. Can you picture a time when, instead of the gentiles focusing on Rome or Geneva, there would—in Nanos' terms—be an "incoming of the gentiles to Zion"? The restoration of non-Jewish believers to their roots among the people of Israel would honor Israel's God and Israel's covenants, especially the Torah. The people of Israel, seeing that this Good News and the Good News of the Torah are one and the same—and, therefore, for them—would be freer to embrace Yeshua. In the end, this gentile restoration to Israel would verify the fact that "the continuity of salvation history is maintained through the restoration of historical Israel to which gentiles are now attached through faith in Israel's God."[103]

Today's body of Messiah is like one big separated family, desperately in need of healing. Beloved, we believe that this healing of one of the greatest divorces that has ever occurred— between the remnant from among Israel and that from among the nations—can be accomplished. As the remnant of Israel commits itself to living by the covenant God gave us at the foot of Mount Sinai, we can begin to attain to the identity and calling planned for us by the Holy One. At the same time, this healing also starts with *you*, the remnant from among the nations.

As we Messianic Jews begin to fulfil our covenantal responsibility, we humbly invite you to "take hold" of our fringes and walk with us. It will be a rather shaky walk at first, because much of this is new for us too. Nevertheless, by the authority of God's Word, we can promise you that it will be the most adventurous and blessed walk on which you will ever embark. As you journey with us, we will pursue our mutual inheritance together. Here is how the Holy One states it:

> Stand by the ways and see and ask for the ancient paths, where the good way is, and walk in it; and you shall find rest for your souls.... (Jeremiah 6:16)

In actuality, Jeremiah 6:16 (quoted above) finishes by saying, "...But they said, 'We will not walk in it'." Let us be different from our ancestors! Let it not be said of us that we would not walk in His ancient paths. After all, we today through the revelation of the Brit Hadasha, possess the added advantage of knowing more clearly who we are as the redeemed of God.

Why do we follow Torah? Why endeavor to pursue our inheritance with the Land, the People, and the Scriptures of Israel? We do so because it is a part of who we are as new creations. When we read of the redeemed person as described by the precepts of Torah, we are, in reality, reading a description of who God has made us to be in the Messiah.

A beautiful picture of this is described for us in James 1:22-25. Here we learn the importance of being doers of the Word instead of listeners only. The illustration is of a person looking at himself in a mirror. What is this mirror? The Torah! (Though translated "law" in nearly every English translation [verse 25], it should actually be rendered *Torah*.) He who does not do the Word is like one who looks at his face in the Torah and immediately forgets what he looks like. In that state, therefore, he does not do the Word. The person who sees himself in the Torah and *remembers* that this is who he is, this is the one who does the Word.

When we look into the mirror of the Torah, our reflection is that of a redeemed person as described therein. The individual teachings, in essence, describe what the redeemed one looks like. Because it is Yeshua who has made us new, made us the righteousness of God (2 Corinthians 5:21), all that is left for us to do is to choose to walk in that new life—the righteous life of Yeshua—the life of Torah.

What would happen if we were all looking into the same mirror?

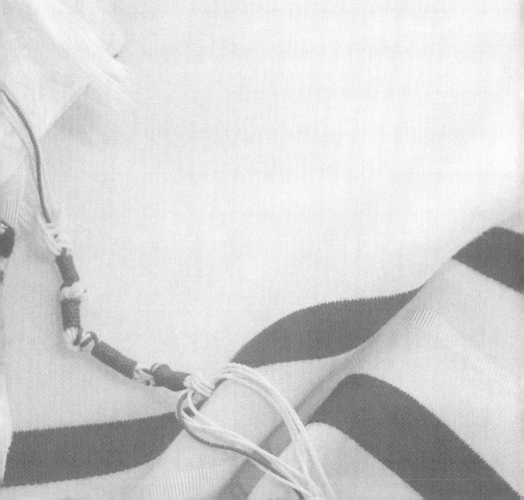

Appendices

Appendix A

Questions and Answers

Take Hold is just a beginning. We hope that the book will serve the body of Messiah at this particular time. This appendix has been included to help answer some of the questions and/or objections which may arise after reading this book. In this section are some of the most commonly asked questions concerning the relationship between Jewish and non-Jewish believers in Yeshua, as well as some frequently asked questions about the place that the Torah has in the life of the believer.

Index of Appendix A

A Brief Hermeneutic Reminder

Before we deal with questions, we would like to provide the reader with a short reminder of some basic hermeneutic principles. Much of this is taken from our previous work entitled, *Torah Rediscovered.* The reason we are touching on the subject of hermeneutics (the science of interpreting) is that we believe that many of the questions posed to us can easily be answered if certain basic interpretative principles are consistently followed. This will not be an exhaustive treatise on hermeneutics. Rather, we will only touch upon that which applies to the particular area of concern in this book.

One of the most frequent objections to some of our ideas, especially concerning the Torah, is the writings of Sha'ul (Paul) of Tarsus. A quick survey of his letter to the Galatians, for instance, often leaves one with the impression that Sha'ul is against any Torah observance on the part of believers in Yeshua. It is our opinion that if we apply some of the basic hermeneutical principles to Sha'ul's writings, we will reach a much different opinion.

One must bear in mind two basic hermeneutical principles when seeking to understand Sha'ul. The first is the concept of keeping *the harmony of the Scriptures* intact. In other words, Scripture cannot contradict Scripture. For example, the events recorded in Acts 21 occurred after Sha'ul had written Galatians and, possibly even the letter to the Romans. In Acts 21, Sha'ul is clearly portrayed as a rather staunch follower of the Torah of Moses, as were the tens of thousands of other Jewish believers in Yeshua! Please note particularly verses 15–26. Someone with the leadership status of Sha'ul of Tarsus would not live in a manner contrary to his teachings; that is, he would not have lived according to Torah while teaching other believers that it had no place in their lives. This would have rendered Sha'ul a hopelessly contradictory teacher, causing the Scriptures to be contradictory as well.

The second hermeneutical principle is *context*. Both the immediate context and that of the whole book or letter are important. Let us take Sha'ul's letter to the Galatians as an example. It is essential to know that the context for Galatians concerns people who believed that salvation was dependent upon obedience to the Torah. Because of this heresy, it stands to reason that Sha'ul's letter would contain many rather negative statements concerning such a use of Torah. But such statements should all be interpreted in light of the context of the letter. Sha'ul's primary purpose in Galatians was not to teach on the application of Torah to the life of the believer, but rather to emphasize that one may not live according to Torah in order to earn, merit, or keep one's justification. The same idea would also apply to Romans. If we keep this in mind, many, if not all, of the questions about Galatians will be answered rather simply.

Unfortunately, many interpreters of Sha'ul's writings have not applied these hermeneutical principles in a consistent fashion. Therefore, Sha'ul is portrayed either as mixed up, contradictory, anti-Jewish, or the founder of a new religion called "Christianity." He is none of the above! He is merely the kind of Jewish person God intended the sons of Jacob to be all along, faithfully engaged in bringing the Good News of the Messiah's atoning death and resurrection to the gentiles and properly applying the message to them.

We will deal with the passages in question as they appear in order in the Brit Hadasha. Thus, we will begin with a question from the Gospel of Mark and then proceed through the rest of the passages in the Brit Hadasha. One more preliminary remark: All of the Scripture quotations in this appendix are from the New American Standard Bible. However, we have replaced every reference to Christ with the title, "Messiah," and all references to Jesus we have changed to "Yeshua."

Questions Concerning
The Gospels and Acts

Mark 7:2–23

This story in the life of Yeshua is often cited as a passage in which He declared *the kosher laws invalid. The key verse is 7:19 where the one who was recording this episode inserts into the text the following:* "Thus, He declared all foods clean."

As with all of the rest of the passages with which we will deal, the context is the critical factor in interpreting the passages in question. In this case there is a broad context and an immediate context that must be considered.

The broad context is Yeshua's attitude toward the Torah as a whole. We have already examined the crucial section in Matthew 5:17–19 in which Yeshua taught about His view concerning the Torah. Here we found that Yeshua emphatically endorsed the Torah as a whole, pronounced a reward for those who taught the Torah and practiced it, as well as a curse to those who did not do either.

If we keep Matthew 5:17–19 in mind, we find that there is no logical reason to assume that the "foods" mentioned in Mark 7 are the forbidden foods described in the Torah. It would be totally inconsistent of the Messiah to annul that section of the Torah. Moreover, we are not told that there is something exceptional about food that would warrant the Messiah changing those teachings.

The second context is the immediate context. The story is one where Yeshua's students are rebuked by a group of Pharisees because they did not wash their hands in the ritual prescribed by that particular Pharisaical group. The real issue at hand is not the teaching of the Torah, but rather, "the traditions of the elders." That phrase is somewhat of a catch phrase in the Gospels referring to the accepted oral tradition, passed down by word of mouth. It is because the students of Yeshua did not utilize the same ritual hand-washing as this particular group of religious leaders that their hands were said to be "unclean" and, consequently, the food eaten from those same hands was declared to be "unclean."

Yeshua used this incident as an opportunity to express some of His estimation of the oral law or "traditions of the elders." Part of His conclusion is that whenever the oral tradition is used to negate or supercede the written Torah, it is wrong. God's Word is perfect. The oral tradition is not God's word, but man's traditions.

In the end, Yeshua taught that the food eaten by His students whose hands were not washed according to a certain oral tradition was food that was permitted to be eaten. His opponents, of course, disagreed with that conclusion and would have insisted that such foods were unfit to eat. Yeshua countered that the foods in question were biblically permitted foods. The hand washing ritual did not make them suitable or unsuitable for eating because these foods are already suitable to eat according to God's decree.

Now comes the most important part. When the writer of Mark expresses in 7:19, "Thus He declared all foods clean," he would not have been referring to the forbidden foods found in the Torah. Those foods were not the ones in question. The foods in the context were the ones that Yeshua's followers were eating (which would have been kosher foods) without having performed the handwashing ritual that this particular group of Pharisees were insisting upon. Thus, all of the food that Yeshua's disciples were eating was declared "clean", in the sense that foregoing a man-made ritual such as handwashing did not make it unclean. His message was that no one should be in bondage to a ritual created by man, yet propagated as God's law. There might be a simpler way to interpret this passage. All we have to do is simply understand that the items forbidden in Leviticus for people to eat are not even foods at all! It might even be a mistake for us to refer to them as "forbidden foods." To the Jewish mind, the word "food" is something that is permitted to be eaten according to Leviticus chapter 11. Other things are simply not foods. We may also want to take this understanding to our study of Acts 10 below.

Acts 10:9–20

And on the next day, as they were on their way, and approaching the city, Peter went up on the housetop about the sixth hour to pray. And he became hungry, and was desiring to eat; but while they were making preparations, he fell into a trance; and he beheld the sky opened up, and a certain object like a great sheet coming down, lowered by four corners to the ground, and there were in it all [kinds of] four-footed animals and crawling creatures of the earth and birds of the air. And a voice came to him, "Arise, Peter, kill and eat!" But Peter said, "By no means, Lord, for I have never eaten anything unholy and unclean." And again a voice *{came} to him a second time, "What God has cleansed, no {longer} consider unholy." And this happened three times; and immediately the object was taken up into the sky. Now while Peter was greatly perplexed in mind as to what the vision which he had seen might be, behold, the men who had been sent by Cornelius, having asked directions for Simon's house, appeared at the gate; and calling out, they were asking whether Simon, who was also called Peter, was staying there. And while Peter was reflecting on the vision, the Spirit said to him, "Behold, three men are looking for you. "But arise, go downstairs, and accompany them without misgivings; for I have sent them Myself.*

This passage, like the previous one from Mark, is often used to demonstrate that the dietary teachings of the Torah have now been cast aside, i.e., believers in Yeshua have no responsibility to live by them. We do not agree with this traditional Christian understanding. Rather, we hope to demonstrate that the dietary teachings are not even in question in this passage.

First, note that Peter is put into a trance whereupon God gives him a vision. It is obvious that God is intending to teach him something very important. But the context implies that the instruction that he is about to receive is intended for his immediate situation.

The vision, as the text indicates, is one where a cloth is spread out with all sorts of unkosher foods on it, somewhat like a picnic blanket coming down from heaven. A voice from heaven accompanied the food, bidding Peter to eat it. In the vision, Peter responded that he had never eaten such food and that he was not about to do it now!

Fortunately, the Spirit of God provides for us the correct understanding of the vision Peter received. Verse 19 tells us that Peter took a while thinking about the vision. He did not understand what it meant. Surely, if it was really intended to teach him to change his eating habits, this perceptive man of God would have realized it. But the Spirit of God had something else in mind. Just as Peter was contemplating the meaning of the vision, we read in verse 19, "The Spirit said to him, 'Behold, three men are looking for you. But arise, go downstairs, and accompany them without misgivings; for I have sent them Myself."

The Spirit of God interrupted Peter's attempts to figure out the vision by giving him the correct interpretation. While Peter may have been thinking that the vision was about his eating habits, in reality, the vision was about people! Up to this point in his life, Peter—like so many Jewish people—was accustomed to avoiding any table fellowship with gentiles. Non-Jews were, more or less, treated as if they were unkosher food and to be avoided. Now, however, God wanted Peter to have close intimate fellowship with a gentile, a Roman army officer named Cornelius. Peter would have naturally been very reluctant to do such a thing. To encourage him to pursue this relationship—even to the point of entering Cornelius' house— God gave this vision to Peter. The meaning was not for Peter to change his eating habits, but to change his fellowship attitudes. God wanted Peter to do what many Jews of the day would have considered the unthinkable—visit with a gentile. The meaning of the vision is summarized in verse 28 where we read, "And he said to them, 'You yourselves know how unlawful it is for a man who is a Jew to associate with a foreigner or to visit him; and {yet} *God has shown me that I should not call any man unholy or unclean'*." (italics ours) Notice that, at this point, Peter is very clear concerning the meaning of the vision he received from God. God told him "not to call any man unholy or unclean." Therefore, the issue was people and not food.

Unclean foods are still unclean foods. The point of the vision was to teach Peter to understand and relate to people in a way that he had not previously understood. This passage does not teach that the dietary instructions of the Torah be changed. Rather, it is a passage in which God was teaching Peter to reach out to non-Jews for the sake of the Messiah. At the same time, Peter is never told by the Holy One to change his own eating customs and practices.

Questions Concerning
The Book of Romans

We received many questions about Sha'ul's letter to the Romans. People wanted to know about the passages in Romans which seem to be teaching against believers in Yeshua living according to the Torah. We will deal with some of the most commonly cited passages.

Romans 2:28-29

For he is not a Jew who is one outwardly; neither is circumcision that which is outward in the flesh. But he is a Jew who is one inwardly; and circumcision is that which is of the heart, by the Spirit, not by the letter; and his praise is not from men, but from God.

The question from this passage is, "Who is a real Jew?" Moreover, it seems to be teaching that anyone whose heart is circumcised is a Jewish person. Thus, the thinking goes, gentile believers in Yeshua, having their hearts circumcised, are "spiritual Jews."

We do not interpret this passage to mean that gentile believers in Yeshua are "spiritual Jews." The reason is simple. In the context, Sha'ul is addressing the physical descendants of Abraham, Isaac, and Jacob, or the physical Jewish people. Gentiles were addressed in 2:1–16. Beginning with 2:17, Sha'ul began to speak directly to Jewish people.

In that light, Sha'ul is making an important distinction in this passage. He is saying that although the descendant of Jacob is circumcised (in the flesh) that alone does not make him the kind of Jewish person God designed him to be. To prove his point, Paul makes a play on the word "Jew." The readers understood that the word "Jew" is a derivative from the word "Judah" (Yehuda), which means "one who praises God." Hence, Sha'ul is saying that a descendant of Jacob who praises God from a new creation heart is a true worshipper of God. Mere physical circumcision does not make one's heart circumcised. It is clear from the context that Sha'ul was saying that the only way to receive this circumcision of the heart circumcision was to submit to God and receive His righteousness as a gift of grace through faith in Yeshua the Messiah. Any Jewish person who has done this is a spiritual, as well as physical, descendant of Abraham.

Romans 3:19–31

Now we know that whatever the Law says, it speaks to those who are under the Law, that every mouth may be closed, and all the world may become accountable to God; because by the works of the Law no flesh will be justified in His sight; for through the Law {comes} the knowledge of sin. But now apart from the Law {the} righteousness of God has been manifested, being witnessed by the Law and the Prophets, even {the} righteousness of God through faith in Yeshua Messiah for all those who believe; for there is no distinction; for all have sinned and fall short of the glory of God, being justified as a gift by His grace through the redemption which is in Messiah Yeshua; whom God displayed publicly as a propitiation in His blood through faith. {This was} to demonstrate His righteousness, because in the forbearance of God He passed over the sins previously committed; for the demonstration, {I say,} of His righteousness at the present time, that He might be just and the justifier of the one who has faith in Yeshua. Where then is boasting? It is excluded. By what kind of law? Of works? No, but by a law of faith. For we maintain that a man is justified by faith apart from works of the Law. Or is God {the God} of Jews only? Is He not {the God} of gentiles also? Yes, of gentiles also, since indeed God who will justify the circumcised by faith and the uncircumcised through faith is one. Do we then nullify the Law through faith? May it never be! On the contrary, we establish the Law.

In this section, Sha'ul appears to say that the purpose for the Torah (rendered "law" in just about every English translation) is to give one a knowledge of sin (3:20). That is true. However, that is not the only purpose for the Torah. This is where many Bible teachers become confused. The reason that Sha'ul says in this passage that the Torah reveals sin is because he is teaching that no one may be justified by living according to the Torah. If one were to attempt to do so, the Torah could only do two things for him: 1) help to make him aware that he is sinful and desperately in need of God's righteousness instead of trying to establish his own, and 2) reveal the Messiah to him.

Verse 28 states the issue clearly when Paul declares that justification is a gift from God and has no connection whatsoever to what a person does, especially what a person does concerning Torah obedience.

In verse 31, Sha'ul affirms the validity of the Torah. He says that the Torah itself teaches the principle of justification by faith and faith alone. Receiving God's gift of salvation (justification) is perfectly consistent with the Torah's teaching on the matter (see Genesis 15). Because of this, believing in Yeshua does not "nullify" the Torah; rather it upholds its teachings.

Romans 4:13–16

> For the promise to Abraham or to his descendants that he would be heir of the world was not through the Law, but through the righteousness of faith. For if those who are of the Law are heirs, faith is made void and the promise is nullified; for the Law brings about wrath, but where there is no law, neither is there violation.

Here is another passage that appears to teach the purpose of the Torah. Like the previous section from Romans, many Bible students read, "for the Law brings about wrath" and assume that, along with revealing sin, the purpose of the Torah is to bring about wrath. Our comments for this passage are similar to those made for Romans 3. The only things the Torah can do for an unbeliever who relies upon his adherence to a set of rules in order to earn his righteousness, is help to reveal his sin, warn him of the impending judgement of God's wrath, and point him to the Messiah.

This passage is not in a context that speaks about following the Torah as a lifestyle for believers. Like most of the passages in Romans, the context is a refute against the attempt to use the Torah as a means of justification.

Romans 6: 14

For sin shall not be master over you, for you are not under Law, but under grace.

Those who insist that a believer in Yeshua should not live by the Torah of Moses often use this catch phrase from this verse, "We are not under law but under grace." We think that there is a better way to understand this passage. First, let us quote a respected Bible scholar on the meaning of the phrase in question and then we will finish with our own comments.

C. E. B. Cranfield has shed much light on the meaning of this Greek phrase, helping us to perceive what Sha'ul actually meant as well as to understand more fully his true stand on the Torah. Because Cranfield's remarks are so pertinent we will quote him at length:

> It will be well to bear in mind the fact (which, as far as we know, had not received attention before it was noted)... that the Greek language of Paul's day possessed no word-group corresponding to our "legalism," "legalist," and "legalistic." This means that he lacked a convenient terminology for expressing a vital distinction, and so was surely seriously hampered in the work of clarifying the Messiahian position with regard to the law. In view of this we should always, we think, be ready to reckon with the possibility that Pauline statements, which at first sight seem to disparage the law, are really directed not against the law itself but against that misunderstanding and misuse of it for which we now have a convenient terminology. In this very difficult terrain Paul was pioneering. If we make due allowance for these circumstances, we shall not be so easily baffled or misled by a certain impreciseness of statement which we shall sometimes encounter.

We encounter the same dilemma in the Hebrew language. There are no Hebrew words which can easily convey the concepts of "legalism" or "legalist." Thus Sha'ul, whether using his Hebrew-oriented mind or his Greek language, was hindered in his attempts to explain that legalism was not what God intended. From our understanding of the true nature of the Torah and Sha'ul's theology, it is our opinion that he did an excellent job of overcoming this language barrier.

Based on this understanding of the Greek in Romans 6:14, we can say, then, that this verse is teaching us that because God regenerated us and caused us to believe in Yeshua, we now have an entirely new relationship to sin. We no longer rely on our legalistic efforts to earn God's righteousness. Instead, we rely on the grace of God. Legalism and grace never mix! Or, to put it in slightly different terms, law and grace never mix. But Torah and grace go hand in hand.

One of the many implications of trusting in the grace of God is that we become new creations in Messiah. This means, among other things, that we now have a new relationship to sin. It is just as 6:14 states, "sin is no longer our master." For the new creation person, this is most definitely true! Relying on legalistic methods to attain salvation could never change our relationship to sin. Only trusting in the grace of God could effect such a change. For those of us who are now new creations by virtue of the new birth, our relationship to sin is forever changed. The Torah is not a legalistic document. It describes the lifestyle of the Redeemed, and it was never God's intention that obeying it would achieve salvation.

Romans 7:1–12

Or do you not know, brethren (for I am speaking to those who know the law), that the law has jurisdiction over a person as long as he lives? For the married woman is bound by law to her husband while he is living; but if her husband dies, she is released from the law concerning the husband. So then if, while her husband is living, she is joined to another man, she shall be called an adulteress; but if her husband dies, she is free from the law, so that she is not an adulteress, though she is joined to another man. Therefore, my brethren, you also were made to die to the Law through the body of Messiah, that you might be joined to another, to Him who was raised from the dead, that we might bear fruit for God. For while we were in the flesh, the sinful passions, which were {aroused} by the Law, were at work in the members of our body to bear fruit for death. But now we have been released from the Law, having died to that by which we were bound, so that we serve in newness of the Spirit and not in oldness of the letter. What shall we say then? Is the Law sin? May it never be! On the contrary, I would not have come to know sin except through the Law; for I would not have known about coveting if the Law had not said, "You shall not covet." But sin, taking opportunity through the commandment, produced in me coveting of every kind; for apart from the Law sin {is} dead. And I was once alive apart from the Law; but when the commandment came, sin became alive, and I died; and this commandment, which was to result in life, proved to result in death for me; for sin, taking opportunity through the commandment, deceived me, and through it killed me. So then, the Law is holy, and the commandment is holy and righteous and good.

At first glance, this seems like a very devastating passage for those believers who desire to live by the Torah. After all, does it not say, "you were also made to die to the Law through the body of Messiah?"

Indeed, this is a tricky passage. Keeping in mind two things will help to open up this passage for us in a more accurate way. First, as always, notice the context. These verses fall in the larger context of Romans 5–8. In this section of Romans, the rabbi from Tarsus is discussing some of the practical effects of being justified by grace through faith. As we stated in the previous verse, one of these effects is that a believer in Yeshua now has a completely different relationship to sin than he had before. He has died to sin and sin is no longer his master.

Second, verses 10–12 provide us with an insight into what Sha'ul really thought of the Torah. As we can readily see from those verses, the Torah was not the problem. Sin was the real culprit in man. Let us see how this unfolds from the passage.

In 7:1–2, it becomes clear that before we trusted in Messiah, our problem was not the Torah, but sin! Sin is that which wrecked havoc with our lives. One of the miracles of the new birth—as this passage is pointing out—is that a believer does not relate to sin the same way any longer. Consequently, Sha'ul says in verse 11, "for sin, taking opportunity through the commandment deceived me, and through it killed me." Sin, not Torah was the problem.

Hence, when Messiah comes into our lives we are released from our bondage to sin and any legalistic relationship we may have previously had with God's teaching. That is what the Sha'ul means in verse 4 when he says that we were made to die to the law. Before, we related to the Torah in a legalistic way. The only thing the Torah could do for us in those circumstances was to condemn us by revealing our sin to us. That relationship to both the Torah and to sin had to change.

Thank God that in Messiah it did change! As far as sin is concerned, it was circumcised from us and relegated to our flesh (7:17, c.f. Colossians 2:11–13). As far as the Torah is concerned, once our relationship to sin was changed through our becoming a new creation, the real value of the Torah for the believer began to come to light. Accordingly, Sha'ul says several very positive things about the Torah in verses 10–12.

God's intention that the Torah would be real life for His people can now become fulfilled. It was our own sin that caused the life of the Torah to become death in us. Now in Messiah, God's real intention for the Torah can be fulfilled in us.

God's Torah is holy. There is nothing about it that needs to be avoided. It is not evil. It is not unhealthy for God's people. In fact the scriptures themselves clearly declare, "These words are not just idle words for you, they are your life" (Deuteronomy 32:47). It is a covenant and a set of instructions making clear to God's people how to live out their new creation lives in the righteousness of God.

God's Torah is good. The Greek word translated "good" is *agathei*, αγαθη. It stresses both external and moral goodness, and usefulness and perfection. It can also be rendered "useful."[104] In other words, far from the Torah being a detriment to the believer's life, it is useful and helpful to follow for our spiritual, moral, and ethical well-being.

The Torah is righteous. It is the teaching about God's righteousness. Moreover, being intrinsically righteous, it was meant only for those whom God has made righteous by His grace. It is not a vehicle to attain righteousness; rather it is a book of instruction revealing what God's righteousness looks like and how to live out the righteousness which we now have become in Messiah.

Romans 14–15:6

Now accept the one who is weak in faith, {but} not for {the purpose of} passing judgment on his opinions. One man has faith that he may eat all things, but he who is weak eats vegetables {only.} Let not him who eats regard with contempt him who does not eat, and let not him who does not eat judge him who eats, for God has accepted him.

This will be the last passage which we will examine in Romans. At first glance, this section appears to be teaching that those believers who live by the Torah (in this context, those who live by the teachings on dietary laws) are nothing other than "weaker" brothers. The spiritually strong and mature, this interpretation goes, are the ones to whom food is not an issue. Carried one step further, the spiritually mature, therefore, leave the Torah behind and follow after Messiah according to the Spirit. They do not need the teachings of Moses any longer.

There is an excellent discussion of this passage in Peter Tomson's book, *Paul and the Jewish Law* (see the Bibliography). In essence, the problem here seems to be that people read the word "weak" and apply it to those believers who try to follow the Torah, such as celebrating the mo'adim and eating kosher, etc. Tomson really helps us by drawing our attention to the nature of the Greek word translated "weak." Let us quote Tomson on the matter because his comments are extremely helpful. He says that here we have an instance when a knowledge of Jewish literature, especially that from the late Second Temple and mishnaic periods helps us to understand concepts from the writings of one who was thoroughly trained in rabbinics, Sha'ul of Tarsus. Regarding the Greek word "weak," *astheneis* (ασθενησ), Tomson writes:

> Not only was the Greek word ασθενης [*astheneis*] among the relatively few [words] to be assimilated into Tannaic usage, but it was used specifically in matters of bodily constitution and diet. A mishna dating from the end of the 1st century CE at the latest, informs us of the following detail regarding the ritual bath the High Priest had to take in the early morning of Yom Kippur; "If the High Priest was aged or infirm אסטניס, *astneis,* they made hot water for him..." (m Yom 3:5). The word is more widely attested in later usage. In view of its context in Paul it is quite likely that for him the word had a similar

specific connotation: "infirm, delicate," stressing a restrictive diet rather than a defective faith. We shall translate it here as "delicate."[105]

Establishing the meaning of the word "weak" is only part of our task. We believe Tomson's analysis is correct and helpful. Now we have to establish who are those who have delicate needs. We think that the answer to that question lies in 14:1 where we read,

"Τον δε ασθενουντα τη πιστει προσλαμβανεσθε, μη εις διακρισεις διαλογισμων...And the one who is delicate in the faith, receive; (but?) not for the purpose of discerning opinions" (my translation). It seems clear both from this verse and from the rest of the passage that the person who has sensitive needs is not one who follows the Torah of God or any other part of God's Word; following God's Word is the standard for any believer. Rather, the one who has sensitive needs is the one who has certain convictions about disputable matters. The Torah is certainly not a disputable matter!

These verses instruct believers to relate to one another without passing judgment on each other's opinions, thereby invalidating each other. We can allow one another to have strong yet differing opinions.

People who have individually strong personal convictions about disputable matters are not weak ones in the faith. Rather they are to be regarded as people who have sensitive needs. What exactly are those needs? They need to be treated with respect and as individuals who are in process, attempting to think through the issues of their lives in accordance with where their faith is at any given time. Accordingly, others in the body of Messiah need to recognize each individual as precious to their Abba (Daddy) and to treat one another "delicately"— which is the author's way of exhorting each of us to be sensitive to one another. This really fits the context of

Romans 14 and 15 where Sha'ul is teaching the body of Messiah to learn how to be sensitive to one another, even though we differ from each other.

Romans 14 and 15 describes the right behavior in handling an individual who has strong convictions over a disputable matter. "Delicately" here refers to how the person should be handled while he still has such strong convictions on a matter on which the Scriptures are not clear and therefore where there is likely to be difference of opinion among other believers. We are exhorted to be gracious to such a one. If his strong conviction is not causing any serious problems in the body, give that person space and allow God to move in his life as needed over time (verses 3–4). We should note that according to verses 5–6 believers have room for their own personal convictions that are important to us in our living out our faith. This is proper and good.

Questions Concerning
The Letter to the Galatians

Even more so than the letter to the Romans, the epistle to the Galatians is cited to discourage those in the body of Messiah who desire to live according to the teachings of Moses.

All of the following so-called "problem passages" from Galatians can easily be answered in a Torah-positive way if we simply bear in mind the context of the whole book of Galatians. The context is established in the letter's thesis statement in 2:15–16:

> We {are} Jews by nature, and not sinners from among the gentiles; nevertheless knowing that a man is not justified by the works of the Law but through faith in Messiah Yeshua, even we have believed in Messiah Yeshua, that we may be justified by faith in Messiah, and not by the works of the Law; since by the works of the Law shall no flesh be justified.

The thesis is this: No person may be justified before God by obeying any list of rules or teachings. That is legalism. Rather, justification is a gift of God given by grace to those who rely solely on the person and work of Messiah Yeshua.

One of the problems in the Galatian fellowship was that there were apparently teachers circulating either from within or from without who were saying that justification is achieved by a combination of faith plus works. In other words, they were teaching that a person had to do the Torah in addition to trusting Messiah in order for God to declare him righteous. Accordingly, we can expect to find many seemingly anti-Torah statements in this letter, which we do! If we remember this background then we can realize that Sha'ul is not teaching against the Torah, but against a legalistic observance of the Torah. Let us examine several passages from this oft-misunderstood letter.

Galatians 2:15-16

We {are} Jews by nature, and not sinners from among the gentiles; nevertheless knowing that a man is not justified by the works of the Law but through faith in Messiah Yeshua, even we have believed in Messiah Yeshua, that we may be justified by faith in Messiah, and not by the works of the Law; since by the works of the Law shall no flesh be justified.

As we have already stated, this passage is the thesis statement for this letter to the Galatians. The issue on Sha'ul's mind was God's requirement for our justification.

There is one more point from verse 16 that we would like to make. Looking at the Greek of Galatians 2:16, we find that the definite article before the phrase "works of law" has been left out. It is not, as many English versions translate it, "works of *the* law." If the translator adds the definite article, the reader assumes that "the law" is a reference to the Torah. However, it is not. "Works of law" is a phrase indicating a man-made system of works, of which performance-based acceptance is the core belief. Thus, this phrase is *ergon nomou* (εργον νομου) and should be translated as "works of law."

Accordingly, Galatians 2:16 should read: "knowing that a man is not justified by works of law but through faith in Messiah Yeshua, even we have believed in Messiah Yeshua, that we may be justified by faith in Messiah, and not by works of law; since by works of law shall no flesh be justified."

We encounter the same translation mistake in verse 19, which states, *"For through the Law I died to the Law, that I might live to God."* Here again, in the Greek, there are no definite articles before the words translated "law." Knowing this permits us to translate this verse: "For, I through law, died to law, in order that to God I might live." The point here is that Paul was not saying that he died to the Torah, but merely to "law." We can paraphrase what he was saying in this way: "It was through legalistic obedience to a set of laws that I realized that I was a sinner. For, I found that obedience was not that which would change me. This pointed me to Messiah. I found that it is only through a personal relationship with Him that God grants a new life. My attempt at legalism backfired! Instead of making me closer to God, it only served to emphasize my sinfulness. Therefore, in Messiah, God caused me to die to law that I might live for Him."

The Torah then, was not in question. Our constant need in the flesh to feel good about ourselves by believing that we have earned righteousness is what is in question! Any time that the Torah of God is reduced to a system of works, what we have is no longer Torah but a man-made system of works—law. Man will always try to reduce God's Words to laws to be obeyed instead of the Words of Life—what they truly are. We who are in Messiah have died to exactly this abuse of the Word of God. Now we embrace the Renewed Covenant in our relationship with God as that which is our very life, our new creation life!

Galatians 3:2

This is the only thing I want to find out from you: did you receive the Spirit by the works of the Law, or by hearing with faith?

There are some who use this verse to contrast life in the Spirit against a life of Torah. Their argument is that we did not receive the Spirit of God by following the Torah.

Our suggestion is that the Torah is not even mentioned in this verse. Once again, we encounter the phrase "works of the law." In the Greek it is the same grammatical construction that was in 2:16. Therefore, it should not read, "works of the law," as if it is the Torah that is being referred to, but "works of law." Hence, this verse is saying that it was not through legalism that we received the Spirit of God. We could not earn God's Spirit. Rather God gave us His Spirit by faith, at the moment of salvation. Thus, this verse is against legalism, not against the Torah.

Galatians 3:21–25

Is the Law then contrary to the promises of God? May it never be! For if a law had been given which was able to impart life, then righteousness would indeed have been based on law. But the Scripture has shut up all men under sin, that the promise by faith in Yeshua the Messiah might be given to those who believe. But before faith came, we were kept in custody under the law, being shut up to the faith which was later to be revealed. Therefore the Law has become our tutor {to lead us} to Messiah, that we may be justified by faith. But now that faith has come, we are no longer under a tutor.

Here is a case where the word *nomos* (νομος) is probably being used to refer to the Torah. In the Greek, it has a definite article before it, "the Law" (the Torah). This series of verses concludes a passage where Sha'ul is comparing the covenant with Abraham with the covenant of Sinai. His conclusion is that the Torah was not given to impart life; that was the purpose of the covenant with Abraham. We receive life by faith. He continues to argue that are only two things the Torah can do for those who attempt to receive spiritual life from God by obeying the Torah. First, the Torah can point out their sinfulness (verse 22) and second, the Torah can then point them to the one who removes sin—the Messiah (verses 23-25).

Verses 23-24 represent only one of the many purposes for the Torah. In fact, the Torah has specific functions for both the righteous (the saved) and the unrighteous (the unsaved). As far as the righteous are concerned, 2 Timothy 3:16 states, *"All Scripture is inspired by God and profitable for teaching, for reproof, for correction, for training in righteousness; that the man of God may be adequate, equipped for every good work."* Of course, "all Scripture" would most certainly have included the Torah.

As far as the unrighteous are concerned, our passage in Galatians indicates what the Torah can accomplish for them. It can serve to point out their sinfulness and point them to Messiah. In this capacity, we should note that 3:25 says, "But now that faith has come, we are no longer under a tutor." The "tutor"[106] is, in context, the Torah. When a person comes to Messiah and receives Him by faith, that particular function of the Torah has ceased (i.e., there is no longer a need for the Torah to serve as a tutor to lead the person to the Messiah). At that point, the Torah begins to function in a totally different capacity—the capacity for which it was originally designed; it describes the lifestyle of the Redeemed.

Galatians 3:28

There is neither Jew nor Greek, there is neither slave nor free man, there is neither male nor female; for you are all one in Messiah Yeshua.

This verse has often been cited to show that there is no place in the life of a believer in Yeshua for the Torah or anything pertaining to Israel. It has often been said that in Messiah there is no room for Jewishness because we are new people in Messiah.

We would like to call on Messianic leader Dr. Daniel Juster to comment on this verse for us. Juster remarks, "Paul is not saying that all distinctions between men and women have been obliterated...It is precisely the same with Jew and non-Jew in the Messiah. Both may be called to different styles of life and witness, to different fields of service, yet they are spiritually one in the Messiah...Note as well, non-Jews are called (in v. 29) not spiritual Israel, but the offspring of Abraham by faith."[107]

It is interesting how most believers have applied this verse over the years. Erroneously thinking that this verse teaches that there is to be no more Torah expression ("neither Jew..."), many believers have lived non-Torah oriented lifestyles. In doing so, however, they have not realized that they did not practice the second expression of the verse that says, "there is neither Jew *nor Greek*." (italics ours) They did not realize that much of their lifestyle reflected that of gentile non-believers. For example, in their attempt to practice the "neither is there Jew" part, they replaced explicit Torah teachings with man-made traditions propagated by some church leaders decades after the Brit Hadasha was written. In this process, they have failed to realize that such practices, would then, also violate the second phrase, "neither is there Greek (gentile)."

In so doing, they have espoused a decidedly culturally non-Jewish life style (and have pressured Jewish believers to do the same).

This verse actually speaks nothing about Torah observance or non-observance. Rather, it merely emphasizes the spiritual equality of Jewish believers with believers from among the gentiles.

Galatians 4:21–31

Tell me, you who want to be under law, do you not listen to the law? For it is written that Abraham had two sons, one by the bondwoman and one by the free woman. But the son by the bondwoman was born according to the flesh, and the son by the free woman through the promise. This is allegorically speaking: for these {women} are two covenants, one {proceeding} from Mount Sinai bearing children who are to be slaves; she is Hagar. Now this Hagar is Mount Sinai in Arabia, and corresponds to the present Jerusalem, for she is in slavery with her children. But the Jerusalem above is free; she is our mother. For it is written, 'Rejoice, barren woman who does not bear; break forth and shout, you who are not in labor; for more are the children of the desolate than of the one who has a husband.' And you brethren, like Isaac, are children of promise. But as at that time he who was born according to the flesh persecuted him {who was born} according to the Spirit, so it is now also. But what does the Scripture say? 'Cast out the bondwoman and her son, for the son of the bondwoman shall not be an heir with the son of the free woman.' So then, brethren, we are not children of a bondwoman, but of the free woman.

This passage is a midrash developed by Sha'ul in order to illustrate the difference between those who trust Messiah for their righteousness and those who are relying on a legalistic observance of the Torah or any set of laws for their salvation.

In our opinion, the key to understanding this midrash is to remember the context in which it is found. The immediate context begins in chapter 3 where Sha'ul begins to compare the two covenants—the covenant with Abraham and the covenant of Sinai. In this midrash, Sha'ul relates what happens when people reverse the proper theological order of the covenants. In other words, theologically, as well as historically, God made the Abrahamic covenant before He enacted the covenant of Sinai. It had to be that way because in the Abrahamic covenant, the promises of God were to be received by faith, while the second covenant was basically one in which those promises would only be fully enjoyed with fruitfulness through obedience.

Abraham's relationship to Hagar and the subsequent fruit of that bond (Ishmael) is compared to those who put the covenant of Sinai first before the covenant of promise (Abrahamic). Through Hagar, Abraham was attempting to secure the promises through his own efforts instead of relying on God's Word and trusting in God's promises concerning Sarah. Thus it is with those who try to earn their righteousness from God by obeying the Torah. Faith always must precede obedience. In addition, saving faith always *results* in obedience.

The midrash illustrates what it is like when people place obedience before faith. We can write this all in a "formula" where G=Grace, F = Faith, W = Works/Obedience, and S = Salvation.

Man's way, the way of "Hagar" is: $S = W + F$

God's way, the way of "Sarah" is: $S = G$ through $F \rightarrow$ Works

Galatians 5:1–6

It was for freedom that Messiah set us free; therefore keep standing firm and do not be subject again to a yoke of slavery. Behold I, Paul, say to you that if you receive circumcision, Messiah will be of no benefit to you. And I testify again to every man who receives circumcision, that he is under obligation to keep the whole Law. You have been severed from Messiah, you who are seeking to be justified by law; you have fallen from grace. For we through the Spirit, by faith, are waiting for the hope of righteousness. For in Yeshua the Messiah neither circumcision nor uncircumcision means anything, but faith working through love.

This will be the final text from Galatians that we will study. It appears to be a devastating blow to our whole argument, stating that if anyone practices circumcision (or any part of the Torah, for that matter,) he will be severed from Messiah.

The key to the proper interpretation of this passage is the following italicized phrase in 5:4 where Sha'ul states, "You have been severed from Messiah, *you who are seeking to be justified by law*; you have fallen from grace." (italics ours) This phrase indicates the motive behind the circumcisions being performed among the Galatians, which were the focus of Sha'ul's criticisms. It tells us that some people were being circumcised in order to be justified by God. In other words, legalism was the problem, not circumcision.

We need to remember that Sha'ul of Tarsus lived according to the Torah (Acts 21). He would never have taught against the Torah. Since circumcision was one of the many teachings of the Torah, we can safely conclude, therefore, that Sha'ul was not arguing against circumcision per se. In fact, we might recall that he had Timothy circumcised (Acts 16:3).

Sha'ul's problem with circumcision in Galatians was that some were doing it in order to earn or keep their salvation; they were seeking to be justified by it. Herein was the core of the problem. He had no problems with practicing circumcision provided it was done with the proper biblical motive (i.e., as the sign of the covenant between God and Israel).

Verse 4 presents the stark contrast between law and grace. One either attempts to earn or keep his salvation by what he does or he relies solely on the grace of God for salvation. The two concepts, law and grace, do not and never can mix. Sha'ul said that whenever a person begins to trust in what he does to gain (or keep) his salvation, he has ceased practicing the principle of grace and has gone over to law. In fact, some people even attempt to make a law out of the Torah (by practicing circumcision, in this context). The plain truth is that whenever someone relies on his works to gain righteousness from God, he has ceased to function according to grace. No one can be saved in this manner. Salvation is solely by grace through faith in the person and work of Yeshua.

Questions Concerning
Other Pauline References

Colossians 2:13–14

And when you were dead in your transgressions and the uncircumcision of your flesh, He made you alive together with Him, having forgiven us all our transgressions, having canceled out the certificate of debt consisting of decrees against us {and} which was hostile to us; and He has taken it out of the way, having nailed it to the cross.

There are some who assume that the subject of this passage is the Torah and that the Torah was nailed to the cross with Yeshua, thereby rendering it either inoperable or canceling it altogether. They get that impression by the surface reading of the words, "having canceled out the certificate of debt consisting of decrees against us {and} which was hostile to us; and He has taken it out of the way, having nailed it to the cross." According to this interpretation, the Torah is represented by the words "certificate of debt consisting of decrees."

This passage, however, provides us with a classic example of how necessary it is to study the Scriptures in their original language along with their original cultural context. In being faithful to this hermeneutic, it becomes quite clear that the Torah, as a document, is not the subject of this passage. Taking this into account, we can come away from this passage with a completely different impression than many receive reading it in English, without reference to the Greek.

The Greek in question is the phrase which is commonly translated, "certificate of debt...having nailed it to the cross." According to scholar, Adolf Deissmann, "Some ancient customs connected with the law of debt must be at the root of the celebrated passage in Colossians 2:14 where the technical expression "handwriting" (=bond) is employed in a religious sense and brought into a remarkable connection with the cross. Christ, says the apostle, has forgiven us all the debts incurred by our trespasses." Finding himself unable to specify specifically the custom to which Sha'ul refers, Dr. Deissmann, nevertheless, comments, "If we are unable to point to the source of the 'bond nailed to the cross,' it may be at least allowed in passing to refer to 'the cross on the bond'. We have learnt from the new texts [he is writing in 1922!] that it was generally customary to cancel a bond [a debt] by crossing it out with the Greek cross-letter Chi (χ)."[108] In essence, the χ stood for the phrase, "I cross out."

In short, what Sha'ul appears to be saying here is that the certificate of debts consisting of decrees against us that was being canceled was all of the debt of sin that we owed to our Father. This is what was being nailed to the cross. It was, in a sense being cancelled with a big X on it, as other debts were cancelled in the ancient Greek world.

Colossians 2:16–17

Therefore let no one act as your judge in regard to food or drink or in respect to a festival or a new moon or a Sabbath day—things which are a {mere} shadow of what is to come; but the substance belongs to Messiah.

Some people refer to this verse to say that believers in Yeshua should not practice the mo'adim taught in Leviticus 23.

We begin our analysis with Sha'ul's statement in verse 5. Here he writes how delighted he is to see how orderly they are and how firm is their faith in Messiah. He follows this praise with an exhortation to continue to live in Him in this manner and to see to it that no one takes them captive through hollow and deceptive philosophy, which depends on human tradition and the basic principles of this world rather than on Messiah. This is hardly a description of Torah!

Continuing on through the passage, this description of the apostle's warning is coupled with the rest of his warnings found in verses 16–23. When we make this connection, we have an exact description of man's age-old tendency of creating from God's words an intricately complicated system of do's and don'ts to which one is held accountable. This system is then accompanied by a sophisticated philosophy designed to awe the hearer into accepting these pious reasons for submitting themselves to these burdensome laws.

Please note that here Sha'ul reminds them of their original doctrine. Their doctrine is the reason why they are not to embrace any reasoning that leads to any form of man-made rules and regulations, no matter how clever the presentation may be (verses 9–15). Verse 16, then, picks up with, "Therefore do not let anyone judge you by what you eat or drink, or with regard to a religious festival, a New Moon celebration or a Sabbath day—these things which are a {mere} shadow of what is to come; but the substance belongs to Messiah."

It is possible to render verse 17 in a slightly different manner by translating it "These things are a shadow of what is to come, the body of Messiah." We know this is quite a different translation that which is found in most English versions. However, it is perfectly consistent with the Greek text (although not consistent with many people's theology!). The second phrase, το δε σωμα του Ξριστου, is that which is in question. The particle δε is usually rendered as a contrasting particle, such as "but" or "however." Yet, it does not have to be understood in that way. In fact, sometimes, it is not even translated.[109] Granted, the word order in this phrase might imply that a contrast is intended. However, we do not see it that way. The next words are rather simple. They mean literally, "the body of Messiah." Putting this verse together, then, we can understand it to mean that the practices of the Torah described in Colossians 2:16 are shadows of that which was to become a reality, the body of Messiah. Having the real thing with us is, of course, the best. However, although the Torah illustrates or foreshadows realities of the body of Messiah, that does not make it useless or unimportant. We are merely to interpret it with its fullest intended meaning, that is, with the understanding that it pictures the person and work of the Messiah and life in His body.

Thus, rather than imploring believers to cease obeying the Torah, Colossians 2:16–17 provides us with the real motive for obeying the teachings of the Torah. We are to obey them with the intention of seeing the Messiah in them. We are not, however, to use them as a club with which to hit those on the head who do not obey them! In other words, we are not to judge others in their practice of Torah.

1 Timothy 1: 8–11

But we know that the Law is good, if one uses it lawfully,
realizing the fact that law is not made for a righteous man,
but for those who are lawless and rebellious, for the ungodly
and sinners, for the unholy and profane, for those who kill
their fathers or mothers, for murderers and immoral men
and homosexuals and kidnappers and liars and perjurers,
and whatever else is contrary to sound teaching, according
to the glorious Gospel of the blessed God, with which I have
been entrusted.

Whenever we have written concerning the Torah we have
stated that the Torah was given to the Redeemed and describes
their intended lifestyle. This passage seems to teach the
opposite. Sha'ul states that "the law was not made for the
righteous..." Should we adjust our position concerning
the Torah?

Not at all! The correct understanding of this passage
requires noting a subtle difference between two different
usages of the word "law" (nomos). The first time it is used is in
verse 8, where we read, "But we know that the Law is good, if
one uses it lawfully." Here, we can observe two things about
the word "law." First, it is used with a definite article ("the") in
the Greek. This would imply that the Torah is in view, and not
the legalistic concept of "law."

Second, Sha'ul describes the Torah as "good." He says that
it is good if it is used properly. What was a proper use of it?
Sha'ul's relationship to Timothy can provide a good example
of proper usage. As noted above, Sha'ul encouraged Timothy—
who was already made righteous through the blood
of Messiah—to be circumcised. Moreover, he also writes to
Timothy that the Torah (as well as the rest of the Tanakh) is
profitable for, "teaching, for reproof, for correction, for

training in righteousness; that the man of God may be adequate, equipped for every good work." These were, indeed, proper usages of the Torah. The letter to the Galatians is an example of how the Torah can be misused—as a means of attempting to earn or to keep one's salvation. Changing the Torah from God's Words of Life to the Redeemed and making it into "law" would be a misuse of Torah.

This leads us to the second usage of the word "law." Verse 9 tells us that "law is not made for a righteous man." Here, there is no definite article in the Greek before the word "law." Judging from the previous uses of this grammatical construction, there is a good chance that the Torah is not in view here, but that pernicious theological concept called "law." Indeed, "law" is not for righteous people. They have nothing to do with law. Instead, they have been given the Torah!

On the other hand, sinners are associated with law. Not only do they always approach God by means of legalism, but the only things God's laws can do for them is to condemn them and point them to Messiah. At that point, God's Torah takes over and instructs them in their new identity as new creations constituted in the righteousness of God through their new birth.

Questions Concerning
The Book of Hebrews

This is the last set of verses that we will study. In chapters 7 to 10 there appear to be several verses which some people have used to teach that the Torah has come to an end or has been rendered inoperable. Therefore, we will take a closer look at these verses.

First, however, let us say a word in general about Hebrews 7–10. We need to remember that the theme for this passage is the sacrificial and priestly system. The writer is communicating that there has been a fundamental change in the sacrificial system and everything related to it. When a specific change is mentioned it is only in reference to the sacrificial system, and to nothing else in the Torah. Knowing this will put many of the so-called "problem passages" in a completely different light. Let us see how this unfolds.

Hebrews 7:11–12, 19

Now if perfection was through the Levitical priesthood (for on the basis of it the people received the Law), what further need [was there] for another priest to arise according to the order of Melchizedek, and not be designated according to the order of Aaron? For when the priesthood is changed, of necessity there takes place a change of law also. For the One concerning whom these things are spoken belongs to another tribe, from which no one has officiated at the altar. For it is evident that our Lord was descended from Judah, a tribe with reference to which Moses spoke nothing concerning priests. And this is clearer still, if another priest arises according to the likeness of Melchizedek, who has become [such] not on the basis of a law of physical requirement, but according to the power of an indestructible life. For it is witnessed [of Him], "Thou art a priest forever according to the order of Melchizedek." For, on the one hand, there is a setting aside of a former commandment because of its weakness and uselessness (for the Law made nothing perfect), and on the other hand there is a bringing in of a better hope, through which we draw near to God.

These verses speak of a change. Accordingly, we are told, "For when the priesthood is changed, of necessity there takes place a change of law also" (verse 12). Moreover, that which underwent a change was "weak and useless" in its former state (verse 18). In addition, the new thing brought on a "better hope" (verse 19).

It is obvious that the things that changed were the provisions in the Torah. However, not all of the Torah was changed. Only those teachings that were associated with the sacrifices, the priests, and other related matters. The reason was the sacrificial atonement and High Priesthood of Yeshua. Since He was God incarnate, it stands to reason that compared to Yeshua, the priestly system described in the Torah was not capable of accomplishing that which Yeshua accomplished. In fact, the sacrificial system and the priesthood were never intended to accomplish that for which the Messiah was sent. In addition, since His sacrifice was perfect, it stands to reason that after it there would be a change in the use of animal sacrifices.

It is only in these areas that the Torah's provisions were—by comparison with Yeshua the Messiah—"weak and useless." They were not weak and useless to accomplish all that they were designed to accomplish. They were designed to be the "shadow" (a "mirror reality") of all that we have in Messiah. But they were, of course, weak and useless for accomplishing that which they were not designed to accomplish—the work that only Messiah Himself could do!

(What do we mean by "mirror reality" in this discussion? God created His physical creation to "mirror" what is true in the spiritual realm. This concept is aptly illustrated by the way that bodies of water on the earth "mirror" the skies of the heavens.)

Hebrews 8:13

When He said, 'A new [covenant]' He has made the first obsolete. But whatever is becoming obsolete and growing old is ready to disappear.

To fully understand this verse, we must refer to the concept of a renewed covenant. By this, we refer to an earlier quote from Dr. John Fischer: "One covenant does not set aside another; one does not invalidate another so as to nullify its stipulations. Rather, it renews, expands, adapts, up-dates."[110]

In addition, the Renewed Covenant, like all biblical covenants made with Israel, incorporates all the provisions of the previous covenants. The renewal incorporated an "update" to the previous covenant, made necessary by the historically accomplished sacrifice of Yeshua. Hence, let us render the phrase "New Covenant" as "Renewed Covenant," understanding that the only updating necessary or intended was that of the sacrificial system and related matters. Other than that, the Torah is still in effect as a covenant and its provisions are still God's instructions for the righteous. In this, all of the Torah is our "mirror" through which we discover what our righteous behavior should look like. Even the passages of Torah expounding on the sacrificial system and the priesthood teach us how to understand who we are both as "living sacrifices holy and pleasing to God" (Romans 12:1) and as the "royal priesthood," described in 1 Peter 2:9.

Hebrews 10:1-9

For the Law, since it has [only] a shadow of the good things to come [and] not the very form of things, can never by the same sacrifices year by year, which they offer continually, make perfect those who draw near. Otherwise, would they not have ceased to be offered, because the worshippers, having once been cleansed, would no longer have had consciousness of sins? But in those [sacrifices] there is a reminder of sins year by year. For it is impossible for the blood of bulls and goats to take away sins...He takes away the first in order to establish the second.

Once again, the key to properly understanding this passage is the same one that we have used all along in the book of Hebrews. This passage teaches that the Torah is "a shadow" (a "mirror reality") of all that we have in Messiah. Calling the teachings of the Torah "shadows" does not negate the importance of living them out. By living out the shadow (or "mirror reality") one can more easily be helped to remember the truths of the real. For example, by living out a weekly Shabbat, we can more easily practice on a daily basis what it means to live in the reality of the Shabbat rest we have through the finished work of Messiah.

Finally, when we are told that, "He takes away the first in order to establish the second," it merely means that the Renewed Covenant replaces the previous one. However, we need to remember that the provisions of the Renewed Covenant are very similar to those of the covenant with Moses. In fact, the provisions of all the covenants are incorporated into the Renewed Covenant (that's why it is called "renewed"). The teachings that are different are those that relate to the sacrifices.

Seeing the New Covenant as a Renewed Covenant really helps clarify the proper place of the Torah both in the Scriptures and in the lives of the Redeemed.

Questions Concerning
Miscellaneous Subjects

Sunday or Shabbat?

Question: How do I politely and without offense answer the question why one observes Saturday as the Shabbat instead of Sunday?

We offer this suggestion: There is nothing wrong with worshipping on Sunday. There is nothing biblically wrong with going to a place of worship on a Sunday and becoming as much involved as one desires.

It is, however, biblically incorrect to call Sunday, or any other day than the seventh day, "Shabbat." God included the Shabbat as one of the mo'adim—His specially appointed times. Therefore, its placement on the seventh day of the week is very important and should not be diminished. It can be honored fully, even if one worships on Sunday or any other day of the week. Moreover, In Leviticus 23, God taught that the Shabbat is the day when the holy community gathers together in a special way to honor Him.

Thus, we suggest that you merely inform your friends (nicely, of course!) that you do not have a problem with worshipping on a Sunday just as long as they do not insist that it be called "the Sabbath."

"Harsh" Commandments

Question: If we are supposed to follow the Torah, what about the commandments that seem unreasonably harsh, e.g., capital punishment for less than capital sins?

First of all, we need to watch our use of the label "unreasonably harsh." How can any of God's teachings be labeled "unreasonably harsh? You are correct in placing the word "seem" before it. It is we humans who label such teachings as harsh because we either fail to understand God's mind or do not trust in His wisdom.

The Torah was given to be followed by the community which lived in the land of Israel. We would like to emphasize that it was supposed to be followed by the entire community. We now find ourselves living in an entirely different situation. We are not a theocratic community living in the Land of Israel. Therefore, we will find that some of the commandments are impossible to perform. It goes without saying that the situation will be completely rectified when Messiah returns.

Seasonal Commandments?

Question: Are there any laws that were designed for a particular time in history but not for now?

God's teachings have applications for all ages of history. The problem with some of them is that they were intended to be carried out to their fullest when done in the land of Israel and within a community. Since following the Torah is not a matter of salvation, it does not hurt to forego doing those teachings that relate only to living in the land of Israel or relate only to doing them within a community. Moving to Israel may not be an option for some. But we strongly urge all of our readers to be in some kind of Torah community. It could be your church, a local Messianic synagogue, Bible study or where none of the above are available, just a small home fellowship.

Yeshua's Prophecy about the Church

Question: If there is such a continuity between the kehilah of the period of the Tanakh and the church (ekklesia) of the present era, then what did Yeshua mean in Matthew 16:18 when, speaking in the future tense, He said, "I will build My church?"

It is true that the future tense is used in Matthew 16:18. However, both in Greek and Hebrew there are several usages for the future tense. We must remember that in all likelihood, the original language spoken by Yeshua—and even written by Matthew—was a Semitic language. That being the case, it is quite possible that Yeshua was using the "continuous future" in this verse.[111] If so, then here is what we think that Yeshua was saying. He was teaching that He will continue to build his kehilah as He always had been doing. However, that which will be the basis of its growth and expansion will be the fact that He is the Messiah.

Circumcision and Baptism

Question: You mentioned that both Jewish believers and gentiles are circumcised. This question is in two parts: a) How are both circumcised? b) Is not the requirement to be physically circumcised a sure sign that gentiles—even gentile believers—may not participate in Passover (therefore signifying that Passover and perhaps other Torah observances are only for the physical descendants of Israel)?

Since both questions relate to circumcision, we decided to give an extended explanation of our viewpoint concerning circumcision. Baptism is also a related subject, so we thought that we would include some of our thoughts on both subjects here. Please note, however, the following is not to be construed as the final word on the subject. This is neither the time nor place for a complete treatment. That will have to wait for another book or booklet.

Circumcision

In order to understand circumcision in the Scriptures, we need to get a grip on how it functions as a Torah picture. The original Torah picture which Israel as a nation portrayed was the reality that each person is either a part of the Kingdom of God or is not. Anything which is outside the "boundaries" of the Kingdom of life is death and therefore unclean. This Torah picture also makes it clear that any individual who is not a legitimate part of that Kingdom cannot participate in it. In Israel (which was designed by God to be the teaching picture of God's Kingdom) the sign that an individual is a part of God's people has always been circumcision.

The Torah Picture

The physical act of circumcision pictures for us what it means to be spiritually circumcised. Physical circumcision is performed when the thick outer flesh of the male organ is cut in such a manner so as to separate it from the body and the head of that organ, thus making visible both the body and the head, as they are without a veil of flesh to cover them. This is an exact picture of what takes place spiritually when an individual is born again, as is referred to in Colossians 2:9–13. Physical circumcision is the sign of the covenant with Abraham. The new birth, which takes place through faith and faith alone, results in an individual being declared righteous by God because of his faith in the Messiah of Israel. As

Abraham was chosen to be the father of the children of God physically, so also is he declared to be the father of all who are spiritually the children of God. Just as physical circumcision is the sign of the covenant with those physically born into the people of God (Israel), so is spiritual circumcision the sign of the covenant with those born spiritually into the people of God.

What does it mean to be one of the physical descendants of Abraham? Such a physical descendant is one who is physically born into that family and who is circumcised on the eighth day. Who are the spiritual descendants of Abraham? Those who are spiritually born into the family of God and spiritually circumcised. Circumcision, therefore, is one of the keys that unlocks the door to understanding the depths of the good news in the Messiah of Israel.

In fact, the Greek verb translated "was circumcised" in Colossians 2:11 is in the *aorist* passive. The aorist tense stresses the fact that it was a once for all action done in the past. The passive voice indicates that man did not do it. Rather, God did the circumcising. God's works are always perfect and complete; this also applies to circumcision. The circumcision of Colossians 2:11, then, is that separation of all that is our "flesh" from who we are as a new creation hidden in Messiah, one with the Father and seated with Him in the heavenlies. It was a once for all action done by God, and it is absolutely permanent. Now this is good news!

Why the eighth day? Obviously, eight follows seven. Being circumcised on the eighth day finishes out the message of the Good News. All the days of our striving to attain merit with God, to establish our own righteousness based on performance-based acceptance models, come to an end when we trust in *the finished work* of the Messiah of Israel. At that point we have actually entered "the seventh day" or "the Sabbath Rest" spoken of in Hebrews chapter 4. Our "six days of labor" has come to an end and having now entered our "seventh day," we now live the rest of our lives in that Seventh Day—in the "Sabbath rest" of being a finished new creation in Messiah. When our life comes to a close, that which follows the "seventh day," will be "the eighth day." In Judaism eight is the symbol of the *Olam Habba*, the world to come. In that "day", the "flesh" as well as the sins of the flesh will be removed forever. (By "flesh" we do not mean the human body but "the mind patterned after this world.")

Anyone who is born again through faith in the finished work of the Messiah has entered the "Sabbath Rest" of Hebrews 4 and is also circumcised with the circumcision done without hands described in Colossians 2. During our lives in our bodies here on earth, all that is our flesh still exists and yet it is cut away, separated from our truest self. That means that it no longer even touches our new creation self, who is now hidden in Messiah and actually already seated in the heavens with Him in Glory! The realities of our "eighth day" are already ours now, for we are seated in the heavenlies in Messiah. Thus we have in the Good News the end of our "six days of labor" and the joint realities of both living in the "Sabbath Rest" (being a new creation) and in the circumcision of our flesh.

Since we are new creations, living as though we were uncircumcised, causes a "veil of flesh behavior" to obscure the true body of Messiah, who is supposed to lift the Head of the body, Messiah Himself. With Messiah lifted up, rivers of *mayim hayim* (living water) will flow, bringing forth life from within that flow!

Walking in the Spirit

Walking in the Spirit and not in the flesh entails knowing for sure that "it is no longer I who live but Messiah who lives in me. The life I live in the body, I live by faith in the Son of God, who loved me and gave Himself for me" (Galatians 2:20).

Walking in the Spirit is knowing that it is truly His life that now dwells within us. At any point in time that we choose to yield the parts of our body to Him who indwells us, it is His life in us that then will flow out from us—His life in us which is "circumcised from our flesh." This is the meaning of the Scriptures which declare, "He who believes in Me, as the Scripture said, 'From his innermost being shall flow rivers of living water [mayim hayim]'" (John 7:38).

Let us be clear, the Scriptures declare that after we are born from above, our old man remains in the grave (Romans 6:1-6). Sin, however, still dwells in the "flesh." As new creations, we are now "constituted the righteousness of God in Messiah" and are "circumcised" (separated) from our "flesh." At this point, we must take care to understand the place of sin in our lives. The Scriptures are clear that a regenerated individual still carries out sin through his members (the parts of his physical body). We are given the responsibility to "take every thought captive," and subsequently, to "yield our members to righteousness instead of to unrighteousness." We are now freed from the bondage of sin and are free to choose to yield to righteousness. Let us therefore know the truth that sets us free and choose righteousness! In so doing, we are then "walking in the spirit."

If we understand the above we are also able to more fully comprehend what Sha'ul teaches in Romans 7:17ff, "When I sin, it is no longer I who sin, but sin that dwells in my members." Do not miss the full impact of the words; we are responsible for our sin but no longer are we (our truest selves—our new creation selves) guilty and/or condemned! For, "There is therefore now no condemnation for those who are in Messiah Yeshua" (Romans 8:1).

Knowing all of this is one of the most important components of living our daily walk where dealing with our flesh is concerned. What is the key to dealing with our flesh?

The key is understanding the truth that as part of our new identity, we are "circumcised" from the flesh. That flesh is no longer part of our identity. That flesh has been separated from our truest self and we are now free to consider ourselves dead to the sins of our flesh, because in truth we are dead to sin and alive to Messiah. To allow Messiah's life in us to be concealed by our flesh is to "walk in the flesh." To refuse to allow our flesh to conceal His life in us is to choose to walk in the Spirit. If we do so, the Scriptures promise us that mayim hayim will flow from our innermost being. And wherever the river of life flows, there will be life!

Continuity

There is another important implication we can draw from the concept of circumcision. Circumcision of the heart is a basic aspect of the Gospel. Moreover, it is a spiritual reality of all individuals who are born from above—both Jewish and gentile believers. Although gentile believers do not share physical descendancy from Abraham, nonetheless, they all share in the spiritual descendancy and, therefore, they are all spiritually circumcised. There is one Gospel and one family and one Messiah who is head over all. Therefore, even though there are different callings within the body of Messiah, there is no separation.

If we have been successful in painting for you the Torah picture of circumcision, the sign of the covenant of faith, it will now be easy to see that anyone who is born again (and therefore circumcised with the circumcision done without hands) is in every way a legitimate participant at the Passover Seder. Why? Simply because they are legitimate participants in the Kingdom of God, for they are ones who have "crossed over" from one kingdom to the other. They are "in life", having been redeemed by the blood of the Passover Lamb. They are Redeemed. They are circumcised. They are citizens of the Kingdom.

Considering the Torah picture of circumcision for the Redeemed, should then any male who is born again also be physically circumcised as a sign of their being participants in the covenant of faith? Certainly, God would not deny any male believer the permission to carry in his body the beauty of this picture, but he does not share the same *responsibility* to do so as does his counterpart who is also one of the physical descendants of Abraham. The key is in the word "responsibility." Sha'ul never taught that non-Jewish believers in Yeshua must be circumcised. But neither did he teach that they were prohibited from doing so. He merely instructed that anyone who wanted to be circumcised was not to do so for the hope of meriting or keeping his salvation.

The fact that God used the term "circumcision" when describing the change that occurred inside a person's heart when he became a believer is no accident. In our opinion, it clearly establishes a connection to the physical circumcision practiced among the children of Israel. Therefore, a spiritually circumcised believing gentile should be permitted to fully participate in the Passover table. By virtue of his spiritual circumcision, this person is considered an equal part of God's holy Redeemed community and therefore fully qualified to participate.

Therefore, as we see it, the circumcision done by God himself qualifies regenerate gentiles to fully participate in that which is now rightfully theirs—citizenship with Israel and partaking in the covenants of promise. However—and this is a big however—if any non-Jewish believer desires to undergo physical circumcision and, thereby, to participate in that Torah picture with his brothers and sisters from among the descendants of Jacob, we think that he has complete divine permission to do so—just as long as he realizes this important truth. He must firmly believe that his act of circumcision neither earns salvation nor wins merit with God.

Baptism

There is one last thought that we would like to communicate about circumcision. For several centuries there have been many in the church who have propagated the idea that baptism now replaces circumcision as the sign of being part of God's people. If the Scriptures had been interpreted with the background of the Land, the People, and the Scriptures of Israel, perhaps this faulty theology would never have developed.

The belief that baptism has replaced circumcision has two problems. First, it confuses two significant but individual Torah pictures. As explained above, circumcision carried with it its own important Torah picture, illustrating what it means to be circumcised in the heart. Baptism on the other hand is derived from a completely different source and consequently carries with it its own teaching picture and meaning. It is derived from the Torah practice of water immersion, in which the water symbolized both the grave and the womb. As one entered the water (the mikveh), it signified entering the grave. As he emerged from the water, he was like one "born again." The water, therefore, is also a picture of the womb. The immersed person, coming up out of the water, knows himself to be a new person in Messiah and free to walk in newness of life. Moreover, like the other Torah practices, immersion itself is not efficacious, that is, it is only symbolic and does not contribute to our salvation.

Hence, the origin and biblical theological development of baptism (immersion) runs along a different track than that of circumcision, although it is complimentary to it. It would not be theologically or biblically correct, therefore, to confuse the two practices. In addition, if we were to accept that one practice has replaced the other, a whole body of precious and significant biblical symbolism would be hopelessly confused and veiled. As important as the mikveh is, circumcision and not the mikveh was designed by God as His choice to be the sign of the covenant of promise/faith.

The second problem is that the theology which teaches that baptism replaces circumcision is also a theology that assumes that God has stripped the covenant nation of Israel of its God-given calling . It assumes that the Church replaced Israel as God's covenanted people. In fact, it was out of the seed-bed of the "Replacement Theology" of some of the early church fathers that the confusion of circumcision and baptism began. They believed and taught that Israel was cursed and that the Church had replaced it.

Appendix B
Those Who Have Taken Hold

The purpose for the following appendix is twofold. By now we hope that the Lord has used this work to reveal to you that you do have a significant and intimate relationship with the Land, the People, and the Scriptures of Israel. Having come into this understanding—which will eventually be followed by practice, you will need fellowship, community and friends that are searching and striving with you, committed one to another to walk in the light of God's Word. This is the first reason for this section—to let you know that you are not alone, and to give you strength and encouragement in realizing that you are a part of large worldwide community and family.

Second, and more importantly we want you to realize that this is a unique move of the Spirit of God. We trust that by reading these testimonies you will see the power and magnitude of this revelation and the impact it has had on the lives of these believers. We believe that as the body of Messiah begins (by His grace) to align itself with the Torah it will change and be re-shaped—preparing and unifying the ancient people of the Book and those grafted in from among the nations into His bride. This alone is far beyond the ability of any man or ministry. We, by no means lay claim to establishing this move or creating the desire of the Body to follow and understand Torah. By God's grace, and that alone, were our hearts prompted to search for our own relationship to His entire Word. The personal background of each one of us at First Fruits of Zion is similar to those of whom you will be reading—raised with little understanding of God and devoid of any teachings concerning His Torah.

Like the story of the man from India in our introduction, we have literally seen hundreds, if not thousands of people from every part of the world returning to this understanding. From remote islands in the Pacific to the closed and hostile gates of China, we have seen and received testimonies of an amazing thirst and desire to return to a lifestyle ordained and sanctioned by God, not man, found only in His written Word— these are just a few of those testimonies.

It is our hope that the testimonies in this appendix will strengthen you as you endeavor to apply the Torah to your own walk. We would also like to hear your testimony and include it in a "testimony book" which has been started here in our Jerusalem office. Your testimony would be a wonderful contribution. As people from among the nations come up to Jerusalem, they will be able to see and read for themselves the Lord's calling on all who have "taken hold."

Testimony One
In Australia's "Sunshine State" They're Taking Hold!

It was in 1991 when Christian life as I knew it came to a halt. I had been born again 15 years earlier; before that I had been raised a Roman Catholic.

As a Christian, my life was very full. I ran a youth group numbering over 100, as well as establishing refuges for homeless youth. I often spoke at seminars and in schools about the reality of God and Jesus. My life before becoming a Christian was not so good—I had a story to tell.

Around 1985, I became interested in Israel and the history of the Jewish people. I went to hear speakers, such as Jan Willem van der Hoeven, who really impacted my life. For the first time I noticed what the Bible said about the Jews and the promises and covenants God gave them. It all happened very quickly, as God made me aware of His plan for the Jewish people and Israel, as well as showing me the century-old lies which were still inhabiting the Church. I understood that it was a root problem, a "replacement theology" foundation on which the

Roman Church had been built, sixteen centuries ago. And yet, even with breaking away from Rome, many denominations continued to follow many of its ordinances.

In 1989, I had been ordained as a minister with a Pentecostal denomination in Australia, one of three women this denomination had ordained in the whole country. But because my thinking had changed so much, my role within the Church added to my crisis. There was much teaching and many practices I could no longer follow. On this night in 1991, which certainly became "different from all other nights," I was sitting at the kitchen table, desperately trying to figure out where I belonged.

In the midst of this, the Lord spoke one word to me— "Ruth." At first I thought God had just mixed me up with somebody else and reminded Him my name was Luana, not Ruth. Then it came again, "Read Ruth." So I got my Bible and began to read, and from that time on, things began to drastically change. In the context of this, I will share with you what it meant for me to "take hold."

When I read the words which Ruth, a gentile, spoke to Naomi, it was like she expressed everything I wanted to say to the Jewish people: "Don't urge me to leave you or to turn back from following you. Where you go I will go and where you stay I will stay. Your people will be my people and your God my God. Where you die I will die and there will I be buried. May the Lord deal with me, be it ever so severely, if anything but death separates me from you" (Ruth 1:16,17). I wanted to go where they were going; I wanted to be part of that family; I wanted to know God in their way. I knew that association with the Jewish people would inevitably create problems, but I wanted to be in covenant with them. This is what Ruth was saying to Naomi, a Jewess: "I want to be in covenant relationship with you; I want to 'take hold' of everything that belongs to you." And so I set out to do exactly just that.

Fortunately, I had some Jewish friends with whom I could speak openly. They were gracious enough to listen and give me the time to talk things through. I had much to learn and unlearn. Slowly, as they explained the God of Israel and His Word to me, and as I listened, willing to lay down my doctrines and learn from them, my thinking began to change. Sometimes it was very difficult, and we had some heated arguments, but there was no way I was going to be like Orpah who, after going with Naomi part of the way, decided to turn back.

The more I learned, the more excited I became. I wanted to know more of what it was like to be a Jew and how, after all they had been through, they still had faith in God. There were some who were very bitter and had lost faith, but for the most part, they still believed. I spent time listening to Holocaust survivors and recording their stories on video.

How was it that this people, whom the Church had declared apostate, could still recite the "Shema" on the way to the gas chambers? How was it that they were prepared to sit and talk to me, a gentile? I was so overwhelmed that I organized large functions where Holocaust survivors could come and speak to Christians. Their stories had to be heard. The offerings we received at these functions went to help Soviet Jews return to Israel. Hundreds of Christians came to hear and responded. Petitions for the release of Refuseniks were signed and thousands of dollars raised. Many Jews attended also, overwhelmed by the response.

Soon I began to ask the question, "Why me, Lord? Why are you revealing these things to me—so much that I can hardly contain it?" He answered me with another part of the Book of Ruth.

The story says that while Ruth was working in the fields, Boaz noticed her and called her to himself. In 2:10, Ruth says to Boaz, "Why have I found such favor in your eyes that you notice me—a foreigner?" Boaz replied, "I've been told about what you have done for your mother-in-law.... May the Lord repay you for what you have done. May you be richly rewarded by the Lord, the God of Israel, under whose wings you have come to take refuge." I wasn't expecting any reward for my enthusiasm in working for the Jewish cause, and yet the reward was great. Now I knew why! J.C. Ryle wrote in the 19th century: "Is there anyone who desires God's special blessing? Then let him labor in the cause of Israel and he shall not fail to find it."

Like Naomi, my Jewish friends (whether they realized it or not) revealed to me the Jewishness of the Messiah: "Is not Boaz, with whose servant girls you have been, a kinsman of ours?" (Ruth 3:2). Realizing the Jewishness of "Jesus" and coming to know his true identity—Yeshua—was a real turning point. Like Ruth, I too could become a part of the family of the Kinsman Redeemer! This is what Paul meant in Romans 11 about being grafted in. I didn't have to remain a gentile in either my thinking or my lifestyle.

By now, I had left behind the paganisms introduced by the Roman Church. I also understood that God had only ever worked within *one* framework—the household of Israel. There was only *one* "betrothed unto Him" and He had not given His Name to another. Yet although I kept the biblical feasts and had come a long way in my thinking, I still felt something was missing.

On my fortieth birthday, my wanderings would end. I retraced my 'journeying' as a believer in Messiah Yeshua and thought about the decisions I had made. As it said in Zechariah 8:23, I had taken hold of the Jewish people. What was missing? I read that Scripture again and saw for the first time that it was not so much 'the Jew' who I was to take hold of, but the *fringes on his robe*! Bingo! I had read a few books on the tzitzit and knew that the fringes represented Torah. That is what was missing! I felt as though I had almost reached "the Promised Land," but had forgotten to make a major stopover—Sinai. So back I went and received Torah.

On this day, my wanderings did end and life has never been the same. At Sinai, I not only received God's instruction for my life, but I also met the Bridegroom in a way that I had never known Him before—He is the "Living Torah."

Although I didn't fully understand the reasons behind all of God's commandments, I knew they were His instructions for my life, for the purpose of being holy—set apart. This is where God has called Israel to be and where Yeshua came and where the early Messianic community was born and lived— within the framework of Torah. This is where all the promises and covenants are. This is the place which God has redeemed.

In embracing this new understanding it has been overwhelming and life giving, but like most who have walked the same road, it has been far from easy. It is not popular, particularly among Christians, to keep God's Torah, but for me, I have found many spiritual rewards in it.

Like Ruth, I have "taken hold of my inheritance with Israel" and am grafted into the household of God.

Luana Fabry
Queensland, Australia

Testimony Two
Christian Life Church Pastor Takes Hold

As a gentile, brought up in a fairly strict surrounding of Christianity, it is amazing that I have just come to the conclusion of another Shabbat—observed with my family. My wife and I looked at each other this afternoon and commented on what a rich and rewarding experience Shabbat has become for our family. Over the last three years we have enjoyed the unique presence of the Lord in doing things His way.

For the past eight years I have been pastoring a church in Jacksonville, Florida. This church has a rich history, as it is one of the oldest in our community, dating back to about 1890. Its past has been made up of people trying to force other people to stop swearing, dancing, drinking, chewing, and quite a few other things. To say that we might have had a few religious spirits hanging around would have been an understatement. It is in this setting that, by the grace of God, He has chosen to begin revealing to us the meaning of a true biblical, godly lifestyle.

I am a preacher's kid, so in my early life practically everything was centered around the church. This knowledge and experience, while instrumental in guiding me to accept Yeshua as my Messiah, left leaving me feeling like there must be more to living for God than "going to church." I was discouraged by the lack of a spiritual structure to hold people to a consistency in their walk with God. I had seen the overall effects of trying to force people to be godly and knew that while we might be pleased with the outward results, the real problem was that the person's relationship was usually shallow. I began praying and asking the Lord to show me what was missing in the way most Christians were trying to live for Him.

One day I heard a statistic that startled me and which God used to prod me in a direction I had never considered. The statistic was that in the Florida penitentiary system, there was one group of people that was grossly under-represented: the Jews. The fact that there were only a handful of Jews in prison, was contrasted with an over-representation of those that claimed to be Christians or had grown up in Christian homes. Coupled with this was the recent statistic from a Christian pollster that reveals Evangelical Christian couples are now more likely to experience divorce than secular couples. I refuse to believe that the God of our faith is that weak—so the problem must lie with how we relate to our God.

Shortly after I saw the prison statistic, the Lord began leading me into situations where I was learning more about the culture and lifestyle of Yeshua, and especially how He lived His life in observance of the Torah. My "discovery" of these things produced in me a contentment and joy that had been missing in my personal life. It also gave me the assurance that this was what the gentile Christian church has been missing for nineteen hundred years. This break with our biblical roots is fairly easy to verify, as most encyclopedias have enough information to give the rather stark anti-Semitic history of our forefathers.

Learning about our biblical heritage and allowing the Spirit of the Lord to reveal the richness of the Scriptures has radically changed my role as pastor. I have seen that God has called me to pastor *this* flock, not to be looking over fences to see if there are more desirable flocks to watch over. I have been able to focus on doing what God has placed in my heart, which is to teach people His ways. The satisfaction that I experience as we move into learning Hebrew, studying Jewish history, and seeing the importance of the cultural setting of Yeshua is extremely rewarding. It has opened up the awesomeness of God to us and helped us to realize that He really does care about every little thing, and will use us if we are willing.

One of the main differences for our family has been our decision to personally honor God with His Sabbath. As parents, we have seen the difference it is making in our own lives, but the added blessing is seeing our children grow up with this as a part of their heritage. We all look forward to this weekly time, and our hearts rejoice as we hear our four-year-old ask us, "Just when is Shabbat coming?"

We believe we can see we are doing the right thing. As I began sharing these things with our local church, there was an initial acceptance and excitement that most shared in and accepted as truth. However, after a couple of years, when it became obvious that we were not playing with a fad, but were serious about allowing God to change our lifestyles, our congregation went through a pruning process.

That is really what it all boils down to. Do we want to live the way we have grown accustomed to and are comfortable in, or do we want to make the biblical changes that will allow us to see the glory of the Lord in our lives and the lives of our children?

Bobby Carswell
Senior Pastor
Christian Life Church

Testimony Three
Embracing Shabbat Observance
as Our Household Covenant with Abba

During the first two years after proclaiming Yeshua as my Messiah, our elder shared with us the Spirit's prompting to "consider our biblical roots." From time to time, he would share material from various Christian organizations with a love for Israel. We also discovered Marvin Wilson's book, "Our Father Abraham," which was the fuel for the fire that would be sparked by the Spirit.

One night the teaching was on Ephesians 2, regarding who gentiles are in being brought near to the promises of God, and how the dividing wall was torn down by Messiah. At this point our elder stated how wonderful it would be to be one with God's people, to be familiar with the worship and life of the redeemed people, so that a Jew could come among us and be at peace with our praise to God. He said, "Wouldn't it warm a Jew's heart to hear a gentile say, '*Baruch haShem Adonai*' (Bless the name of the Lord)? It does mine!"

From that moment my heart was opened to God's people, sensing the longing that Abba has for His redeemed creation to be one in Messiah. But how do we live, how do we learn about our place in the spiritual community of Yeshua? I could see from Acts that gentile believers went to the synagogue to learn from their Messianic brothers, but how could my wife and I do this, here in Michigan?

The answer came in the form of a simple-looking newspaper entitled, "First Fruits of Zion." The contents and the spirit of the writers said, "Come, let us go up to the house of the Lord—together." This publication became our long-distance correspondence course in Torah. My wife, Deborah, and I were blessed by the truth shared about Torah, and we knew we needed to put this truth into practice in our lives.

The first application of Torah in our lives was to embrace Shabbat observance as our household covenant with Abba. The first obstacle was my work schedule. Working second shift, my week wouldn't end until Friday night; hours after sunset. We saw no way out of this situation. Nevertheless, we prayerfully petitioned the Lord to consider the intentions of our hearts and accept our Shabbat meal, which would take place on Saturday night. All day Saturday was set aside to the Lord, studying Torah and learning *zimrot* (songs) that we would sing together on Shabbat. Later we added Messianic dance. The promise of Abba's rest in the Shabbat soon became real to us as we began to look forward to Shabbat. I would feel spiritual relief after the last work day, closing the door on the outside world and turning my heart to the Lord of the Shabbat. My wife cherishes these moments and the growth of our relationship together through the Shabbat and Torah.

We began to recognize the fruit of our Shabbat covenant with God by the response of family, friends and strangers who would visit our home. To the natural eye, our home was nothing spectacular, yet non-believers would say, "This home is so peaceful," and would not want to leave. We could only bless God for His promise of all that His shalom means in the midst of His redeemed: comfort, contentment, tranquillity and well-being.

Some of our own family members—believers—criticized this Torah-observant life we were living. Yet, they would tell us they sensed this same "*shalom beit*" (peaceful home), and that they could see a character change in us. The Lord is faithful to all His promises: Blessed are they who keep His statutes and seek Him with all their heart.

Dennis & Deborah Harold
Harbor Springs, Michigan
USA

Testimony Four
I heard the *Barchu* and I Took Hold!

Most people say they want to be close to God, yet most are content to stand at the Temple gate. Since my childhood, I have wanted to stand at His feet, wrapped up in the folds of His robe. I wanted to live life on His terms. Whatever lifestyle was important to God, that was the lifestyle I wanted to live.

Raised in a Christian home, I read the Bible often, examining the characteristics of lives that pleased God. It became evident early on that God established Israel for this very reason, to show to all of humanity the way to Him. They were to live in a way that was pleasing to Him, and it was available to anyone who could read the Torah that He gave to them.

I also read about Ruth and her decision to join with Israel. I considered the revelation that a gentile could join with Israel, and be pleasing to God. I discovered that even in Torah He made provisions for non-Jews living in Israel to be considered as part of Israel, as long as they turned to God and lived on His terms.

I fell in love with and married a Catholic girl. I began to search within the Catholic tradition for depth and meaning. I found much history and tradition. Liturgically there were many similarities to Judaism and that piqued my curiosity.

Then I discovered Hebrew Christianity. For a while, there seemed to be a great deal of spiritual and historical depth. I had studied Israeli Hebrew in college and the minimal liturgy gave me an outlet to use it in religious practice. The worship services were expressively "calm" enough for my Catholic wife to enjoy.

Within a few years, however, I had devoured as much "Hebraic" material as was available. Hebrew Christianity was too reminiscent of the "Christian culture" I had left. Whenever I tried to inquire about Torah observance, my inquiries were met with uncomfortable responses from the leadership.

I was hungry now for Torah. But Hebrew Christianity was not going to give me Torah. Here I was, at the gates of the Temple and it looked as if I wasn't going to get inside. I decided that as long as *HaShem* ("The Name," a reference to God) was letting me enter the Temple grounds because of my faith in His Mashiach, Yeshua, then I wanted in. All the way in.

We found Messianic Judaism. Now, there was Torah in abundance, expressive worship, the festivals—all of them, not just Passover—community, lifestyle, a sense of awe and holiness. That sense of awe was palpable during worship services. Every time I heard the *Barchu* (blessing) calling my soul to worship, I could feel the *tallit* (prayer shawl) around my shoulders, and I knew the very robe of the Lord was being wrapped around me.

In our home, my wife and I had been minimally observing Shabbat. Now, we began to fully observe Shabbat, not just lighting candles on Friday evening. Like Ruth in Scripture, we were taking hold of our inheritance and joining with Israel. Now I was becoming part of the community that had diligently kept these ways for thousands of years. I found the depth that had been missing.

I have now come to a place where my personal t'shuvah (return or repentance) is both an inward journey and an outward reflection. My motives are based on the inward passions of my heart. My practices are outward reflections of this inward passion for HaShem and for His righteousness. And along the way, the outward reflections stand out to others as a witness. I believe HaShem designed Torah observance for that reason: to teach us balance, to reveal our motives, and to catch the attention of others around us.

Torah observance provides me with reminders and tools for staying on the path of t'shuvah, walking back to God, on His terms. My new understanding of Torah and the ways of God deepens my understanding and love for the Scriptures. It provides me with a community of other believers who are on similar journeys.

Above all, I long to see Yeshua return in glory to Zion, my adopted homeland.

Christopher (Dov-Yatziv) Page
Thousand Oaks, California USA

Testimony Five
"Si Señor"—I've Taken Hold!

A member of the Roman Catholic Church by birth, at 25 years of age I wanted to know the origin of my faith, so I became a friend to a priest where I lived in Mexico City. He started me studying the doctrine of the "sacred mother Church" with Jesuit theologians. As I learned, I began to question my teachers: Where did so many of the doctrines come from? They answered that they came from the Bible and the pronouncements of the Church Fathers.

Then I began to read the Word of God. This was where my problems began, because the doctrine didn't harmonize with the Bible. My teachers answered my questions by saying that I shouldn't get involved in the sacred mysteries of God, because many who had tried ended up crazy.

If I wanted what God had for me, I would have to leave my land, my house, my kin, the Catholic Church and religion! So I came out from the religious world, and for six years I entered the world of meditation, self-improvement, philosophy and Rosicrucianism. With so much of a useless load on me, and about to be shipwrecked, I read the New Covenant writings about the God who revealed Himself to His people Israel. If only He could manifest Himself to me, as He does to His own people!

Without God and without hope, at 30 years of age I opened a business in Tijuana, a place where many people came who claimed they knew God: Jehovah's Witnesses, Mormons, Seventh-Day Adventists. But they didn't convince me with their doctrinal interpretations. At that time I came to know an evangelist of an independent Presbyterian church. He invited me to study the Scriptures, which were presented in an open and simple form. He took me all through the Bible, answering the questions which at that time were essential to me. And then it pleased God to reveal His Son to me!

It was an indescribable experience, finding myself in front of the burning bush which wasn't consumed, before the Holy One of Israel, the Redeemer of His people, in front of this purifying fire, and finding that there was no place to hide. This is how I came to hate the sinfulness of sin. I had been born again!

In my new life from God, I began attending the Presbyterian Church, and then I entered seminary in order to learn more. There my problems began anew. Many of the teachings were not in agreement with the counsel of the Lord. By that time, I had been elected to the church board. However, I wanted to be faithful to the word I had received, so I resigned to follow the way that God had put me on. I had left Ur of the Chaldeans, so why couldn't I also leave Egypt?

I wandered for ten years in the desert. But in this desert, I also met the sovereign God, and saw His faithfulness toward Israel, and His grace revealed in giving the Torah, so that Israel would become a holy nation, different from all other nations. I had to trust in the Lord, get out from this desert, and gather with His people to enter into the Promised Land!

I began to follow the footsteps of the Pastor of pastors and I saw that He entered a synagogue on Saturday as was His custom. How could this custom be on Saturday? Another day, He spoke with a woman of Samaria, and said to her: "You worship what you don't know, because salvation comes from the Jews." How could gentiles not know how to worship, but Jews have the key to salvation? On one occasion, many Jews followed Him, and they were zealous for the Torah. This was indeed strange: Jews who believed in the Messiah and who were zealous for the Torah? At that I proclaimed: "Lord, you rejected your people, I am your spiritual Israel. I am no longer under the Torah, but under grace. I am under the New Covenant!"

I was 47 years old, and it was like starting all over again. It was like searching between the wheat and the tares. I began to put into practice all that my Rabbi Yeshua and His Jewish followers did, since I didn't want to rebel against the heavenly vision. I called the Israeli Consulate to find a synagogue in Tijuana. They gave me the address of the Tijuana Jewish Community Center, and I immediately made an appointment with the Rabbi.

That day I had so many questions. How am I to properly keep the Torah and what was my part with the God of Abraham, Isaac and Jacob? How was it that God had revealed to Moses that there was only one Torah for both the Jew and the gentile who wanted a part in Jacob's inheritance? Lord, you haven't rejected your people but rather you have grafted *me* into them: your olive tree! There is only one spiritual Israel, and by your grace and Spirit you have written your Torah in my mind and heart!

At my first appointment with the Rabbi, I explained the reason for my visit, and he gave me a writing with the seven Noachide Laws for the gentiles. On my a appointment, he told me very kindly that they were a closed group and could not accept me among them.

I continued searching for the remnant which God has been preserving for the glory of His name, asking my Heavenly Father if I had found grace before Him, to be worthy of being in that small remnant. Then my son, César, brought me an address he had found in the American Yellow Pages, which invited Jews and gentiles to enjoy their Messiah together. We immediately made an appointment with the Rabbi.

We began to attend the Messianic synagogue together with my family. The first year, we only attended once a month. The following year, we become a full part of that Messianic Fellowship.

If at the end of my days, someone asked me if it was worth living, I would respond by quoting the Scripture found in Ecclesiastes 12:13-14, "Now all has been heard and here is the conclusion of the matter: Fear God and keep his commandments, for this is the whole duty of man. For God will bring every deed into judgment, including every hidden thing, whether it is good or evil."

We pray that this testimony will be an encouragement to you and we ask you to please pray that our Spanish speaking brothers here in Mexico and South America will soon realize as we have that there is much life to be realized in the Messiah when one takes hold of his relationship with Israel—not Rome!

Manuel Martínez
Tijuana, Mexico

Testimony Six
A Country Music Star and His Family Take Hold

We had been attending a church in Phoenix for thirteen years. The pastor taught the Scriptures verse by verse. His sermons were evangelical, intellectual, and inspirational. We grew by leaps and bounds in our walk with God.

Then God began to teach us about the biblical festivals outlined in Leviticus 23. We were amazed to learn that the festivals were actually God's appointed times, "prophecies" which the Messiah would fulfil. Yeshua fulfilled the first four festivals and there are three to go. When I saw the Messiah in the festivals I thought: "Why haven't I been taught about these things? Why have we been wasting our time doing bunnies and eggs and trees?" God gave us these festivals to teach us about the redemptive work of His Messiah and said that He would meet with us during these appointed times throughout the year. We wanted this for our family.

We began trying to incorporate the festivals into our lives. Because we were not raised Jewish, this required much study. I found Barney Kasdan's book, "God's Appointed Times," and "Celebrating The Sabbath the Messianic Jewish Way," by Ariel and D'vorah Berkowitz. They were a great help to us.

Celebrating the festivals was a fantastic teaching tool for our children. Suddenly all of the Scriptures, both in the *Tanakh* (Old Testament) and the *Brit Hadasha* (New Testament), began to blossom before our eyes. We were understanding the Hebraic background and thus our knowledge of the Scriptures seemed to double and then triple. We were so excited!

We began to share the things we were learning with our friends. I remember being so excited that I would almost hyperventilate. "Let me tell you what I learned today!" Then I would talk for an hour about Yeshua proclaiming that He is the light of the world in the context of the Sukkot or Feast of Tabernacles celebration, during which there were four great torches—called the "light of the world"—that burned in the courtyard of the Temple. This festival was all about Yeshua! I couldn't stop talking about the Lord: It just kept overflowing out of me, like rivers of living water (also Sukkot terminology)!

I started a Bible study with about fifteen women, meeting in our home to study the festivals. We were all blessed beyond belief! We started a Torah Study *Chavurah* (Fellowship), and hosted a Passover Seder Celebration for our friends. We have never had more fun!

I began to study church history and saw how we were severed from our Jewish roots. I read "The Messianic Jewish Manifesto" by Dr. David Stern, "Jewish Roots" by Dan Juster, "Our Father Abraham" by Marvin Wilson, and then someone gave us a copy of a "First Fruits of Zion" magazine. The light went on! I had now discovered my true identity in Messiah. Not only am I a new creation, born of the Spirit of God, but I have been grafted into Israel (Romans 11) and am now part of the commonwealth of Israel (Ephesians 2). I am a joint heir and partaker in the covenants. God has always made a provision in the Torah for the non-Jew, the "stranger (*ger*) within your gates."

I am not Jewish. But is God the God of the Jews only? No, He is the God of the whole world. If I have to become Jewish to be saved, God is reduced to being the God of the Jews only. If the Torah applied to the "stranger" then, how much more should it apply to me now?

We thought the Old Testament was just a history book. Now we know it is our family album that shows us who we are in Messiah as a people of God. The very God who identifies Himself as the God of Abraham, Isaac and Jacob is our God.

The revelation that the Torah has not been abolished and that it has a place in my life has been a blessing, and it has caused me to "take hold" of my roots, and come into a fullness which I never knew existed for my life.

Therefore, remember your former state: you gentiles by birth—called the Uncircumcised by those who, merely because of an operation on their flesh, are called the Circumcised—at that time had no Messiah. You were estranged from the national life of Israel. You were foreigners to the covenants embodying God's promise. You were in this world without hope and without God.

So then, you are no longer foreigners and strangers. On the contrary, you are fellow-citizens with God's people and members of God's family (Ephesians 2:11–12,19 Jewish New Testament).

If God said in Exodus 12:49: "One law (Torah) shall be for the native-born and for the stranger who dwells among you," how much more so, now that I am a fellow citizen and member of the commonwealth of Israel, the household of God? I freely embrace the Torah, it is my marriage covenant with the Lord. I do it because He has written it on my heart and I love Him.

"'But this is the covenant that I will make with the house of Israel after those days,' says the Lord, 'I will put My Torah in their minds, and write it on their hearts; and I will be their God, and they shall be My people'" (Jeremiah 31:33). The "new" or "renewed" covenant was made with the house of Israel. Are we non-Jews a part of Israel or not? Has God written His Torah on our minds and hearts or not?

Not only is God saying *shema* (hear!) to Israel, but He is saying it to the nations as well. The church must repent of its anti-Jewish, anti-Torah bias and take hold of the wonderful inheritance that God has so graciously given us in His Torah through His Messiah, Yeshua!

The revelation that the Torah has not been abolished, that it has a place in the life of the believer has been a blessing, but there have been difficulties as well. We have been misunderstood by many fellow Christians who are ignorant of their Jewish roots and who misunderstand the writings of Paul. However, as they see us live out Torah in freedom and love, through time their fears have been dispelled. The hardest thing has been to find a fellowship that already understands that the Torah is a perpetual covenant rather than an abolished one. I am hopeful that this book, especially the section on difficult passages, will help our brothers and sisters in the Lord realize that if we look into the Torah, we can see what the body of Messiah should look like and how it should behave. The New Covenant contains over 1,050 commands, which are halackic in nature. They do not take away from it or replace the Torah, but expand and explain it.

What is in the Torah that I would not want to do? Now for the first time in my life I can say with King David: "May Thy compassion come to me, that I may live, for Thy Torah is my delight" (Psalm 119:77). We have found a place of peace, grace and happiness in our new understanding and application of the entire Word of God to our lives. We pray that you will as well.

Glen and Kim Campbell
Pheonix, Arizona

Testimony Seven
An Afrikaner Takes Hold

June 1981: It was almost midnight when my three year old daughter and I stepped out of the EL-AL plane and hesitantly took our first steps onto the soil of the land of Israel. I had no idea, other than knowing that I was being obedient to the Lord's voice, why I was coming to this particular place. The Jewish people and the physical land of Israel had not even been part of my frame of reference up until that point in time. How odd—is it not?

For 33 years, the latter part of which I had been born-again, I had been a faithful and respected member of the Church and yet, when I got off that plane, to my mind there was no difference between Israel, South Africa or the Bahamas. Knowing that I only had a one-night hotel reservation in Jerusalem, I looked up into the clear summer sky. "As the stars in heaven…"—I vaguely remembered something about Abraham being the father of our faith, who had left all behind and set out in pursuit of his inheritance. Little did I realize that my journey had just begun. Maybe I would have made a U-turn right there and then had I known that my whole foundation as a Christian was going to be hit by an earthquake measuring 8.5 on the spiritual Richter scale.

With the gung-ho attitude of a newly saved believer who had completed every "How to" course that was available in the Christian market place, I was ready to "take-on" this little country and its people. How gracious the Lord is when we charge headlong forward with our zeal for Him—zeal sometimes based on ignorance and pre-conceived ideas. Nonetheless, He shut me up for almost my first two years in the Land by putting me in a kitchen, which became my school of learning while I was peeling onions and potatoes. I took His admonition seriously, and knew that I had nothing to give to the Jewish people unless I understood His heart for them and this Land.

I began to realize that I didn't even know much about the Jesus that I was so eager to present to them. At that time in my life, He was only a caricature of who He truly is—the Lion of the tribe of Judah, who came, and will return in fulfillment of the Hebrew Scriptures, God's prophetic Word spoken in the Old Testament, of which I knew nothing. And so, the first tremors of the earthquake were experienced as I came to the realization that the "Old" is not as old as I had been led to believe. Such joy gripped me as I started discovering how relevant God's prophetic Word is for our day and age. I no longer had to accept an allegorized approach to the Hebrew Scriptures like the teaching I had received thus far. Yeshua standing on the Mount of Olives according to Zechariah 14 no longer meant to me that He comes to stand with His feet in my heart when I pray the sinner's prayer and invite Him into my life. I had never gotten round to asking that teacher what becomes of "all the saints" that accompany the Lord to the "mountain"—according to his interpretation! What a relief it was to discover that our God indeed is the same, yesterday today and forever. That He *is* a covenant-keeping God and that

He did not change His mind or His purposes concerning this Land and this nation, and that therefore I can put my trust fully in Him and His Word.

But, as I was soon to discover, getting on a spiritual high about prophecy was not an end in itself. It is a useless exercise unless it brings one to a place of identification with God's redemptive purposes for Israel. And even in addition to that, to realize that I, as a gentile, owe a spiritual debt to the Jewish people which should effect a response from me in terms of my relationship to them and my involvement with them as a nation.

In response to this, I thought I had all bases covered when I returned to South Africa and launched a project aimed at linking groups and churches there with Messianic believers living in Israel. But discovering the amazing truths of Romans 11 and Ephesians 2 & 3 shook me right out of my belief system founded on Replacement Theology. It confronted me with a scary question: If I am a wild olive branch grafted into the cultivated olive tree, but have been walking in ignorance, arrogance and apathy towards that tree, how much of the nourishing sap from that tree have I gained access to? Which sap was I being nourished by? And from which tree? Have I been part of a different tree and consequently robbed of my true inheritance as a "fellow-citizen" with Israel? The answer sent further shock waves through my little world as a Christian.

The appalling history of anti-Semitism, persecution and murder of the Jewish people sanctioned by the institutionalized church through the centuries and a systematic moving away from the Jewish roots of our faith, gave rise to a sense of panic as I began to feel that for me it was becoming a matter of life and death spiritually. How, for instance, could the faithful believing remnant of Israel, the cultivated olive branches celebrate one set of festivals, and we, the wild branches in yet the same tree, claim a different set according to our own calendar? At the entrance to a shopping center in South Africa I read "Happy Passover" on one pillar and "Happy Easter" on the other. Ezekiel 43 flashed through my mind, "When they placed their doorpost next to my doorpost...with only a wall between them and Me, they defiled My Holy Name". I started recognizing the doorposts based on a thin veneer of truth, but which are in fact "traditions of men" springing from the fertile soil of Replacement Theology and anti-Semitism, causing the church in many instances to put her roots down into pagan soil.

It was December 1992. I found myself on a tour standing at the Egyptian obelisk on the square in front of St Peter's church at the Vatican. And I knew there was no turning back. I read verses from Romans 11 and Ephesians 2 and 3. Then, in a simple prayer, a friend and I declared before the Holy One of Israel that we had no desire to be part of a tree that did not originate with Him, or with man who says, "We will serve You, but we will do it our way!" We repented for not having heeded God's warning recorded in Deuteronomy 12:30, "Do not inquire after their gods saying, 'How did these nations serve their gods? I will do likewise.' Thou shall not do so unto the Lord thy God. What ever I command you, observe to do that." My friend and I flew from there to Egypt. It was again, in Alexandria, where the lie of Replacement Theology was nurtured by church fathers like Origin and from there found its way into the church worldwide. We again spent time repenting before the Lord and praying for a way of escape for the bride of Messiah out of the Babylon of man-made religion.

Our journey continued by bus, crossing the Red (Reed) Sea by ferry and reaching Jerusalem twenty minutes before a conference called "The Jewish Roots of Our Faith" was due to start! I did not anticipate that the battle within me would intensify. But in spite of many severe after tremors of the earthquake, there was now a sense of joyful anticipation and excitement as the Lord led me, and by now many others that I was acquainted with, along the path of entering into our inheritance. The Lord started drawing individuals out of the woodwork in my homeland of South Africa and groups like "Bat Tzion" in Johannesburg and "B'nei Tzion" in Pretoria, as well as many others which I gradually heard about, were meeting together, rediscovering the Word of God and sensing the Lord bringing forth "one new man," Jew and gentile, one in Messiah Yeshua.

As we started meeting at the "appointed times" to celebrate the festivals of the Lord, not even being sure exactly how to go about it, my faith was strengthened and enriched as gradually the nourishing sap started seeping through to us as gentile believers. But then the inevitable happened. What about the Lord's Sabbath? I discovered that it was mentioned first in the list of His appointed times, that it was so pivotal that it was to be a *weekly* celebration, and that the Sabbath, the seventh day, was fixed as a day of rest *already* at the time of creation. What is more, God set His calendar and His mo'adim in place on the forth day when He created the sun, moon and stars as lights and for seasons—mo'adim.

The God of Abraham, Isaac and Jacob is restoring His cycle and His mo'adim, including the Sabbath, to be as fixed as the sun and the moon in the sky, not to be tampered with. What's more, the Creator God determined that His Son, Yeshua, would be "Lord of the Sabbath." The blessing resulting from obedience to God's Word far outweighs the feelings of rejection when labeled with, "She is going back under the Law, you know!" Yes, I thought, God's wonderful Law—the Torah. I stood appalled that day when the Spirit of God put His light on my defiant, irreverent attitude toward His Torah! But what joy I experienced as the Lord graciously began to and continues to give me more access to the nourishing sap from the olive tree: the tallit, the Mishkan, Pesach and Yom Kippur, etc. Everything from Genesis to Revelation points toward God's plan of salvation for all of mankind and testifies to the truth of that all-encompassing declaration: "Hear o Israel, the Lord our God, the Lord is One."

What an amazing God we serve! Watching Him at work in South Africa, where recently I was able to share this message with many groups, including 700 black brothers and sisters, fills one with awe and delight. I will always remember that when the dust has settled after the earthquake, only that which is of Him remains!

Jo Tait
Pretoria, South Africa

Glossary of Terms

We have chosen to use the Jewish form of certain names and phrases in this book for specific reasons. Foremost among these is to maintain a Jewish sensibility so that the book may be "user friendly" for Jewish readers. We have provided this glossary for those readers unfamiliar with Jewish terminology.

It is sometimes difficult to transliterate words from one language to another. Accordingly, we have encountered certain problems in transliterating some words from Hebrew or Greek into English; hence, we have listed variant spellings in cases where more than one rendering is possible.

BCE, CE—This is the Jewish way of dating or reckoning the centuries. BCE = Before the Common Era (BC), and CE = Common Era (AD). By using these terms we are in no way attempting to diminish the centrality of Yeshua in our lives, or to deprive Him of His due honor. We are merely endeavoring to be sensitive to Jewish feelings.

Church fathers—The Christian scholars and leaders who preached and wrote between approximately 100 to 450 CE.

Counting the Days—This is a period of time specified by Leviticus 23, falling between Pesach and Shavu'ot. We are merely told to "count the days."

First Jewish Revolt—The First Jewish Revolt was a Jewish rebellion against Roman rule occurring between the years 66-73 CE. The results were a defeat for the Jews and the total destruction of the Temple in Jerusalem.

Gemarah—"Completion." This is the second and longer of the two pieces of literature which comprise the Talmud. The Gemarah completes the Mishnah by functioning as its commentary.

Haftarah—To complement the Torah portions, the Prophets and the Writings have also been divided into weekly readings and are read following the Torah portion.

Halakha—Derived from the Hebrew word meaning "walk," this is the way one is to walk out or live one's life, based on the teachings of both written and oral Torah. In a sense, halakhic Judaism is rabbinic or traditional Judaism. A halakha is also a specific legal decision in a given area of life which a person is to follow.

HaMakom—"The place" —Although this word is used in common everyday Hebrew, it also has sacred overtones to refer to the place where God dwells, or in some cases, to God Himself.

HaShem—"The Name" — Shem is also used in everyday Hebrew to speak of anyone's name. However, HaShem is specifically used in Jewish religious literature to refer to the sacred Name of God reflected in the tetragrammaton, (יהוה). The rabbis have chosen to use the phrase "HaShem" instead of writing or speaking the tetragrammaton because they are trying to be careful not to desecrate the Name of God by pronouncing it incorrectly. Moreover, in the days of the Second Temple, the only time the tetragrammaton was pronounced was on Yom Kippur by the High Priest. Today, we do not know how it is correctly pronounced, despite the many attempts there are either to transliterate it (YHWH, etc.) or to say it.

Hebrew names for the books of the Torah:

Hebrew Title	In Hebrew	Translation	English Title
Bereshit	בראשית	In the Beginning	Genesis
Shemot	שמות	Names	Exodus
Vayikra	ויקרא	And He Called	Leviticus
Bemidbar	במדבר	In the Wilderness	Numbers
Devarim	דברים	Words	Deuteronomy

Ketubah—A Jewish marriage contract, derived from the Hebrew word for "writing."

Kosher—Kosher means "fit to be eaten according to Jewish dietary laws." The noun derived from it is *kashrut*, the system of Jewish dietary laws.

Megila, Megilot (plural)—A scroll of one of the following Five Books of the Bible: Esther, Song of Solomon, Ruth, Lamentations, and Ecclesiastes.

Mezuzah—Mezuzah literally means "doorpost." It refers to the small parchment of Scripture which the Torah commands to be placed on the doorpost of our houses.

Midrash—(1) A method of interpreting the Tanakh, stressing the allegorical method of interpretation. It also is a homiletic way of looking at a biblical text, as opposed to a scholarly or literal approach. (2) The name of certain specific collections of commentaries which have employed the midrashic method of interpretation. The best known is called the *Midrash Rabbah*, which is a commentary on the entire Torah plus the five megilot. Although compiled sometime between the fourth and fifth centuries CE, this Midrash includes some material from Yeshua's time and even before.

Mikvah—A ritual immersion pool.

Mishkan—A Hebrew word derived from the word "to dwell" (a sister word to "shekhinah). It refers to the tabernacle, the place where God dwelt in a special way among His people.

Mishnah—This is an authoritative collection of oral Torah. It was compiled by Rabbi Yehudah haNasi (Rabbi Judah the Prince) around the year 200 CE. The Mishnah also comprises the smaller of the two pieces of writing that make up the Talmud.

Mitzvah, mitzvot (plural)—A commandment.

Mo'ed, mo'adim (plural)—Literally, "appointed time." A mo'ed is a Holy Day, either a feast or a fast. A list of the mo'adim is found in chapter 23 of Leviticus.

Niddah—The term used to refer to the period of separation between husband and wife during the menstrual period.

Parasha, parashot (plural)—The weekly Torah portion. Presently, the Torah is divided into 54 portions which are read and studied each week for one year. In ancient times, the Torah-reading cycle lasted three years. A parasha (portion) is sometimes also called a *sidra*.

Passover, Pesach (Hebrew)—This is the biblically commanded festival in late March or early to mid-April which celebrates the Israelite exodus from slavery in Egypt.

Rabbi Yehudah haNasi—One of the greatest rabbis of all time, credited with compiling the traditional oral teachings into the writing called the Mishnah, circa 200 CE. In the Talmud he is simply referred to as "the Rabbi."

Rabbi Yochanan ben Zakkai—This important sage was one of the pharisaic survivors of the First Jewish Revolt against Rome. He led his disciples from Jerusalem to Yavne (near present day Tel Aviv), where they set out to establish a

Judaism which could exist without the Temple. He is often credited with firmly establishing rabbinic Judaism.

Sha'ul—This is a Jewish way of referring to Paul. His Hebrew name was Sha'ul (Saul), and because of his position as a teacher and his training in rabbinic thinking, we have given him the honorary title of "Rav."

Second Jewish Revolt—This was another revolt against the Roman occupation of Israel, taking place between 132–135 CE. This rebellion, led by Simon bar Kochba, also failed. The result was that Jews were no longer permitted anywhere near Jerusalem, whose name was changed by the Romans to Aelia Capitolina. This is technically the *Third* Jewish Revolt, but it was the second that took place in what the Romans called Palestine.

Seder—This word means "order." It is frequently used in reference to Passover when the family sits down and conducts an ordered meal including a celebration of the Passover event. Because there is a definite plan to the observance and the meal, it is, therefore, called a "Seder."

Sefer Torah—The Torah scroll.

Segulah—This Hebrew word means "precious treasure."

Septuagint—The translation of the Hebrew Scriptures into Greek around the year 250 BCE. This was the first known translation of the Tanakh. It is often abbreviated "LXX."

Shabbat—The seventh day of the week. In English it is often called the Sabbath, or just Saturday.

Shavu'ot, Pentecost—The fiftieth day after the Pesach Shabbat. In Judaism, Shavu'ot is the time when we remember the giving of the Torah on Mount Sinai. It is also a firstfruits holiday. It was on Shavu'ot that the Spirit of God came upon the early Jewish followers of Yeshua as they were worshiping in the Temple.

Shekhinah—This is a rabbinic term for the residing glory of God in the tabernacle. It is derived from the Hebrew word that means "to dwell."

Shofar—A ram's horn blown on Rosh Hashanah and other special times.

Sukkot—The Feast of Tabernacles. This is the biblically commanded festival in late September or early to mid-October when Jewish people live in temporary booths for one week and celebrate the provisions of God.

T'shuvah—This is a Hebrew term meaning "repentance."

Tahor—Being in a state of ritual purity. This is a very difficult concept to render into English. The person who is tahor has been removed from a declared state of ritual impurity and declared by God to be free of the vestiges of his or her contact with the realm of sin and/or death. The means of changing the outward state from "tamei" to "tahor" usually involved offering the prescribed sacrifice and/or purification through water.

Talmid, talmidim (plural)—A "learner," or student. A talmid was really a student who was also a disciple: he did not just learn facts, he also learned life from his teacher.

Talmud—The two-part authoritative compendium of oral law. The main but shorter part is the Mishnah. After each Mishnah is quoted, it is followed by the second, longer part called the Gemarah (a commentary on the Mishnah). There are actually two Talmuds. The more authoritative work is called the Babylonian Talmud, because it was compiled by sages living in or near Babylon sometime around 500 CE. The second, known as the Jerusalem or Palestinian Talmud, was compiled by sages living in what was then called "Palestine" by the Romans—*not* in Jerusalem. The date is also uncertain, but many believe it was finished slightly earlier than the Babylonian

Talmud. The English edition by Soncino Press takes up over two feet on a bookshelf!

Tamei—Being in a state of ritual impurity. Like *tahor*, this is a difficult concept to render into English. The person who is tamei has come into contact with the realm of sin and/or death. However, it does not always mean that the person has sinned.

Tanakh—An acronym for the Old Testament. T = Torah; N = Neviim (Prophets); Kh = Ketuvim (Writings), the threefold division of the Tanakh.

Tzitziot—The "fringes" on a four-cornered garment worn by observant Jewish men. In biblical times, these fringes were worn by both men and women.

Ya'acov—The Hebrew name translated in English as Jacob and James.

Yeshua—The Hebrew name translated in English as Jesus.

Yom Kippur—Day of Atonement.

Yom Teruah—In traditional Judaism, this Holy Day (mo'ed) is known as Rosh Hashanah. biblically, it is the day set aside for a special blowing of the shofar.

Endnotes

1. Understanding the nature of the new birth will also provide the key to understanding the complicated issues known as *halakha* (the practical application of Torah truth)—specifically, how the Torah is lived out in the daily life of the redeemed.

2. Babylonian Talmud Sanhedrin 59a.

3. Abraham Cohen, *Everyman's Talmud*, p. 63.

4. For a fuller discussion of this issue, please read *Torah Rediscovered* by Ariel and D'vorah Berkowitz (First Fruits of Zion Publications).

5. All quotations in this paragraph are taken from Rabbi Louis Jacobs, *The Book of Jewish Belief*, p. 42.

6. There are two versions of the Talmud, the Babylonian Talmud, compiled about 500 CE, and the Jerusalem Talmud, compiled about 400 CE. They both have the same Mishnah, but have different Gamarahs. The Babylonian Talmud, which has a longer Gamarah, is considered to be the more authoritative of the two.

7. Thomas Edward McComiskey, *The Covenants of Promise*, p. 10.

8. Geoffrey W. Bromiley, gen. ed., *The International Standard Bible Encyclopedia* ("ISBE"), Vol. 1, p. 790.

9. Ibid., p. 790.

10. Geerhardus Vos, *Biblical Theology*, p. 33.

11. ISBE, op. cit., p. 791.

12. Nechama Leibowitz, *New Studies in Bereshit*, p. 86.

13. Please refer to our previously published book, *Torah Rediscovered*, for more details on the specific comparisons. See also ISBE, Vol. 1, pp. 790–791.

14. Clarence E. Mason, Jr. "Biblical Introduction," *Hermeneutics*, p. 19.

15. McComiskey, op. cit., pp. 140–141.

16. Ibid., pp. 72, 73, 75.

17. John Fischer, "Covenant, Fulfillment & Judaism in Hebrews," an unpublished paper, p. 3. This quotation is, in reality, a quote that Dr. Fischer has made from J. Barton Payne, *The Theology of the Older Testament* (Grand Rapids: Eerdmans, 1972), p. 79.

18. Fischer, op. cit., p. 4.

19. Ibid., p. 6, quoting Samuel Schultz, *The Prophets Speak* (New York: Harper and Row, 1968), pp. 46–47.

20. Ibid., p. 7.

21. Ibid., p. 8.

22. Ibid., p. 13.

23. Ibid., p. 14.

24. Ibid., p. 8.

25. McComiskey, op. cit., p. 23.

26. For an excellent introduction to the mo'adim, see *God's Appointed Times* by Barney Kasdan (Lederer Publications).

27. Spiros Zodhiates, *The Complete Word Study Dictionary of the New Testament*, entry # 2219.

28. Barney Kasdan, *God's Appointed Times*, p. viii.

29. The Hebrew word translated either "stranger" or "alien" is not the usual word ger (גר) but *ben nekher* (בן נכר). According to Brown, Driver, and Briggs, it has to do with "foreignness, that which is foreign" and "of another family, tribe, or nation." The rabbis interpret this word to mean converts. (See Rosenberg, Rabbi A.J., *The Book of Isaiah*, Vol. 2 (New York: The Judaica Press, 1989.) However, the usual rabbinic word for converts is ger (גר). In both cases, in this author's opinion, the rabbis are reading their own theology back into the words of the Tanakh, assuming that all foreigners had to have been converts to Israel in the same sense that there are converts of the rabbis.

30. Hobart E. Freeman, *An Introduction to the Old Testament Prophets*, p. 337.

31. David Bivin and Roy Blizzard, Jr., *Understanding the Difficult Words of Jesus*, p. 152–155.

32. Some valuable sources of information on this subject are: S. Safrai and M. Stern, *The Jewish People in the First Century*, Vol. 2, pp. 1007–1064; *Biblical Archaeology Review*, "Did Jesus Speak Greek?", by Joseph A. Fitzmyer, September/October 1992, pp. 58–63; and Bivin and Blizzard, op. cit. The original language of Yeshua in the Gospels was most certainly not Greek—it was Semitic, either Hebrew or Aramaic. There is a large debate concerning whether Yeshua taught His students or even spoke on an everyday basis in Hebrew or Aramaic. Both of these Semitic

languages are very similar in thought. Moreover, the word "commandment" has definite religious overtones, reminding all readers knowledgeable of the Torah and rabbinic literature of the Torah concept of *mitzvot*, commandments.

33. Marvin Wilson, *Our Father Abraham*, p. 21. This wonderful treatment of Jewish-Christian relations provided us with a great deal of inspiration in writing *Take Hold*. Not to take anything away from the scholarship and impact of Wilson's book, we think, nevertheless, that we go a step further. We are attempting to demonstrate that gentiles are not only spiritually related to the Jewish people, but part of Israel itself; as such, they have the right to follow the Torah. Wilson begins by quoting E.P.Sanders, *Paul and Palestinian Judaism*, p. 422.

34. S. Safrai and M. Stern, *The Jewish People in the First Century*, Vol. 2, p. 878.

35. From an unpublished paper by Patrice Fischer entitled "Modern-Day God-fearers: A Biblical Role Model for gentile Participation in Messianic Congregations" (N/D), as well as from a private conversation with her. This excellent study is certainly deserving of publication.

36. David H. Stern, *Jewish New Testament Commentary*, p. 257.

37. Patrice Fischer, op. cit., p. 2.

38. Ibid., p. 2.

39. Ibid., p. 8.

40. For a more complete treatment of the place of the so-called Noachide Laws have in gentile salvation, please read Dr. Louis Goldberg's excellent booklet, *Are There Two Ways of Atonement*? (see Bibliography)

41. D. Stern, op. cit., p. 278.

42. Peter Tompson, *Paul and the Jewish Law*, p. 230.

43. Patrice Fischer, op. cit., p. 8.

44. Richard Longenecker, *Acts* (The Expositor's Bible Commentary), Vol. 8, p. 486.

45. Wilson, op. cit., p. 14.

46. Ibid., p. 13.

47. William F. Arndt and F. Wilbur Gingrich, *A Greek-English Lexicon of the New Testament*, p. 781.

48. Colin Brown, gen. Ed. *The New International Dictionary of New Testament Theology*, Vol. 1, p. 644.

49. F. F. Bruce, *The Epistle of Paul to the Romans* (TNTC), p. 217.

50. Ibid., p. 218.

51. Ibid., p. 218.

52. Wilson, op. cit., p. 15.

53. J. H. Moulton and G. Milligan, *The Vocabulary of the Greek New Testament*, p.

525.

54. Arndt and Gingrich, op. cit., p. 550.1

55. Tim Hegg, "What Does plhrwsai Mean in Matthew 5:17, Ephesians 2:14–15—An Application of the Study." An unpublished paper presented at the Northwest Regional Evangelical Theological Society on February 28, 1998, p. 12, n. 49.

56. Ibid., p. 13.

57. Ibid., p. 18

58. Ibid. A good portion of Hegg's rabbinic sources are found in the Mishnah (Pesachim 8:8; Shecklim 8:1; Oholot 18:7, 9; Shabbat 9:1; Avodah Zerah 3:6).

59. Ibid.

60. Many of these thoughts on the middle wall of partition were gleaned from a personal interview with Dr. John Fischer on 15 May 1997 in Jerusalem as well as from Tim Hegg's unpublished paper delivered at a session of the Evangelical Theological Society. See the Bibliography for details.

61. Safrai and Stern, op. cit., p. 866.

62. P. Fischer, op. cit., p. 4.

63. Hegg, op. cit., p. 18.

64. Ibid., p. 17.

65. Ibid., p. 18.

66. Arndt and Gingrich, op. cit., p. 802.

67. NIDNT, op. cit. vol. 4, p. 504.

68. Mason, op. cit., p. 15.

69. J. Barton Payne, quoting Dr. Louis Berkof in *Encyclopedia of Biblical Prophecy*, p. 9.

70. Vos, op. cit., p. 15.

71. For some excellent treatments of this whole subject, we recommend that you read the following books, all of which have had a profound impact on these authors' lives: 1) *Birthright*, by Dr. David C. Needham; *Lifetime Guarantee*, by Dr. Bill and Annabel Gillham, *Commentary on Romans*, by Dr. John Murray; and *Romans: The New Man (An Exposition of Chapter 6)*, by Dr. D. Martyn Lloyd-Jones.

72. David C. Needham, *Birthright*, p. 61. we have changed the word "Christian" in his quotation to the word "believer."

73. There are many excellent books on this subject, written from both Messianic Jewish and non-Jewish believing points of view. We particularly recommend those by Dr. Daniel Juster, Dr. Gene Getz, Dr. Francis A. Schaeffer, Dr. Ray Steadman, Dr. John A. MacArthur, Jr., and Ralph W. Neighbour, Jr.

74. Colin Brown, gen. ed., *Dictionary of New Testament Theology*, Vol. 2, p. 292.

75. Boice, *God and History,* op.cit.

76. James I. Packer, Merrill C. Tenney, and William White, Jr., eds. *Everyday Life in the Bible,* p. 177.

77. Leon J. Wood, *The Holy Spirit in the Old Testament,* p. 65.

78. Ibid., pp. 67–68, 70.

79. Luke 2:25–38.

80. Chaim Richman, *The Holy Temple of Jerusalem,* p. 10.

81. "Shekhinah," Encyclopedia Judaica, Vol. 14, p. 1351.

82. Ibid., p. 1351.

83. cf. Richman, op. cit., p. 10.

84. Henry C. Thiessen, *Introductory Lectures in Systematic Theology,* p. 409.

85. Danny Litvin, *Pentecost is Jewish,* p. 31. Danny has passed away since this book was written. His wife, Rivi, has carried on his teaching ministry; being a native Israeli, she knows many of the nuances of Hebrew better than most. She is also very well versed in the Jewish background of the Brit Hadasha and runs an educational center in Israel dedicated to teaching people that background—a goal to which she and her husband were dedicated before his sudden death in 1986.

86. Ibid., p. 30.

87. Babylonian Talmud Shabbat 87b.

88. This information was gleaned from a Yeshiva class taken in Jerusalem.

89. Jack Finegan, *Light From the Ancient Past,* Vol. 1, p. 69.

90. Ibid., p. 69.

91. This idea did not originate with us. We first heard it while studying with a rabbi in the USA. He was teaching a class that had a good percentage of non-Jews in it.

92. This viewpoint was first heard while taking a class in a school for Jewish Studies in Worcester, MA. When we presented this meaning of the word "Jordan" to two native Israeli Hebrew professional translators, they confirmed the possibility of this interpretation.

93. Actually, there is good evidence to suggest that both Yeshua and Joshua were the same Hebrew name. Historically, the name Joshua (Yehoshua) began to be shortened over the years into the form of Yeshua. In English, this may be compared to Thomas becoming Tom or Richard becoming Rick.

94. These comments are from First Fruits of Zion's Torah Club commentator, Moshe (ben Shaya) Morrison, during a conversation the publication staff had with him in February 1998 at our home in Jerusalem.

95. We again urge you to read *Torah Rediscovered* (available from this ministry) to become familiar with the true nature of the document called the Torah.

96. Cohen, op. cit., p. 62.

97. Walter A. Elwell, ed., *Evangelical Dictionary of Theology*, p. 340.

98. C. E. B. Cranfield, *Romans (ICC)*, p. 575.

99. Boaz Michael, director of First Fruits of Zion ministries, has suggested a position very close to what we are proposing through Professor Nanos. It was his suggestion which prompted additional investigation into this passage from Romans 11.

100. Mark Nanos, *The Mystery of Romans*, p. 267.

101. All of the Nanos quotes in this paragraph are from Ibid., p. 267.

102. We are being kind by using the word "attitude" here. In actuality, the trait that the Scriptures warn against in Romans 11 is "arrogance." Indeed, arrogance has been and continues to be the prevailing attitude that a great number of non-Jewish believers have toward the Jewish people.

103. Mark Nanos, quoting Jacob Jervell in Nanos, Ibid., p. 269.

104. Ardnt and Gingrich, op. cit, pp. 2–3.

105. Tompson, op. cit., pp. 194–195.

106. The Greek word translated "tutor" is actually the word "pedagogue". Here are some appropriate comments about this concept, most of which are a quotation from *Torah Rediscovered (p. 22–23)*: "Sha'ul was drawing upon a very familiar illustration from the ancient Greco-Roman world of which he was a part. Well-to-do families often hired someone to serve as a protector for their children when they sent them to their teachers. The protector was not the teacher, but merely someone who made sure that a child would safely reach his or her teacher. Sha'ul uses this kind of language in Galatians 3:22ff. to illustrate how the Torah functioned as a protector. How does God preserve such people? One way He has chosen to do so, though certainly not the only way, is through the Torah. According to Galatians 3:22ff., the Torah can function as a *pedagogue*, as the Greek word for tutor should be translated (verse 24). This pedagogue's duty was to conduct the boy or youth to and from school and to superintend his conduct…he was not a teacher. (Arndt and Gingrich, p. 608) Please note that the definition of the Greek word *paidagogos* differs from the modern English usage of pedagogue. Hence, he was something of a bodyguard to help ensure the student's safety on the way to his teacher. In verse 23, Sha'ul explains this protective concept with a slightly different image. There he uses a word which has usually been translated as kept in custody. However, by rendering the Greek verb *sugkleio* in such a manner, translators have unwittingly cast a negative shadow on the Torah, depicting it as something that holds people captive, like prisoners. But the word can have a slightly different connotation. It can also be rendered close up, hem in, or enclose in a positive sense. Seen in this light, the verse emphasizes protection rather than imprisonment. Furthermore, this translation also fits well with the concept of the pedagogue.

Thus, the Torah was intended to preserve the mental, moral and social safety of the environment into which an individual was born and raised. The person was protected 'until the date set by the Father' (Galatians 4:2) when the Spirit of God would lead them to the Teacher, the Messiah."

107. Dr. Daniel Juster, *Jewish Roots*, pp. 111–112.

108. Adolf Deissmann, *Light From the Ancient East*, pp. 332–333.

109. Arndt and Gingrich, op. cit., p. 170.

110. Fischer, op. cit., p. 14

111. H. E. Dana and Julius R. Mantey, *A Manual Grammar of the Greek New Testament*, p. 192.

Bibliography

Arndt, William F., and F. Wilbur Gingrich. *Bauer's Greek-English Lexicon of the New Testament and Other Early Christian Literature*. Chicago: The University of Chicago Press, 1957.

Benhayim, Menahem. *Jews, gentiles, and the New Testament Scriptures*. Jerusalem: Yanetz, Ltd., 1985.

Berkowitz, Ariel and D'vorah. *Torah Rediscovered*, second ed. Littleton, CO: First Fruits of Zion, 1996.

Bivin, David and Roy Blizzard, Jr. *Understanding the Difficult Words of Jesus*. Austin, Texas: Center for Judaic-Christian Studies, 1984.

Boice, James Montgomery. *Ephesians: An Expositional Commentary*. Grand Rapids: Zondervan, 1988.

—— *God and History*, volume IV of the series "Foundations of the Christian Faith." Downers Grove, IL: InterVarsity Press, 1981.

Bromiley, Geoffrey W., gen. ed. *The International Standard Bible Encyclopedia*, in four volumes. Grand Rapids: Eerdmans, 1979.

Brown, Colin, gen. ed. *The New International Dictionary of New Testament Theology*, Vols. 1 and.2. Grand Rapids: Zondervan, 1975, 1979.

Brown, Francis, S. R. Driver, and Charles A. Briggs. *Gesenius' Hebrew and English Lexicon of the Old Testament*. Oxford: The Clarendon Press, 1966.

Bruce, F. F. *The Epistle of Paul to the Romans* (TNTC). Grand Rapids: Eerdmans, 1963.

Cohen, Boaz A. *Everyman's Talmud*. New York: Shocken Books, 1975.

Cranfield, C. E. B. *Romans (ICC)*, Vols. 1 and 2. Edinburgh: T & T Clark, Ltd, 1979.

Dana, H.E. and Mantey, Julius R. A *Manual Grammar of the Greek New Testament*. Toronto: The Macmillan Company, 1927, 1955

Deissmann, Adolf. *Light From the Ancient East*. Grand Rapids: Baker, reprint 1978.

Edersheim, Alfred. *The Temple*. Grand Rapids: Eerdmans, 1978.

Elwell, Walter A., ed. *Evangelical Dictionary of Theology*. Grand Rapids: Baker Book House, 1984.

"Covenant." *Encyclopedia Judaica*, Vol. 5. Jerusalem: Keter Publishing, N/D.

Finegan, Jack. *Light From the Ancient Past*, Vol. 1. Princeton: Princeton University Press, 1946, 1974.

Fischer, John. "Covenant Fulfillment and Judaism in Hebrews," an unpublished paper.

Fischer, Patrice. "Modern-Day God-Fearers: A Biblical Role Model For Gentile Participation in Messianic Congregations," an unpublished paper.

Fitzmyer, Joseph A. "Did Jesus Speak Greek?" *Biblical Archaeology Review* 18 (1992): 58–63.

Freeman, Hobart E. *An Introduction to the Old Testament Prophets*. Chicago: Moody Press, 1971.

Gaebelein, Frank E., gen. ed. *The Expositors Bible Commentary*, Vols. 9 and 10, *John* and *Acts, Romans, 1 Corinthians, 2 Corinthians,* and *Galatians*. Grand Rapids: Zondervan, 1981.

Goldberg, Louis. *Are There Two Ways of Atonement?* Baltimore: Lederer Publications, 1990.

Hegg, Tim. "What Does πληρωσαι Mean in Matthew 5:17, Ephesians 2:14–15—An Application of the Study." An unpublished paper presented at the Northwest Regional Evangelical Theological Society on 28 February, 1998.

Kasdan, Barney. *God's Appointed Times*. Clarksville, MD: Lederer Messianic Publications, 1993.

Jacobs, Louis. *The Book of Jewish Belief*. West Orange, NJ: Behrman House, Inc., 1984.

Juster, Daniel. *Jewish Roots*. Rockville, MD: DAVAR, 1986.

Leibowitz, Nechama. *New Studies in Bereshit*. Jerusalem: Hemed Press, N/D.

Liddell, Henry George and Scott, Robert. *A Greek-English Lexicon*. Oxford: The Clarendon Press, 1893, 1985.

Litvin, Danny. *Pentecost is Jewish*. Orange, CA: Promise Publishing Company, 1987.

Mason, Clarence E., ed. "Biblical Introduction," *Hermeneutics*. These are class notes published by and for use in conjunction with the class by the said name and teacher at Philadelphia College of Bible, 1970.

McComiskey, Thomas Edward. *The Covenants of Promise*. Grand Rapids: Baker Book House, 1985.

Moulton, James Hope and Milligan, George. *The Vocabulary of the Greek New Testament*. Grand Rapids: Eerdmans, 1930, 1982.

Murray, John. *The Covenant of Grace*. London: 1954.

Nanos, Mark D. *The Mystery of Romans—The Jewish Context of Paul's Letters*. Minneapolis: Fortress Press, 1996.

Needham, David C. *Birthright*. Portland, Oregon: Multnomah Press, 1982.

"Noachide Laws." *Encyclopedia Judaica*, Vol. 13. Jerusalem: Keter Publishing, N/D.

Rabbinowitz, J., trans. *Midrash Rabbah: Devarim*. London: Soncino Press, 1983.

Packer, James I., Merrill C. Tenney, and William White, Jr., eds. *Everyday Life in the Bible*. New York: Bonanza Books, 1980.

Payne, J. Barton. *Encyclopedia of Biblical Prophecy*. New York: Harper and Row Publishers, 1973.

Richman, Chaim. *The Holy Temple of Jerusalem*. Jerusalem: The Temple Institute & Carta, 1997.

Rosenberg, Rabbi A. J. *The Book of Isaiah*, Vol. 2. New York: The Judaica Press, 1989.

Safrai, S., and M. Stern, eds. *The Jewish People in the First Century*, Vols. 1 and 2. Philadelphia: Fortress Press, 1976.

Simpson, E. K. and Bruce, F. F. *The Epistles of Ephesians and Colossians* (NICNT). Grand Rapids: Eerdmans, 1957, 1984.

"Shekhinah." *Encyclopedia Judaica*, Vol. 14. Jerusalem: Keter Publishing, N/D

Stern, David H. *Jewish New Testament Commentary*. Clarksville, MD: Jewish New Testament Publications, 1992.

Tenney, Merrill C. *New Testament Survey*. Grand Rapids: Eerdmans, and Leicester, England: Inter-Varsity Press, 1961, 1988.

The Babylonian Talmud, English Edition. London: The Soncino Press, 1938.

Thiessen, Henry Clarence. *Introductory Lectures in Systematic Theology*. Grand Rapids: Eerdmans, 1949.

Tomson, Peter. *Paul and the Jewish Law*. Minneapolis: Fortress Press, 1990.

Voss, Geerhardus. *Biblical Theology*. Grand Rapids: Eerdmans, 1948, 1973.

Waskow, Arthur I. *Seasons of Our Joy*. New York: Summit Books, 1982.

Wilson, Marvin R. *Our Father Abraham*. Grand Rapids: Eerdmans, and Dayton, OH: Center for Judaic-Christian Studies, 1989.

Wood, Leon, J. *The Holy Spirit in the Old Testament*. Grand Rapids: Zondervan, 1976.

Zodhiates, Spiros. *The Complete Word Study Dictionary of the New Testament*. Iowa Falls, Iowa: World Bible Publishers, 1992.

Bibles

BH *Biblia Hebraica Stuttgartensia*. Stuttgart, Germany: Deutsche Bibelgesellschaft, 1990.

GNT *The Greek New Testament*, Third Edition. Stuttgart, Germany: United Bible Societies, 1983.

JNT Stern, Dr.David H. trans. *The Jewish New Testament*. Jerusalem, Israel: Jewish New Testament Publications, 1989.

JPS *The Tanakh—The Holy Scriptures, The New JPS Translation*. Philadelphia: The Jewish Publication Society, 1988.

NASB New American Standard Bible, *The International Inductive Study Bible*. Eugene, OR: Harvest House Publishers, 1993.

NIV *The New International Version*. Colorado Springs, CO: International Bible Society, 1984.

Index A
Words and Terms

Index B

Scriptures Referenced

Index C
Author Index

IndexD
Greek / Hebrew Words

Greek Words Used

agathei 215

aorist 245

astheneis 216

de swma tou xristou 232

ekklesia 142-144, 158, 243

ergon nomou 221

hagiois 143

ho perateis 171

koinonia 105

mysterion 126

nomos 25, 101, 223, 233

phoboumenoi 89

politeia 111

politeis 111

religio illicita 102

seboumenoi 89–90

sugkoinonos 105

theon 90

xenos 112

Hebrew Words Used

amim 66

astneis 216

avar 171

baruch hashem 49, 265

bayit 165

beit hamikdash 164

ben nekher 298

brit 18, 19

chadash 33

chazak 72

dan 176

ger 279, 298

goy 5, 71, 93

habayit 21, 165

haMakom 156

har habayit 165

kanaf 71

kashrut 291

kehilah 141, 166, 177–178, 193, 243

ketubah 153–154

nevi'im 162

ohel mo'ed 50, 160

olam habba 246

qahal 142

qol 142

segulah 154

sh'lichim 162

shekinah 153, 160–161, 301, 308

talmidim 51, 84, 294

tamei 294-295

tzitzit 72, 100, 190

xenos 112

zimrot 266

Torah Rediscovered
Challenging Centuries of Misinterpretation and Neglect

Ariel and D'vorah Berkowitz. This book will clarify many of the difficult issues relating to the Torah which have been misinterpreted throughout years of abuse and neglect by Jewish and Christian leaders. Torah Rediscovered paints a clear picture of how the Torah can be honored by Jewish and non-Jewish believers. (See page 16 for additional information.)...$13.95

The Mezuzah
A Visible Reminder of Who You Are

This booklet will teach you the scriptural basis for the tradition of the Mezuzah, its history, purpose and contents. Experience the full meaning and purpose of this reminder as you participate in this wonderful tradition.
Also included: A beautiful, high quality wooden mezuzah and a Messianic ceremony for affixing it to your doorpost. Celebrate this special ceremony with family and friends...$15.95

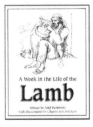

A Week in the Life of the Lamb

A speculatory fiction that brings the reader into the life of Ya'akov — a bystander at the events during the week of the crucifixion of Yeshua. This book gives its readers a perspective on the historical, cultural and spiritual lives of Yeshua and His followers during His ministry here on earth. Although not a factual account, this book is based upon many respected resources on this time era and lifestyle............................$4.95

Hanukkah
In the Home of the Redeemed

Hanukkah reminds us to use the weapon that combats assimilation—the Word of God. What is it that in every generation stands up against the godlessness, lawlessness, and corruption of man? It is the Torah of our God, entrusted to us that we might live it out. Learn from the model of the Maccabeans of old. A Daily guide for a great celebration. Everything you need to know and do! $8.95

Jot & Tittle
Introducing the Hebrew Alefbet through the Weekly Torah Portions

Use Jot & Tittle week-by-week to learn Hebrew straight from the Bible, you'll be amazed at what you can learn! Each Torah portion has a quick two-page lesson. By the end of a year, you can know all 54 names of the weekly portions, what they mean, and what goes on in that chunk of scripture. Spell out each name, one letter at a time, then sound out the syllables as the vowel points are added. Practice tracing block and cursive writing, right in the workbook. You can even learn alphabetical order and extra vocabulary. Each time you finish a book (Genesis, Exodus, etc.), word puzzles give you a fun chance to review everything you've learned. $12.95

First Fruits of Zion *Magazine*

First Fruits of Zion
"A Promise of What is to Come"

First Fruits of Zion publishes this bi-monthly magazine from the Land of Israel. The Magazine features teachings on the relevance of a biblical Torah lifestyle, the Hebrew language, the Land and People of Israel. **Included in every issue are commentaries on the weekly Torah Portions**. To receive a FREE sample of the magazine, or to purchase a year's subscription, please use the form at the end of this book.

US & Canada...$27.00
International..$38.00

The Torah Club
Weekly Torah Study Program

The Torah Club is a teaching, training and discipleship program designed to help God's people understand and walk in His ways (the Torah). Study how the Torah is the key to a greater understanding of the Messiah Yeshua and His teachings.

Volume 1 — Torah Treasures
Volume One takes you through the entire Torah, introducing you to the world of Jewish thought through the anointing and inspiration of our talented Torah teachers. This Volume lays the foundations which enable one to fully enjoy and understand Volume Two. $35.00 per month.

Volume 2 — Yeshua in the Torah
Yeshua stated that every word written in the Torah pointed toward and spoke of Him. Volume Two examines the Torah with this challenge in mind. How is Yeshua pictured in each portion? Take a revealing look at how Messiah's love, grace and redemption are intertwined in each passage. $35.00 per month.

Volume 3 — The Prophets
The Prophets proclaimed three major themes: the end of the age; the return of God's people to His Torah; and the anticipated Messiah. Volume Three closely examines the contents of the Haftarot, and is an invaluable resource for preparing God's people for the end of the age, as we return to His Torah in the fullness of Messiah. $35.00 per month.

Each Volume includes...
- Extensive written teachings on each Parasha, with notes and study questions, by Ariel Berkowitz.
- A high quality and attractive full-color binder, with Parasha dividers for your study notes, glossaries, and explanations of the teachings.
- Audio Teachings, 45 minutes per Parasha, by Moshe Ben Shaiya, Messianic leader in Israel, and Dr. David Friedman.

- Beautiful cassette binders containing your Audio Lessons.
- A subscription to our magazine
- 10% discount off all books in this Resource Guide
- Conference registration fee discounts.

First Fruits of Zion is a non-profit organization dependent on the participation of our faithful supporters. From your $35.00 per month membership fee, you receive a tax credit of $25.00 per month. Thank you for supporting our ministry!

Binders

Audio Teachings

Written Notes

First Fruits of Zion *for Children*

Children's Torah Club
Weekly Torah Study Program

The Children's Torah Club is a wonderful way for you to teach the weekly Torah Portion to your children. Designed to work in conjunction with the adult Torah Clubs (Can also serve as stand-alone study). As a parent you would do your personal studies in Torah Club One or Two and then use what you learned to share the truths with your child. The activities and teachings in the Children's Torah Club will impart His timeless Torah truths and give hours of enjoyment and pleasure to your children as they study. $20.00

Children's Torah Club includes...

- Beautifully illustrated activity and lesson books based on the Parasha Hashavuah.
- Each Parasha is an eight-page booklet, individually bound and drilled with three holes for easy insertion into the notebook.
- A Hebrew lesson in each study.
- A beautiful full-color notebook binder to hold all lessons and activities.

First Fruits of Zion *Discipleship*

HaYesod (Hebrew meaning: The Foundation) is a new fourteen-week discipleship course designed for small home groups. Each week, material based on significant biblical principles is presented for study. *HaYesod* results in added depth of understanding and practical application of Scripture.

Examples of Leadership and Student Manuals, Notes and Visuals

HaYesod
A Discipleship Series on the Foundation of the Faith

Equally Sharing In God's Work

Our central purpose is to facilitate the teaching of timeless Torah truths. To achieve this, we need to both prepare quality materials/resources and establish dedicated and equipped leaders who will utilize these materials. Only by working together as one team can we hope to be effective in sharing the truths of God's Word that He has entrusted to all of us. In doing so, our desire is to strengthen the love and appreciation of all Believers in the Body of Messiah for the Land, the People, and the Scriptures of Israel.

HaYesod Program Purpose

- HaYesod is a professional and well organized program. The materials are designed to equip you, as a leader, with the ability to teach and impart with confidence, the powerful life-changing biblical concepts in small home group settings.

- By focusing on the foundational truths of Scripture, congregations and fellowships will be strengthened together in the Word of God.

- More details are outlined in the HaYesod brochure.

How you can be a part of HaYesod

HaYesod is a structured, carefully planned program. The methodical, clearly presented information and helpful illustrations and charts are designed to adequately equip you in teaching and encouraging students in the foundational truths of the entire Word of God. For HaYesod to be fruitful and effective, we need the help of those who share this vision and who will work with us in the important role of teaching this valuable material. At what level can you be a part?

Congregational Leaders

As a congregational leader, you can effectively use this program in your cell groups, mid-week Bible studies or discipleship classes.

Regional Leaders

Representatives with a vision for this program are needed. You will be responsible for helping to promote the program, training area leaders and the overseeing of groups.

Group Leaders

Individuals who are called and have a desire to teach are needed to co-ordinate and teach the 14–week program in small, home-group settings.

For more information visit the HaYesod Web site, www.hayesod.org or to receive a Leadership Application Form, call 1–800–775–4807, or write: PO Box 620099, Littleton, CO 80162, USA

First Fruits of Zion

Resources

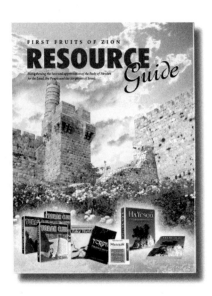

It is the calling of First Fruits of Zion to provide you with books, teaching tapes and other resources to assist you in your understanding of the unique relationship you have with the Land, The People, and the Scriptures of Israel. First Fruits of Zion is not a business. We are a non-profit organization called to disseminate information about the misunderstood and often neglected first five books of the Bible, the "Torah."

The First Fruits of Zion Resource Guide is published periodically to benefit you in gathering this information. The Resource Guide is FREE to all.

Write for your copy today!

PO Box 620099
Littleton, CO 80162
USA

Torah Club (A Weekly Study Program)

☐ VOLUME 1, Torah Treasures $35.00 / MONTH

☐ VOLUME 2, Yeshua in the Torah $35.00 / MONTH

☐ VOLUME 3, The Prophets $35.00 / MONTH

Please enroll me in the marked Torah Club Volume

☐ I am a new Torah Club Member, please give me my 50% discount off the first month's teaching.

Children's Torah Club

☐ VOLUME 1 $20.00 / MONTH

First Fruits of Zion Magazine

☐ Please send me a ONE Year Subscription to FFOZ Magazine

☐ Please send me a FREE sample issue

☐ Please send me .... issues every month on your Bulk Magazine Program at the appropriate price.

Bulk Magazine Program

5	–	10	Magazines......................$2.00 each
11	–	20	Magazines......................$1.85 each
21	–	50	Magazines......................$1.60 each
50 Plus		Magazines......................$1.45 each	

■ Plus Shipping & Handling charges

Other items

I would like to purchase these books:

1 ....$ _____

2 ....$ _____

3 ....$ _____

4 ....$ _____

Shipping & Handling charges for Orders

$ 0	–	$25.00	Add $3.50
$25.01	–	$50.00	Add $5.50
$50.01	–	$100.00	Add $7.50

$100.00 Plus   Add 10% of Order Total

Canada & Mexico..................................Double shipping

Other countries..Triple shipping

■ International Orders are shipped Surface Rate.

ORDER TOTAL...$ _____

Less Applicable Discount...$ _____

Plus Shipping & Handling charges *(see left)*....................$ _____

Total ....$ _____

Payment by

☐ Master Card   ☐ Visa   ☐ Amex   ☐ Disc

☐ Enclosed is a CHECK / Money Order for the above amount

Ship to

Name _____

Address _____

City _____

State _____ Zip Code _____

Country _____

Phone _____

E-mail: _____

Credit Card Number

☐☐☐☐☐☐☐☐☐☐☐☐☐☐☐☐

Expiration Date

☐☐ / ☐☐

Name *(as printed on card)*

_____

Authorized Signature

_____

Send check or money order to: First Fruits of Zion, PO Box 620099, Littleton, CO 80162-0099

Call 1–800–775–4807, Int'l Calls, dial 303–933–2119, Fax 303–933–0997

From: _____

_____

_____

First Fruits of Zion
PO Box 620099
Littleton, CO 80162–0099

USA